# Praise for *Corridors of Contagion*

"With *Corridors of Contagion*, Vikki Law shows how the COVID-19 pandemic, with its largely unheeded calls for decarceration, was a missed opportunity not only to free those for whom there is a structural propensity to be locked up and locked down, but to radically expand the reach of freedom for all. For years, Law's expert investigations and discerning analyses have been indispensable to anti-prison campaigns and to the international abolitionist movement more broadly, and this book is no less so."

—**Angela Y. Davis**, professor emerita at University of California, Santa Cruz, and author of *Freedom Is a Constant Struggle*

"Through piercing prose that will make you want to scream and in heart-rending stories that will make you want to cry, Victoria Law takes readers into the strictest COVID lockdowns in the United States: inside our prisons. Regardless of what they'd been convicted of, more than a million incarcerated Americans were condemned in 2020 to isolation from their families, overcrowded cells ripe for mass infection, and viral death sentences. Though it reads at times like a horror thriller about mass social murder, *Corridors of Contagion* is also a compassionate love letter to and from those who were most lethally affected by the novel coronavirus. A masterpiece in the emerging field of COVID literature, and a roadmap for why prison abolition is paramount to stopping current and future pandemics, *Corridors of Contagion* is a heartfelt must-read for anyone who wants to understand why the richest nation on earth has had the most COVID deaths: because the United States incarcerates more people than any other country, and our penitentiaries are killing cages of viral transmission."

—**Steven W. Thrasher**, author of the award-winning book *The Viral Underclass*

"'Don't look away,' Victoria Law's searing book insists. *Corridors of Contagion* powerfully brings us into the actual lockdown of the pandemic—the experiences of incarcerated people forced to endure COVID behind bars. But this book also vividly demonstrates the ways incarcerated men and women fashioned ways to protect, defend, and educate each other, when the state abandoned them. Law shows how th~~ a wakeup call to the United States—and what

—**Jeanne Theoharis**, author of *The Reb~~

T0182560

"*Corridors of Contagion* will both move and enrage you. Victoria Law uses her exceptional investigative abilities and her immense compassion to expose how the COVID pandemic ravaged prisons and endangered incarcerated people. This book recounts a tragic history, but it also provides a vital glimpse into how mutual aid works behind the walls. The lives and voices of the incarcerated people featured by Law will reverberate long after you have finished reading the book. As they should."

—**Mariame Kaba**, author of *We Do This 'Til We Free Us*

"This powerful text is what we have been waiting for, essential reading if we are to identify and learn from the failures of the recent past in dealing with a deadly pandemic and the fraught political divide that led to denial and mob violence that haunts the present and future."

—**Roxanne Dunbar-Ortiz**, historian and author

"Incarcerated people in America's overcrowded, brutal prisons and jails are the canaries in the coal mine of our nation's waning commitment to civil and human rights. In *Corridors of Contagion: How the Pandemic Exposed the Cruelties of Incarceration* accomplished, journalist Victoria Law bears witness to the coronavirus emergency's tragic impact behind bars. One of the United States' most experienced and well-informed chroniclers of mass incarceration, Law shows in *Corridors of Contagion* how a once-in-a-lifetime moment could have resulted in safe decarceration across the country, but instead imposed human suffering and preventable death on a trapped and desperate population. In the wake of the carceral public health failures of 2020, Law reveals how many harsh and unnecessary coronavirus policies remain in place today, compounding the isolation of the world's biggest prison population."

—**Piper Kerman**, author of *Orange is the New Black*

"*Corridors of Contagion* is a deeply disturbing account of the convergence of the harsh punishment system in the US and the cruel inequities that propelled the COVID pandemic. Victoria Law has, once again, brought her gift as one of the most passionate social justice storytellers to expose the long-term and deadly consequences of carceral policies and politics. The compelling story she tells must be widely read to challenge the mean spirited prison nation and how a pandemic can further the dangers of it."

—**Beth E. Richie**, professor, activist, and author of *Arrested Justice: Black Women, Violence and America's Prison Nation*

"With her characteristic evocative storytelling, compelling prose, and razor sharp analysis, Victoria Law delivers another searing look inside the nation's systems of punishment. Law turns an unflinching eye on the cruel operation of structures of punishment in the context of a global pandemic, in which the prison, jailers, and systemic denial of the most basic forms of health care, information, and agency exacerbate their death-making and disabling functions. Law surfaces critical lessons along with defiant acts of humanity, love, and resilience, inviting readers to not turn away from the horrors of prisons but instead to turn toward futures free of them."

**—Andrea J. Ritchie**, coleader of COVID19 Policing Project, cofounder of Interrupting Criminalization, and coauthor of *No More Police: A Case for Abolition*

"*Corridors of Contagion* is an expertly reported account of the malice and incompetence that defined how US prisons and jails responded to the pandemic. Guided by the voices of incarcerated people, journalist Victoria Law shows incontrovertibly what abolitionists on both sides of the walls insisted in March 2020: prison is incompatible with public health."

**—Dan Berger**, author of *Stayed on Freedom: The Long History of Black Power Through One Family's Journey*

"Victoria Law has meticulously and compassionately documented the often-ignored ways in which the pandemic, in tandem with the brutality of the criminalization system, has wreaked havoc on incarcerated people. Powerfully written and deeply reported, *Corridors of Contagion* is both a heartbreaking chronicle of injustice and a profound celebration of how people take care of each other in dire times. This book is an essential tool in our struggle to avoid repeating a lethal chapter in history."

**—Maya Schenwar**, coauthor of *Prison by Any Other Name*

"Intimate and infuriating, Law—one of our most potent abolitionist journalists—offers a necessary and painful history of COVID behind bars. Reading this book together moves readers to grieve those whom we have lost, to recognize the resistance and ingenuity of people inside and their loved ones, and strengthens our ability to grow movements for people's release."

**—Erica Meiners**, coauthor of *Abolition.Feminism.Now.* and *The Feminist and the Sex Offender*

"*Corridors of Contagion* is a masterpiece only Victoria Law could have written. She has a vast knowledge of the prison system, incredible connections with incarcerated people, especially those in women's prisons, and an unparalleled ability to tell their stories. Victoria Law has given us a work that provides in-depth understanding of how the dehumanizing carceral system operates at the granular level. No work does this better than *Corridors of Contagion*."

—**James Kilgore**, formerly incarcerated activist and National Book Award–winning author

"*Corridors of Contagion* combines impeccable research, compelling storytelling, and unflinching commitment to abolition, persuasively demonstrating that the COVID pandemic can only be understood if we look carefully at how it has unfolded inside US prisons. Examining the data on COVID in prisons, recording the stories of people living through the first years of the pandemic in prisons, and analyzing the impacts murderous policy responses and non-responses undertaken by prison official and other government officials, Vikki Law raises a call to action for abolition that is essential reading right now, as environmental crisis ensures that new pandemics are inevitably on the horizon. *Corridors of Contagion* is yet another invaluable contribution from Vikki Law."

—**Dean Spade**, author of *Mutual Aid: Building Solidarity During This Crisis (and the Next)*

"In *Corridors of Contagion*, Victoria Law insists that Americans reckon with what we otherwise work so hard not to see: the senseless violence of our penal system, in ordinary times and in crises. An important and deeply disturbing report."

—**Eric Klinenberg**, author of *2020: One City, Seven People, and the Year Everything Changed*

"Victoria Law, one of the most important journalistic voices on incarceration, has rendered an urgent mosaic of first-person stories of enduring and surviving the ravages of the coronavirus pandemic in US prisons. Through painstaking research and lucid analysis, *Corridors of Contagion* reveals the devastation of the state's neglect and weaponization of disease behind bars while also illuminating the ways in which incarcerated people fought for their own and each other's lives through acts of caring resistance."

—**Emily Thuma**, author of *All Our Trials: Prisons, Policing and the Feminist Fight to End Violence*

"*Corridors of Contagion* is probably the most vivid chronicle of survival and resistance that we will ever read about incarceration during the pandemic. But this book is no catalogue of atrocities. The story underneath the story is that Victoria Law has devoted her life to building political and personal connections with women behind bars, and so within this book—in fact, the very condition of possibility for this book—is a rehearsal for life after borders and walls."

—**Naomi Murakawa**, professor of African American studies at Princeton University and author of *The First Civil Right*

"It has long been understood that prisons are revelatory of a society's larger structure. Victoria Law's powerful account of prison life during the COVID pandemic forces readers to confront the worst state failures, as well as how much the US—as an international outlier—failed to manage this crisis through decarceration. Thanks to Law, and inspired by the creativity of those who persevered, we should know the way forward. One pandemic might have ended but the other persists."

—**Gina Dent**, coauthor of *Abolition.Feminism.Now.* and professor of humanities at University of California, Santa Cruz

"In *Corridors of Contagion*, Victoria Law brings the horror of COVID-19 for incarcerated people to life. Her deep knowledge of the prison system, her boundless empathy for incarcerated people, and the trusting relationships she has built with incarcerated people over her years of telling their stories make Law the ideal person to report on the spaces where the pandemic hit the hardest—carceral facilities—and to warn us of the devastation that incarcerated people will face if we do not learn the lessons of this pandemic before the next one hits."

—**Leigh Goodmark**, author of *Imperfect Victims: Criminalized Survivors and the Promise of Abolition Feminism*

# Corridors of Contagion

How the Pandemic Exposed

the Cruelties of Incarceration

## Victoria Law

Haymarket Books
Chicago, Illinois

Published in 2024 by
Haymarket Books
P.O. Box 180165
Chicago, IL 60618
www.haymarketbooks.org

ISBN: 979-8-88890-256-1

Distributed to the trade in the US through Consortium Book Sales
and Distribution (www.cbsd.com) and internationally through Ingram
Publisher Services International (www.ingramcontent.com).

This book was published with the generous support of Lannan
Foundation, Wallace Action Fund, and Marguerite Casey Foundation.

Special discounts are available for bulk purchases by organizations and
institutions. Please email info@haymarketbooks.org for more information.

Cover design by Eric Kerl.

Library of Congress Cataloging-in-Publication data is available.

10 9 8 7 6 5 4 3 2 1

# Contents

# Introduction

"If the coronavirus were designing its
ideal home, it would build a prison."

—J. Clark Kelso, federal receiver overseeing
health care in California prisons[1]

L ike millions across the United States, Mary Fish was tired of
sheltering in place by May. For her, though, sheltering in place
didn't mean confining herself to a house or even a small studio
apartment. Instead, for Mary and the 1,122 other women at Mabel Bassett Correctional Center, Oklahoma's maximum-security
prison for women, sheltering in place meant being locked in eight-
by-twelve-foot cells or confined to crammed dormitories all day.[2] It
was a scenario repeated in thousands of jails and prisons across the
United States.[3]

Prisons do not allow internet, so the Zoom calls crisscrossing
the ether weren't an option. Neither were phone calls, which, even
in non-pandemic times, cost twenty cents per minute and strained
the budgets of women earning thirty-five cents an hour. The prison's phones were in the various dayrooms or common areas. That
spring, those rooms were off-limits.

But Mary wasn't totally alone. She had the misfortune of living in one of the prison's dormitories. For the next month, she was

unable to escape the din of dozens of women living less than four feet apart from one another.

Behind bars, everyone dreads the word *lockdown*. Under lockdown, every person in a housing unit, and sometimes the entire jail or prison, remains locked in their cell (or confined to their dormitories) for nearly twenty-four hours a day. They have no access to educational or vocational programs, visits, or calls. Meals are delivered to their cells and shoved through a slot in the door. Lockdowns can last days, weeks, or even months—and are typically a group punishment for events as minor as a dispute between a few people, to as severe as a large-scale fight.

In March 2020, the entire country would become familiar with that term—and come to dread it just as much. That month, the novel coronavirus SARS-CoV-2 skyrocketed in New York City, overwhelming hospitals and overflowing morgues. Shortly after, jails and prisons across the country reported explosions of COVID-19. By May 2020, thirty of the fifty top outbreaks, including the four largest in the country, were inside jails and prisons.[4]

The lockdown at Mabel Bassett was an early—and futile— attempt to keep the virus from spreading. But no explanation was given to the women, leaving many to wonder about what seemed like collective punishment when none of them had done anything wrong.

Mary, however, watched the news each night and guessed that these unexplained restrictions were connected with the terrifying virus that had ripped its way through China and Europe and was now decimating the East Coast.

At the start of April, the deputy warden called together the women on Mary's unit.

"Do you know what coronavirus is?" he asked.

"Beer!" one young woman exclaimed.

The women laughed, but the mood quickly sobered as he told them about the novel coronavirus sweeping the country, inundating intensive care units and morgues. He told them that that they would have to remain locked in their cells for their own protection.

The women were struck speechless. Finally, one woman broke the silence. "How long will we be locked down?"

"I don't know," he confessed.

A chorus of grumbles greeted his response. "We didn't do anything," groused another woman. "Why are we being punished?"

One of Mary's close friends didn't say anything. She simply pulled a laundry cart into her cell and began piling her belongings into it. If she was going to be locked down, she might as well go to the SHU, or "special housing unit." The SHU—or "lock," as it's commonly called in Oklahoma—is the typical punishment for any infraction of prison rules. There, women spend nearly twenty-four hours locked in a cell without most of their belongings.

The COVID lockdown seemed like punishment and, Mary's friend reasoned, if she was going to be punished, she might as well be locked in that unit.

But a supervising officer stopped her. The virus was deadly, particularly for elderly people, he explained. At home, he wasn't letting his mother leave the house except to take walks in their backyard, and even those were brief. And inside Mabel Bassett, he cautioned, prison officials were using the SHU to quarantine women who had recently arrived from county jails.[5]

His explanation mollified her enough to unpack her cart.

Several weeks later, the unit manager, or the woman in charge of the prison's daily operations, brought them into the dayroom for another group announcement. "The coronavirus doesn't take a break," she told them. "Get up and clean."

The women who worked as maintenance workers cleaning the prison's halls, bathrooms, and common areas complained that it was their day off. The unit manager was unmoved, ordering everyone to clean in the hope of preventing surface contamination. They swept and mopped the floors. They sterilized the microwaves, tables, and telephones mounted to the walls in the dayroom. They scrubbed the six working showers meant for over a hundred women.

For the first time, they saw a guard wearing a surgical mask. That day, each woman was issued one mask. "Take care of it," the unit manager advised as Mary signed for it. "It may be a while before you get another."

Anyone leaving her cell without a mask would be sent back and forced to remain inside her cell until she complied. Anyone who refused to mask would be sent to the SHU.

Mary didn't mind wearing a mask. It hid her broken dentures, which she had been unable to get repaired or replaced.

The women were instructed to keep six feet apart—or "socially distance"—an impossibility in nearly every prison. Even in non-pandemic times, they could barely move through the corridors without brushing against each other. At the best of times, the congested conditions led to tempers flaring, arguments, and fights. Now, many feared that a casual bump might lead to death.

Two days later, every Oklahoma prison went on lockdown. At Mabel Bassett, women remained confined to their cells or, if they were unlucky enough to be in a dormitory, on their beds. Each day, they could leave their beds for one fleeting hour. Only then could they stretch their legs or, if they were quick enough, take a short shower and possibly wash their underwear under the nozzle while others waited impatiently just past the green shower curtain.

To curb the pains flaring in her lower back and sciatic nerve from the constant immobility, Mary tried to exercise on her bed, lying flat on her back and bringing her knee to her chest. Sometimes she slid off the bed to the dirt-encrusted cement floor below and, on her pink yoga mat, stretched to relieve the pains. But that wasn't enough—she still felt cramps in her legs and feet. She tried her best to ignore the incessant noise from the women on neighboring beds. Many had their own televisions and, with nothing else to do, watched incessantly. Each one turned the volume higher and higher to compete with the sounds from the surrounding sets.

Mary breathed a sigh of relief when she was moved to a four-person cell in mid-April. Behind the closed steel door, she could stand up, practice yoga without fear of staff reprimanding her, and take several steps past her bunk before reaching the door or her cellmates' beds. She began sewing cloth masks for herself and her cellmates with colorfully patterned fabric left over from the prison's attempts to mass-produce masks.

That was the full range of her motion. For a month, instead of walking to the cafeteria and standing in line for their meals, women received trays wrapped in plastic. The lockdown meant that the women who usually worked in the kitchens remained in their cells while guards cooked the food, wrapped each tray in plastic, then placed it in laundry carts that they tugged over to each housing unit. Food in prison is typically subpar, and meals frequently are too meager to assuage an adult's hunger. With lockdown, the food became even worse. The only edible items were the chicken patties, sometimes arriving cold, and prepackaged cookies. Everything else was unpalatable. For once, however, food was abundant. Sometimes the guards offered women an extra tray of food because many refused to accept the unappetizing meals.

By May 5, when her door unexpectedly clicked open, everyone had endured these conditions for over a month.

That Tuesday evening, dozens of women streamed out of their cells. Some raced to take a hot shower. They formed a line of brown, gray, and white bathrobes slinging their mesh bags, filled with soap, shampoo, and other toiletries, over their shoulders as they waited for one of the unit's fifteen showers.

Others ran to the two microwaves in the dayroom, desperate for a hot edible meal. Soon the unit filled with the smells of meat mixed with onions and garlic as women concocted noodle burritos from the cheese and meat sticks bought at commissary, or the prison's sole store. Still others dragged blue plastic chairs from their cells to the eight phones lined along the dayroom wall, desperate to hear their loved ones' voices after a month of anxieties about the new and unknown virus.

Mary wasn't sure what to do first. She finally decided to join the line for the phones. She was eager to talk to her sons and find out how they were weathering the pandemic. Her sons, too, had worried about their sixty-seven-year-old mother over the past month, but family members are unable to call their imprisoned loved ones. Instead, they must wait for them to call.

After accepting the charges for her collect call, her son's first question was, "Mom, is it warm where you are?"

By the time her fifteen-minute call was cut off, Mary was relieved that her sons were still alive, healthy, and COVID-free. She lined up for the shower, though by the time she stepped beneath the stream, the water had turned cool. At least she was able to shower. Other women were still in line when their hour of relative freedom ended and officers ordered them back to their cells.

Outside, the temperature hovered in the mid-70s, a nearly 20-degree drop from the 93 degrees the previous day. But no one was allowed to venture into the yard to look up at the sky or feel the breeze rippling their hair. Nonetheless, after that long month cooped up in their cells, simply being in the dayroom, talking to family members, and seeing people other than their cellmates seemed like a tiny bit of freedom. "I felt like, I'm free, I'm free," Mary recalled. "It felt wonderful to be out of that cell."

The prison had escaped the early ravages of the pandemic. Mary—and many of the women around her—felt optimistic that the hour of freedom signaled that things were getting better and that soon, prison life would be back to normal.

They had no idea of what was to come.

⁂

From the start of the pandemic, public health and medical officials warned that incarcerated people were uniquely vulnerable to COVID and its most severe complications.

Many people enter prison with a raft of preexisting health conditions. Inside prison, they are unable to physically distance from each other. They cannot adhere to other prevention guidelines issued by the Centers for Disease Control and Prevention, such as frequent hand washing, using alcohol-based sanitizers, and wearing masks. Many prisons did not issue masks for weeks. Officers often threatened to punish those who improvised masks from other pieces of clothing.

Other countries ordered mass prison releases as a precautionary measure. Iran, for instance, ordered the temporary release of 85,000 people in mid-March 2020.[6] Turkey released more than 114,000 people (nearly 40 percent of its prison population), while the Philippines, India, Iraq, and Ethiopia also released tens of thousands of people. Several European nations also ordered mass prison releases.[7]

In the United States, public health professionals, alarmed family members, prisoner rights advocates, and prison abolitionists called repeatedly for similar wide-scale releases.

Public health professionals pointed out that, in confined and often overcrowded spaces, the coronavirus would proliferate, bringing mass sickness and avoidable deaths. Family members worried about their loved ones' chances for survival if, or more likely when, they caught the terrifying new virus.

Prisoner rights advocates pressured state and local governments to decarcerate, or drastically decrease, the numbers of people behind bars.

Decarceration has long been a demand of prison abolitionists working toward a world without prisons. Drawing from the abolitionist movement to end chattel slavery, which seemed like an impossible dream until it became a reality, prison abolitionists have long fought to end incarceration by organizing to both reduce the numbers of people criminalized and incarcerated, and release those who are currently behind bars.[8]

Years before the pandemic, abolitionist organizers had launched state and local campaigns to close jails and prisons and stop the construction of new facilities. But abolitionists weren't simply calling for the end of physical jails, prisons, and other sites of involuntary confinement. They demanded, instead, that state and local governments redirect current carceral funding into resources, such as affordable housing, health care, mental health care, education, and employment, that would prevent people from slipping through the holes in the social safety net.

Over years of organizing, some of these abolitionist campaigns succeeded, some partially succeeded, and some lost. Nonetheless, each time they organized, abolitionists challenged and changed the widely believed narratives about crime and punishment that had propped up decades of prison booms. Many groups also created resources that would address individual and community needs in their own neighborhoods and towns, often on shoestring budgets.

Prison abolitionist Mariame Kaba had long called prisons "death-making institutions." With a contagious new virus ripping its way through the United States, her characterization became a frighteningly accurate prophecy.[9]

Still, widespread fears of the new, highly contagious virus did not result in the same scale of decarceration as other countries. Only a handful of jurisdictions took steps to release people and, relative to the enormous numbers of people behind bars, released a relative few.

Instead, jails and prisons stopped all vocational and educational programs, barred outside volunteers, and prevented groups of people from gathering. They halted visits, cutting off many from their family, friends, and support systems. These measures seemed more like additional punishments than preventive measures, especially since staff continued many practices that required close physical contact—pat frisks, strip searches, cell shakedowns, and escorting people between units. Those doing the frisking, searching, and escorting were guards who came in and out of the prison daily. Each shift change brought a renewed possibility of a viral outbreak.

Experts' dire predictions quickly came true as several jails and prisons emerged as the nation's top hot spots.

By mid-June 2020, the *New York Times* reported that, even as cases were leveling off across the country, the number of COVID cases in prisons had doubled within the previous month to more than sixty-eight thousand people. Prison deaths connected to the coronavirus had also risen by 73 percent since mid-May. "By now, the five largest known clusters of the virus in the United States are not at nursing homes or meatpacking plants, but inside correctional institutions," the paper noted.[10]

Even in the handful of states and counties that reduced their prison populations, the releases were too few to successfully stem the spread once COVID made its way inside.

During the first year of the pandemic, I received hundreds of letters from people imprisoned across the nation about conditions caused by the coronavirus. Many expressed fear and uncertainty. In the early days, prison officials gave virtually no information about the virus, let alone prevention methods. When people began coughing or exhibiting COVID-like symptoms, they were often whisked away—to be mass quarantined in gyms or auditoriums among dozens of other sick people, or to be isolated in solitary confinement. Rarely was anyone offered medical treatment other than a perfunctory temperature check. Meanwhile, they were unable to call home to tell their loved ones what was happening—or to ensure that their loved ones were still alive. In some prisons, people who tested positive were not allowed to bring their belongings, consigning them to fourteen days of mind-numbing boredom locked in a small solitary cell or assigned to a bunk in a dormitory surrounded by dozens of other coughing and sneezing people.

Some were semi-quarantined, leaving their uninfected peers at risk. Sarah Pender was incarcerated at one of Indiana's three women's prisons. In that prison, up to fourteen women share a single cell, sleeping in bunk beds less than three feet apart. In early December 2020, Sarah and six of her roommates tested positive. They were quarantined in their cell for two weeks. So were the five roommates who had not tested positive.

But everyone, regardless of status, still had to leave their cells to use one of the unit's two bathrooms. Staff did not designate either bathroom as one specifically for those who had tested positive. Instead, the unit's 136 women shared both bathrooms. More people tested positive and, days before Christmas, 116 women were under quarantine and another four had been sent to the prison infirmary. The sixteen remaining women stayed in one room. None were tested.[11]

Both in Indiana and around the country, others hid their symptoms and shunned medical attention, hoping to avoid a similar fate. Predictably, their actions led to even wider spread. In prisons that conducted random testing, the results were astronomical: in some places, over half the population tested positive; in others, nearly three-quarters.

As I sheltered at home during those first few months, turning down stories that required travel or face-to-face contact, I could feel the dread, uncertainty, and desperation emanating from each letter that I unfolded. I at least could limit my contact with the outside world—venturing out twice a week for groceries and decreasing my daily forays to the post office, which had become a potential hotbed as lines of customers snaked down the block to mail supplies to faraway loved ones. Twice a week, I held my breath beneath my mask as I strode to the back of the post office and found my mailbox crammed with letters—some paper-thin, others bulging with multiple sheets documenting repeated attempts to seek help. The letters detailed the ways in which people behind bars were unable to take the basic precautions that had now become a routine part of my life. In prison, even receiving mail required close contact with a guard—and many described how the guards wore their masks improperly, if at all. Some of these letters dripping with desperation also included recollections of small acts of resistance, such as talking a cellmate out of a suicide attempt or sharing information about the virus and prevention methods. In prison, people are not allowed to share anything, not even a pen or a flyer. Sharing life-saving information became, in itself, an act of resistance.

Ten months after the pandemic first ravaged the country, the second wave came crashing down. COVID spread through prisons that had, until then, avoided the pandemic, as well as those that had previously been hit (and where administrators had done little to implement measures to prevent a second spread).

By June 2021, state and federal prisons had confirmed more than half a million COVID cases, a rate more than four times as high as among the general public. At least three in ten prisoners had had COVID-19, a figure that correctional health experts widely agree is an undercount.[12] State and federal prisons counted at least 2,715 deaths from COVID, a figure not including deaths in jails, immigration prisons, or juvenile detention.

Ninety of the hundred largest COVID-19 clusters in the United States occurred in its prisons and jails. And, unlike the inhabitants inside, the virus was not bound by walls and bars; each staff member's arrival and departure offered an opportunity to hitch a ride and replicate in a new population.

Six months later, in December 2021, despite rising numbers of vaccinations, another variant hit the United States—and surged. Omicron unleashed a new round of outbreaks throughout the country—and those behind bars were, once again, hard hit. Prisons placed housing units on extended lockdowns with little to no explanation, leaving trails of panic and confusion. Many prison systems canceled in-person visits, which, over a year later, had slowly been resuming. In some states, confusion about vaccination status and testing results caused officers to turn heartbroken children away from visiting rooms. And more people died. By then, however, some prisons had stopped reporting, and sometimes even tracking, confirmed cases and deaths.

By the time that the even more contagious BA.5 variant ripped across the country in summer 2022, the US public had entered a phase described by one incarcerated woman as a "pandemic hangover."[13]

Many people, including those behind bars who had borne the brunt of both the coronavirus and the prison system's punitive approach to the pandemic, had also tired of hearing about or taking precautions to prevent COVID—and many prison systems were all too happy to oblige. By that summer, seventeen state prison systems had stopped reporting active COVID cases. Ten had stopped reporting any COVID-related data at all. While other prison systems continued to report active cases, some did not disclose testing numbers, making it impossible to ascertain whether low numbers reflected low transmission rates or fewer tests.[14]

"Historically, pandemics have forced humans to break with the past and imagine their world anew," author Arundhati Roy wrote in April 2020. "This one is no different. It is a portal, a gateway between one world and the next."[15]

The COVID-19 pandemic laid bare the many failures that could have prevented the mass spread within the nation's jails, prisons, and other carceral institutions which, in turn, fueled outbreaks outside. These were failures caused not only by prison administration and architectural design, but also by long-standing political decisions that could have mitigated the extent of the pandemic—including a refusal to revisit draconian sentencing guidelines keeping people imprisoned for multiple decades; governors who granted a limited number of commutations or sentence reductions; and parole boards that continually denied release to those who had served decades behind bars and posed no risks to public safety. It was a crisis that could have been averted on so many levels—yet again and again, local, state, and federal officials failed to do so.

It was also a lost opportunity to walk through that portal and broadly rethink the nation's addiction to punishment and imprisonment, and reimagine a world that prioritized creating life-affirming resources and support systems.

Each letter was another reminder of this lost opportunity. These crises were allowed to occur because the larger public had remained unaware and largely indifferent about not only what happens inside prisons, but also the many factors that have built the United States into the world's largest jailer. Years and decades of large-scale neglect over these hidden conditions—and willful ignorance about what tough-on-crime policies meant for the millions funneled into the criminal justice system each year—had led to overcrowded, squalid, and life-threatening conditions that quickly became petri dishes for COVID.

For months, the crisis behind bars sparked greater public attention, outrage, and organizing to challenge and change conditions that are too frequently ignored. Now, public attention has again shifted away from prisons, enabling them to resume routine (and even extraordinary) indignities and injustices. The pandemic also allowed jails and prisons to implement more severe restrictions, some of which have become permanent regulations rather than temporary precautions.

As COVID-19 continues to spread and claim lives, even if it is no longer considered a national emergency, the stories of those abandoned as the deadly new virus ripped its way behind bars are more urgent than ever.

Eric Reinhart, a resident physician at Northwestern University's Department of Psychiatry and political anthropologist of public health, has dubbed prisons (and other carceral facilities such as jails, immigrant detention centers, and psychiatric hospitals) "epidemic engines that multiply and spread sickness and death throughout broader communities."[16]

His words are not hyperbole. Studies have shown that prisons alone have contributed to more than half a million additional COVID cases throughout the United States.[17]

But stories from behind the walls continue to remain largely hidden from public view. Writers reporting on what happens inside prisons come across numerous obstacles. Prisons themselves exemplify contradictions in record keeping and historical memory. On the one hand, prisons document and number everything—from the people held within to the number of towels or sack lunches provided. There are numerous documents that trace each person's journey from the streets into prison—arrest records, mug shots, court documents, and prison intake forms. Records may include physical identifiers such as height, hair and eye color, and the location of tattoos. At the same time, incarcerated people are under-documented and under-recorded in many other ways, from their relationships with their families to their multiple roles within their home communities, from their musical proclivities to their love of elaborate meals.

During the first months of the pandemic, I was in emergency reporting mode—investigating and cranking out story after story about conditions in various jails and prisons.[18] There was no time to pause and reflect on the larger picture of a nation where, of the approximately 1.3 million people in state and federal prisons, nearly half a million—or 38 percent—had contracted COVID in 2020 alone.[19] It was not until nine months into the pandemic—as COVID became the new normal and urgency faded into outraged resignation and hopelessness for many behind bars—that I realized that these experiences needed to be documented not as individual instances that happened in discrete locales and jurisdictions, but as a larger, enduring narrative that exposed the systemic failings that led to this deadly crisis behind bars. News articles had sufficed for galvanizing immediate public outrage to this disaster, but what happens two years from now? Or five?

Without a more permanent record, would the general public, once masks and social distancing were discarded, forget about the long genealogy of policies, laws, and conditions that exacerbated the pandemic—and, if left unchanged and unaddressed, would again prove fatally inadequate when the next crisis hit? Or would the public be more likely to support reducing the numbers of people inside jails and prisons, closing places that had quite literally become "death-making institutions," and redirecting the money saved into resources that provided for people's needs? Would they connect the lack of quality health care, food, and financial resources, all of which became even scarcer during that terrifying first pandemic year, with the vast sums of public money gobbled up by our ongoing reliance on incarceration?

Would they be less likely to shy away from the idea of abolition?

I brought the question up to several of the people who had written me numerous letters describing their experiences—including their uncertainties and fears—throughout that first year. All thought that this was a crisis that should not be forgotten—though, as people serving lengthy and life sentences, they were long accustomed to being erased.

More than three years after the novel coronavirus was first detected in the United States, books and other documentary efforts are emerging to document that terrifying first year. But these efforts often don't reach into jails, prisons, immigrant detention centers, and other spaces of confinement, all of which are designed to deliberately obstruct information flow. Julie Golia, the curator of the New York Public Library's "Pandemic Diaries," which collected oral histories of New Yorkers living through the first year of the pandemic, acknowledged that the collection, which spanned nearly three hundred stories, excluded some of the most vulnerable New Yorkers, such as homeless people. "There are so many silences," she reflected.[20]

Those silences also extend to those behind bars, who are often forgotten. As Mariame Kaba has pointed out, prisons don't simply destroy lives. They also destroy records of lives, particularly records of subversion.[21] As abolitionist and historian Angela Y. Davis has repeatedly noted, incarceration serves to disappear social problems from public view. In doing so, incarceration exacerbates, rather than solves, them.[22] This has been true time and again throughout the US history of incarceration—and was proven time and time again during the pandemic.

This book follows the experiences of five people incarcerated during the three years that the United States and the World Health Organization recognized as the COVID-19 emergency. Their experiences illustrate many of the ways in which the pandemic magnified existing outrages and abuses behind bars.

Behind bars, where uncertainty, violence, and chaos are the norm, not many wanted to continually revisit that terrifying and traumatizing first year. Jack, Kwaneta, Malakki, Mary, and Mwalimu all agreed that they could commit to a prolonged correspondence about that first frightening year and the gradual return to the dehumanizing reality that passes for normalcy behind bars. For nearly three years, we wrote letters (and later electronic messages). I accepted phone calls, sometimes scribbling their updates on random scraps of paper or even cardboard torn from curbside recycling. Mwalimu and I attempted to speak via video visit, although after depositing twenty-seven dollars to cover the cost, I could never get the technology to work on my laptop. Malakki and I video-visited once a month. Jack, Kwaneta, and Mary did not have access to video visits.

Although I exchanged letters with several incarcerated trans women before and during the pandemic, our correspondence was more sporadic, and none were able to commit to answering my ongoing barrage of questions in a timely manner. I included three stories specific to the dangers that trans women face, both during the pandemic and behind bars in general: Angel Unique, who faces the continual threat of sexual and physical assault from both staff and incarcerated men; Nancy, who was unable to escape her cellmates' repeated sexual and physical assaults during lockdown; and Heather, who died after prison medical staff failed to take her complaints seriously for a month.

When thinking about my role as the outside writer listening to these painful and harrowing experiences, then transcribing and collating them into a cohesive narrative, I am reminded of the caveat that immigrant justice activist Alejandra Oliva wrote at the start of her memoir about translating for asylum seekers: "While I believe my proximity to the people who are the subject of this book doesn't authorize me to speak over them, I also believe that proximity has enabled me to listen more closely."[23]

This book is the product of years of listening more closely—not just to the five who generously offered their time, experiences, and analyses, but also the hundreds of others who reached out to me about the indignities and abuses they experienced during the pandemic and for many years before.

As much as possible, I sought to highlight the ways in which people behind bars took care of one another, even when physically coming together was impossible. They challenged life-threatening practices and conditions, even when doing so increased their own risks. In a system that demands total subservience, these are not only acts of subversion, but also deeds that embody a central abolitionist principle: "We keep us safe."

The pandemic health emergency has been declared over, with COVID now considered a permanent part of our landscape of diseases. It is easy to forget the mass terror and suffering of those early days, particularly among populations hidden from society. By working to make sure this chapter of the pandemic is not erased, I hope to honor the lives of those millions who lived with and died from COVID behind bars—and to provoke the conversations and changes urgently needed to ensure that a crisis of this magnitude never occurs behind bars again.

# Chapter 1

# The Pandemic Begins

I f she didn't have a radio, Kwaneta Harris would not have known anything was amiss, let alone that a highly contagious virus was heading her way.

The forty-eight-year-old had spent the last four years in solitary confinement at the Lane Murray Unit, one of Texas's ninety-seven prisons. In prison, she has no access to the internet.

In solitary, she does not even have access to a television. Her sole source of news comes from the clear, plastic radio that she bought from commissary for twenty dollars.

Every day, Kwaneta listens to *National Public Radio*, not only to keep up with current world events, but also to block out the constant screaming of women in the other cells. Shortly after the first case was identified in the United States in January, Kwaneta heard about the novel coronavirus.

"Don't worry," staff told her, comparing the new virus to the flu. But Kwaneta, a former nurse, had never known any flu to cause this much uncertainty and chaos.

"Was this the start of a pandemic?" she wondered. "How soon would it come to Texas and then into the prison? Maybe officers, many of whom were constantly coughing and sneezing, had already walked the virus into the prison."

But the new virus was secondary to her years-long legal fight. Four years earlier, Kwaneta had been accused of forging a judge's signature on paperwork shortening her fifty-year prison sentence. To this day, she vehemently denies that charge, maintaining that another woman, who had ties to the Aryan Brotherhood, forged her signature to have Kwaneta, who is Black, punished with solitary.

Kwaneta was determined not to plead guilty. She intended to go to trial—confident that the evidence would clear her of the fraudulent charge. Meanwhile, she sat in "administrative segregation," the prison's euphemism for solitary confinement, and waited for her day in court.

She hoped that once a jury acquitted her, she would be transferred to either a less restrictive unit or general population, where she could call her family, be out of her cell for several hours each day, and return to running regularly in the prison yard. But despite the Sixth Amendment right to a speedy trial, the wheels of justice grind slowly. By 2020, she had been waiting four years.

On March 4, officers woke Kwaneta before sunrise. The laundry officer handed her a two-piece white prison uniform. After she changed, officers cuffed her hands and ankles, attaching both sets of cuffs to a chain looped around her waist, before opening her cell door and walking her to a minivan.

Inside, Kwaneta sat on a metal bench too narrow for her body for the fifteen-minute drive to the courthouse. There, she met her newly appointed attorney.

"She can barely talk—her voice is raw," Kwaneta told me the following week in a handwritten letter. "She's snifflin' like crazy. She says she has 'allergies.' With this virus stuff I'm not comfortable with her sitting beside me—talking low—sitting too close."

But she had no choice but to sit close if she wanted to hear her attorney. Meanwhile, a procession of Black men from neighboring prisons appeared before the judge about additional criminal charges they had incurred while incarcerated. Some seemed nearly catatonic, drooling and staring into space as a result of their medications. All pled guilty. "It's like cattle call—meet 'em and plead 'em," Kwaneta described.

Normally, she focused on the grim spectacle from the jury box where she, as the sole incarcerated woman, waited for her docket number to be called. That day, however, as her attorney continually cleared her throat, Kwaneta paid less attention to the proceedings in front of her or to her attorney's words than to the nagging question, Does she have COVID?

The news on the radio instructed listeners to wash their hands frequently with soap and water, and to wash for a duration of at least twenty seconds, or the time it took to sing the "Happy Birthday" song. But being imprisoned made it difficult, and sometimes impossible, to follow even this basic precaution. In mid-March, the unit's hot water was out for over a week, so Kwaneta and the forty others on that unit could only rinse their hands in cold water. A small handful could afford to pay twenty cents for motel-sized bars of soap. Others had to stretch the domino-sized bars supplied by the prison.

The Lane Murray Unit is one of eight prisons in Coryell County, located in Central Texas a hundred miles from both Austin and Dallas. The county reported no COVID cases until March 24. That number soon skyrocketed—from one case on April 1 to 153 by May 1. Statewide, Texas went from eleven new cases on March 1 to 523 by month's end, prompting Governor Greg Abbott to issue an executive order instructing Texans to stay at home unless they were essential workers or performing essential tasks, such as grocery shopping or seeing a doctor. Jail and prison staff, in Texas and across the country, were considered essential workers and, day after day, were required to go to work.

Officials don't like to use the term *solitary confinement*, which conjures images of a dank, dark dungeon and has become synonymous with deprivation and torture. Instead, they use less charged wording, such as *administrative segregation, punitive segregation,* or *restrictive housing*. Regardless of the name, it's a practice in which a person spends at least twenty-three hours each day locked into their cell.

At Murray, an "ad seg" cell is nine by twelve feet. Kwaneta had been locked in cells that size since January 2016.

One might assume that being locked away from nearly all face-to-face contact would be enough to prevent COVID exposure. After all, millions of people around the world were sheltering at home in the hopes of doing just that. In prison, however, solitary does not remove a person from communicable illness. Prison practices still require close contact and, ironically, segregation requires even more contact during the scant time a person leaves their cell. If she wants to shower, or spend an hour outside in a recreation cage, Kwaneta must be handcuffed and escorted by two officers. Although the CDC and public health officials had repeatedly recommended that people stay at least six feet apart, what is called "socially distancing," the officers were mere inches from her. Often, one of the officers gripped her cuffed hands with one hand and her shoulder with the other, bringing him even closer.

Even staying in her cell doesn't guarantee that she can avoid others' respiratory droplets. Vents connect her cell to the adjoining ones. "I can smell my neighbor passing gas next door," Kwaneta described. "I could smell her morning breath when she called [to] me before brushing her teeth."

Officers deliver meals and mail through the slot in her cell door. And, every three days, staff conduct cell searches to ensure that Kwaneta isn't hiding contraband in her cell. The term *contraband* encompasses not only drugs and weapons, but also any prohibited items, which in her case included a jump rope fashioned from the cord of broken headphones and a shoelace stretched into a makeshift clothesline.

Before each cell search, officers strip-search Kwaneta, a humiliation that requires her to stand within inches of the inspecting officer. They then handcuff and push her out of her cell. An officer grips each arm to ensure that, despite the handcuffs, she will not fight back or attempt to flee toward the locked door at the end of the corridor. While the inspection squad flushes her toilet, turns on the faucets, hits the walls with a black rubber mallet, and rifles through every photo, letter, book, and piece of clothing, the two officers continue to grip her arms.

"They're coughing and sneezing," Kwaneta wrote when she recounted the cell inspections of early 2020. "Sneeze in your elbow! Use that Purell before you touch me!" she fussed at them. Their response was to ask if *she* had the coronavirus.

In segregation, Kwaneta is locked behind a solid metal door that has a vertical opening covered by mesh to allow for communication—a brief consultation with mental health staff, an order from a guard, or a prayer with the volunteer church group that had proselytized on weekends before the pandemic canceled all outside visitors. That long strip of mesh was also porous enough to allow the breath of anyone passing by—officers or another person on their way to the shower or rec cage—to waft into her cell.

"We have no human contact besides guards," Kwaneta pointed out. She knew that, if and when the coronavirus entered the prison, it would walk in with a staff member. From there, Kwaneta knew it would be a matter of weeks, or more likely days, before it proliferated. She also knew, from past experiences, that if she contracted this terrifying new disease, prison medical staff would be unlikely to diagnose it, let alone offer treatment. They might even refuse to examine her. "Most medical complaints are always answered with, 'All those drugs and drinking. You should have taken better care of your body.' When I told them I didn't drink or do drugs, they smile at me. They don't believe us," she wrote.

And that's when medical complaints are answered at all. The first time she got sick in prison was in 2013, when she had been working in Texas's punishing prison fields, where, under the blistering sun, incarcerated people plant, weed, pick produce, and sort cotton. Armed guards keep watch from horseback.[1] Kwaneta calls it "an exercise in time-travel trauma."[2]

During those cold, rainy months in 2013, she wasn't the only one coughing and sneezing. Still, staff demanded that the women continue planting sweet potato slips, digging trenches, and pulling waist-high weeds to clear fields.

One night, after another day of backbreaking work in rain that soaked through her uniform, every part of her body ached. Her cellmate filled plastic water bottles with hot water and placed them around her. She piled every piece of clothing that both women owned on top of Kwaneta. Still, she couldn't stop shivering.

The next morning, Kwaneta couldn't get out of bed or even turn her head. When her roommate used their shared toilet, Kwaneta tried to lift her head to look the other way, allowing her the pretense of privacy, but even that effort was too much. That morning, she did not go to work.

"I don't give a fuck if you got Ebola," the prison's squad boss told her before issuing a disciplinary ticket for refusing to work. It was a charge that could have resulted in her losing the ability to call her family, go to outside for recreation, or shop at commissary to supplement the insufficient and unappetizing meals. If she continued to refuse, staff could punish her with solitary and, years later, the parole board could hold that refusal against her when deciding whether to grant her release.[3]

By the time she returned to the fields, the squad boss had withdrawn his ticket. Instead, he appointed Kwaneta as the striker—or the person charged with keeping the others on track to meet the daily quota. Kwaneta had always avoided the role, knowing that she would spend the day berating and yelling at women to speed up. If they didn't, she was responsible for making up the shortfalls, a responsibility that left her aching even more at the end of each day.

That wasn't all. The Texas prison system charged a fee of $100 to anyone seeking medical care. The cost is a disincentive for most, but Kwaneta was fortunate to have family support and could pay that fee—only to be told that medical staff couldn't see her for another week or two. The other women came to her cell, bearing tea and chicken broth and, because incarcerated people are not allowed to be in others' cells, risking their own disciplinary tickets.

Kwaneta recovered after a week and canceled the medical appointment. The prison still deducted that $100 from her account. It took her several months, many complaints to the medical records staff, and an outburst by another woman who loudly accused medical staff of "stealing everybody's money" before the funds were credited back to her account.

Those experiences left Kwaneta terrified of what could happen if she contracted the virus. She had already survived overt racism throughout her childhood, a kidnapping and sexual assault before puberty, stray bullets and drive-by shootings, a gunshot wound, carjackings, home invasion, multiple pistol-whippings, appendicitis, high-risk pregnancies, childbirth complications, and countless instances of intimate partner violence. "I thought I had survived against the odds with those near-death experiences," she said. But she wasn't sure if she would survive this new potentially lethal illness. "My nine lives were used decades ago."

※

As COVID-19 barreled across the United States, it became an increasingly polarized political issue. In prison, that polarization played out in the ways that staff treated preventive measures. Many officers at Lane Murray were fervent supporters of President Donald Trump. Many refused to adhere to the recommendations by the Centers for Disease Control and Prevention (CDC), such as wearing masks and frequent hand washing. Some believed that the coronavirus was a Democratic hoax. Others stated that the virus was God's punishment of sinners. A handful told the women that masks caused COVID.

But each day, Kwaneta read about the rising numbers of positive cases and statewide deaths in USA Today. She knew that this new virus could be deadly—and these precautions could save her life.

Kwaneta's access to information, particularly in segregation with no televisions and little access to other media, was exceptional.

Many of the women (and trans men) around her—and in prison generally—have no money from either prison jobs or family support. They cannot purchase a prison-approved radio, let alone subscribe to newspapers or magazines. Instead, their sole sources of information are prison staff and other incarcerated people, with nothing to counter any distortions or outright lies.

The advice from government officials, which contradicted effective health care practices, reinforced the prisons' unwillingness to take preventive measures. In late February, in an attempt to preserve the supply of surgical masks for health care providers, the US surgeon general urged the public not to buy masks, stating that they were ineffective at preventing COVID spread. The CDC followed suit and, even as COVID spread across the country, continued to proclaim that healthy people who do not work in medical settings need not mask.[4]

At Lane Murray, the few officers who wore masks to work were sent home by their supervisor. In early April, after the CDC changed its stance and urged the general public to wear masks, Texas prisons required that all staff wear masks.[5] Many did so reluctantly and incorrectly—on their chins or foreheads or dangling off one ear.

Throughout March and well into April, officers laughed when Kwaneta tied a bandanna around her mouth and nose during each cell inspection. She ignored their derision.

Then she noticed that the officer tasked with collecting and returning the beige-colored linens from the laundry to segregation was continually coughing. "You got TB?" Kwaneta asked, half-joking and more than half-scared.

That was when Kwaneta decided to stop leaving her cell to shower, avoiding the required strip search and escort down the hall. Instead, she gave herself bird baths in her cell sink.

When officers delivered her mail, she asked them to throw it into her cell rather than hand it to her, but she could not do the same for the meals served on plastic trays. From past years toiling in a prison kitchen, Kwaneta knew that the trays were never properly cleaned. Unsure whether COVID might live on the tray's hard plastic surface, Kwaneta stopped eating the prison-issued meals, relying instead on ramen and oatmeal bought from commissary.

She used her postage stamps to buy cleaning supplies from the incarcerated people working as janitors, risking a ticket if she was caught with these contraband items. Her walking became limited to three steps from her bed to the steel door and another three steps back to the bed. She would ultimately spend nearly four months without feeling sunlight on her face.

She covered the vents that connected her cell and the adjoining ones with cardboard and, later, with menstrual pads and plastic. The few times she had to interact with staff—when they delivered meals, laundry, or medications—she wore a handkerchief over her face. She even covered the mesh window on her door—another rule violation that could cost her the one hour of outdoor recreation, ability to shop at commissary, or five-minute phone call allotted every three months—until staff told her to remove it.

In prison, Kwaneta must follow orders or risk further punishment. She couldn't refuse to uncover her window or refuse cell inspections, even with the knowledge that each of the two unmasked guards gripping her arm increased her risk of COVID.

I asked what the penalty would be for refusing a cell search.

"If I refuse a cell inspection?" she asked, incredulously. "They will gas my ass."

Those five words illuminate another reality in jails and prisons across the nation—the routine use of pepper spray against incarcerated people. Guards use it to break up fights, subdue a person, or punish them for having a "smart-ass mouth." They also use it when a person refuses to obey one of their orders and even when a person is engaging in self-harm or attempting suicide.[6]

Kwaneta has witnessed guards use gas when they see a person harming themselves—cutting their skin or even attempting to hang themselves. Several times, she has breathed in the aftermath of this response. Some months might go by with no gassing incidents, while others might have as many as six. "On average, we have two gassings a month," she told me. In January 2020, guards gassed women twice. Once was after a woman told them she was feeling suicidal. In April, Kwaneta recalled four gassings. In three of those instances, the woman was self-harming—banging her head against a steel table or cutting herself.

Guards keep the gas canisters, alongside handcuffs, on their belts, which Kwaneta likens to Batman's utility belt. "When someone is threatening to gas us, they unbutton the holder," she described. What comes next perpetually reminds her of the Westerns she watched as a child, but instead of a gun, the guard withdraws the canister.

"That's our clue to take cover," she told me. Taking cover means covering the cell door window with whatever fabric is closest—a towel, a sheet, or clothing. Kwaneta turns her two electric fans on high, pointing one toward the door to blow back any gas that seeps through her makeshift barrier, and the other toward the window to blow out any gas that leaks through the mesh, under or through the sides of the door, or through the vents. She then wets a towel to swaddle around her nose and mouth, tucks her sheets and blankets securely into her mattress, then tucks her face under them.

As guards continued to gas women for minor acts of disobedience or self-harm, Kwaneta worried about not only the noxious chemicals that burned her eyes and throat, but also the danger of inhaling the respiratory droplets from those choking in the adjoining cells.

❋

In early April, the coughing laundry officer tested positive for COVID. The prison instituted a fourteen-day medical lockdown. The mess hall closed as both kitchen workers and the women tasked with delivering food to segregation were locked in their cells.

Prison food is always terrible—and in Texas, officials had already chopped $2.8 million from its food budget by replacing liquid milk with a powdered version, substituting white bread for hot dog and hamburger buns, and feeding people twice instead of three times a day on weekends.[7]

During lockdown, it became even worse. Instead of hot meals of dubious quality on trays, guards delivered "johnnies," or brown paper bags containing cold sandwiches of even more questionable quality and often smaller quantity. The area outside Lane Murray's segregation building teems with feral cats, whom the women sometimes feed from their trays. That spring, the food was so dry and brittle that even the cats refused it.

Mealtimes—always strict behind bars—fluctuated, depending on the number of guards available to deliver the bags. The commissary also closed, leaving Kwaneta unable to stave off hunger with overpriced snacks. One day, she thought she heard thunder and craned her head to look out the window. The noise was her stomach. After a few days, the rumbling stopped. "I guess it got tired of groaning and decided to conserve its energy," she mused.

Adding to the gnawing pangs were the continual water shutoffs. She could not wash her hands or even flush her toilet. Prison toilets lack lids (with the justification that they might be ripped off and used as a weapon), so Kwaneta would fold a blanket or towel into a makeshift lid to mask the smell of accumulated feces, urine, and menstrual blood.

Still, lockdown didn't prevent women from other units from entering and leaving segregation on a regular basis. All prisons employ incarcerated people in various jobs that keep the institutions running. One of these jobs is maintenance—or cleaning the unit's common areas. Although the laundry officer—and her subordinates—stopped working during that first medical lockdown, incarcerated janitors still came to segregation to scrub the showers, sweep and mop the hallway, and pass out toilet paper, feminine hygiene items, and occasionally meal trays. They were issued gloves, masks, and gowns, but even by early April, Texas temperatures frequently soar above 90 degrees, making the additional layers feel like punishment rather than protection. One woman, nicknamed "N.O." because she had lived in New Orleans, continually complained about wearing "all this hot shit" as she swabbed her way down the corridor.

The prison provided no cleaning supplies for individual cells. A handful of guards brought their own supplies from home and, contravening prison rules, shared them with the incarcerated women. But, Kwaneta hastened to add, they weren't motivated by altruism or sympathy. They were afraid that the incarcerated women would somehow give them the virus.

Still, neither the lockdown nor these few guards' efforts kept the virus out. By mid-April, 35 of the prison's 341 employees and 49 of the 1,341 incarcerated people had tested positive.[8]

That was when Jack, a fifty-three-year-old Black trans man in the cell directly below Kwaneta's, reached out to me. Covering three pages in pencil, he described ambulances arriving with EMTs clad in full hazmat suits. Guards told them that they were responding to a suicide attempt. They did not explain why the first responders wore full protective equipment.

Jack saw officers come to work with masks. Even then, he recounted, "no one even told us there was a global-wide pandemic and that people on our unit had tested positive." He, too, relied on *National Public Radio* to stay informed. Otherwise, he would have remained clueless.

From the window of her cell, Kwaneta could also see ambulances pulling into the prison. She watched each time emergency medical technicians arrived, entered one of the buildings, and left with a woman on a stretcher.

In April, she noticed the EMTs emerging in full personal protective equipment (PPE). Kwaneta had worked as a nurse in Detroit before her imprisonment, but this was the first time she had personally seen a medical professional wearing PPE.

Although she had been following the virus's trajectory through the news, seeing the emergency technicians in full protective gear drove the danger—and terror—home.

From the cell below, Jack sought reassurance, shouting through the vent connecting their toilets. "Tell me I shouldn't be scared," he pleaded. Kwaneta could not offer false security. "I'm scared," she responded.

The ambulance visits heightened everyone's fears. The deafening noise of the unit dwindled into an eerie silence, as if everyone were holding their breath. Even the women who constantly argued with the voices in their heads quieted. "What do they do with our dead?" the younger women asked. "What if we don't have family to bury us?"

Shortly before the pandemic began, staff had issued a small strip of cloth to each person in solitary. The cloth was intended as a cooling towel—to be soaked in the lukewarm water drizzling from the cell sink, then laid across a person's forehead. Jack and others began tying them around their mouths and nose. On several occasions, guards ordered them to remove their makeshift masks, telling them that their faces could not be covered for security reasons ("always their go-to answer," noted Jack). Many ignored their orders. "We had already been told that the laundry officer had come up positive for COVID and had most likely infected the entire laundry department [staffed by imprisoned workers]," Jack recalled. "No way were we taking any chances. I was willing to get that disciplinary case if it meant I was protected."

Although he was already in segregation, a disciplinary case might cost Jack his one hour out of cell for recreation or access to commissary, barring his ability to buy stamps, writing supplies, bottled water, or food.[9]

But guards were more likely to informally punish the infraction, clarified Jack. Rather than filling out the paperwork and scheduling the required hearing, they would withhold food, drinking water, or mail, prohibit a person from leaving their cell for their one hour of recreation, refuse to bring them to the shower, or falsely tell medical staff that the incarcerated person had refused their appointment.

"They keep telling us we are on fourteen-day medical lockdown but every few days someone new either gets tested or comes up positive and we start our fourteen days over," Jack wrote in mid-April. "It's been twenty-one days so far. Officers are testing positive, causing their whole shift to be quarantined so there is a shortage of staff right now." More than two years later, many of the limitations first imposed by the pandemic had become routine as the shortages continued.

Even so, medical lockdown did not stop cell inspections and the accompanying strip searches. Jack was subject to six different inspections in April and another seven in May.

※

Kwaneta and I had already been corresponding for nearly a year by the time she first heard the term *novel coronavirus*. But during the first year of the pandemic, dozens of people in other prisons reached out. Every other day, I found envelopes crammed into my small post office box. Nearly all were from people imprisoned across the United States.

While Kwaneta's envelope bore no markings or indicators that they originated from a prison, Mary's envelopes always came stamped with a warning, in faded red ink, alerting me that my correspondent was "an inmate under the custody of the Oklahoma Department of Corrections." I had been corresponding with Mary for years before the pandemic. Unlike Kwaneta, who had never before been arrested before her current incarceration, Mary had spent the majority of her adult life in and out of Oklahoma's prison system. Nearly all her convictions were for crimes that she had committed while drunk or high. By the time COVID-19 came to the United States, the sixty-seven-year-old Creek grandmother had spent her past seventeen birthdays in prison, most of them at the Mabel Bassett Correctional Center, the state's perpetually overcrowded maximum-security women's prison. Like Kwaneta, she was desperate to get out—an urgency heightened by the new highly contagious virus.

In March 2020, prison officials began making preparations for the coronavirus. Mabel Bassett contains the reception area where newly sentenced women are sent before being assigned to a more permanent location. County jails continued to send women; each new arrival was another potential transmission. Staff moved 106 women out of one housing unit, or pod, to quarantine the new arrivals from counties that were hard hit by COVID.

Mary spent the first few weeks of pandemic lockdown sitting on her bed in a loud dormitory with dozens of other agitated and bored women. Then she was moved to a four-person cell.

Among her three new cellmates was Archie, the grandchild of a woman with whom Mary had been incarcerated during the 1980s. Archie, a twenty-eight-year-old trans man, had scraped putty from the cell window to affix a picture of his grandmother to the wall beside his bed. At first, Mary didn't recognize the gray-haired woman as her quiet coworker from the prison kitchen forty years earlier. One evening, Archie mentioned his grandmother's name and that she had been locked up at an older prison, which had since been shuttered. Only then did Mary recognize her as the woman with whom she spent countless hours scraping mold off butter and sterilizing the kitchen. The woman had been released decades earlier—and had never returned. Meeting the boy caused Mary to rue the years she had cycled in and out of jails and prisons, missing milestones in the lives of her sons and grandchildren.

Women (and trans men) at Mabel Bassett in April 2020 were allowed one hour out of their cells in groups of eight. During that hour, they could socialize in the dayroom, take a shower, or use one of ten phones to call home and check on their families. They had to mask for that hour.

Not everyone was happy with the new restrictions. Archie initially vowed to stay in his cell until the mask requirement ended. He occasionally sneaked out, jamming the door's locking mechanism with putty. Then, when the guards were off the floor, he swiped his ID card to unlatch the door and sneak out to shower.

A woman in an adjoining cell used the same trick, but instead of surreptitiously slipping out, she appeared in view of the guards. She was punished with thirty days of solitary.

Afraid that her impetuous cellmate would be sent to lock (the women's term for solitary confinement) as well, Mary sewed him a mask. She spent over six hours on that first mask, one of an eventual eighty-five she created that year. Although the horses in the pattern's fabric ended up upside-down, Archie was pleased with her efforts, especially given Mary's connection to his beloved grandmother. He stopped sneaking out and proudly wore the mask during the approved hour out of cell. "That made me feel a little joy, just knowing that I was appreciated for my ability to sew something that was of value during a scary time," Mary recalled.

By April, Pottawatomie County, where the Mabel Bassett Correctional Center is located, had already had two confirmed COVID cases and one death among its 72,500 residents.[10] The entire state of Oklahoma had 1,327 confirmed cases and fifty-one deaths.[11]

Every day, Mary watched the news on the television that she had bought from commissary. Each day, she noted the rising death toll. She feared for her sons and grandchildren. "Wear your mask," Mary reminded them during her infrequent calls. She mailed them her hand-sewn masks. When the prison began distributing surgical masks on a weekly basis, she mailed some to her sons, hoping, she told me, "they would take this deadly plague more seriously."

Still they refused. "Ah Mom, the news is hyping it up more than what is really out here!" her oldest son told her. (Later, he contracted COVID and lost twenty pounds.)

The youngest even reprimanded her. "Don't put your COVID religion on me!"

☀

Across the country, as health officials urged the public to keep at least six feet apart and cities instituted shutdowns of nonessential businesses and issued orders to shelter in place, forty-seven state prison systems, the federal prison system, and immigrant prisons canceled in-person visits.

Without visits, many families relied on phone calls. Calls are often a lifeline for those in prison, but they frequently come at a high price. In New York, for instance, prison calls cost forty-three cents per minute. In Georgia, a fifteen-minute call ranges from $1.95 to $2.40. Calls from prison are typically limited to fifteen or twenty minutes, terminating abruptly with an automated "Goodbye."

In prison, incarcerated people can call their loved ones, but their loved ones cannot call them. Instead, they must wait and hope that a silent phone does not indicate a disaster.

Cell phones are prohibited in prison. Staff sometimes smuggle them in to sell at exorbitant prices, but most incarcerated people rely on the handful of phones lining the wall of the dayroom. Private corporations contract with prison systems to provide telecommunications services. The corporation sets the cost of calls and video visits. These costs frequently include commissions to the prison, commonly referred to as kickbacks, which can comprise up to 60 percent of each call's cost. The Federal Communications Commission attempted to regulate the cost of prison calls, capping them at twenty-one cents per minute for interstate calls. But the agency's efforts to cap in-state calls, which make up the majority of prison calls, was struck down by a federal court in 2017, leaving many families to choose between paying bills or paying to hear their imprisoned loved ones' voices.[12]

The number of phones varies in each unit, but even before the pandemic, demand was typically high. Some prisons allow people to sign up in advance for a specific block of time. Others have no

such process, requiring people to stand in line. Arguments can—
and frequently do—erupt and some turn physical. In early 2020,
another woman attempted to grab the phone that Mary had patiently been waiting to use. Mary hit the woman in the head with
the receiver and spent thirty days in lock. She was released only to
be locked down again a few weeks later when the pandemic hit the
United States.

Shortly after visits were canceled, some prisons and phone
corporations offered a limited number of free calls—and occasionally a free video visit. Even then, not everyone had access to the
phones. Those in Texas's solitary units, for instance, were rarely allowed access. Kwaneta and Jack could make one five-minute call
to an immediate family member every three months. During those
terrifying early days, they waited for letters from home assuring
them that their loved ones were surviving the pandemic—or, in
some tragic instances, informing them that a beloved relative had
died from COVID.

In nearly half the country, prison telecommunications companies
also provide e-messaging, a crude form of email that allows incarcerated people to correspond with outside family members and friends
but not to access the wider internet. Like phone and video calls,
e-messages aren't free. They typically cost between twenty-five and
nearly fifty cents for one page of approximately five hundred words.

At the start of the pandemic, some companies offered a limited number of free e-messages to people inside. Their outside loved
ones, however, still had to pay the same fees for the responses they
typed. Each company had its own interface and log-in, which, for
me, meant keeping track of and checking three to four different
sites for messages on a regular basis.

As the pandemic dragged on, my email inbox began filling
with notices of messages in these various accounts. All were from

people describing how the prison's response to the coronavirus stifled their limited ability to participate in rehabilitative programming, communicate with family, or even go outside. Many were frightened—unsure how to protect themselves. They saw their peers carted away to quarantine, then returned fourteen days later, often with horror stories. Others described a range of worsening conditions from staff shortages that further limited their ability to leave their cells, to food shortages, to even longer delays in painfully slow medical treatment.

That was what happened to Malakki, who turned fifty-four in a Pennsylvania prison shortly before the coronavirus hit the United States. Malakki and I had not been in touch before the pandemic. We connected in 2022 when I was reporting on the medical consequences of the ongoing crisis.

Prison bureaucracy, coupled with staff shortages caused by COVID, repeatedly delayed Malakki's treatment for multiple sclerosis. His speech and mobility deteriorated, sometimes to the point where he could not talk on the phone. On those days, he relied on e-messaging, and the system in his prison limited him to two thousand characters (fewer than five hundred words) per message.

Unlike email in the outside world, prison e-messages are not received instantaneously, but instead take days to reach the recipient. When I emailed him, several days would pass before I received a notification confirming that my message had been approved and sent to his account.

Then I had to wait for him to sync his prison-issued tablet to the kiosk in the dayroom, download my message, type a response, and sync his tablet again to send it.

My messages to Malakki sometimes took as long as a week to get through. However, they always reached him—eventually. In other states, prison officials rejected some of my e-messages, particularly those with information about COVID, prevention practices, and long COVID. The forty-three to fifty cents I had spent on each message was not refunded.

※

In New York City, existing jail policy added a layer of needless cruelty onto a person's need to connect. Two days after the city had confirmed its first COVID case, Tracy McCarter, a forty-four-year-old Black nurse, was sent to Rikers Island, the ten-jail complex notorious for its ongoing violence, brutality, and disregard for human life.[13] Under normal circumstances, her case would have been brought before a grand jury, which would decide whether to indict her or let her go free. But shortly after her arrest, COVID closed all courtroom proceedings, leaving her stuck in legal limbo in what was to become one of the nation's first hot spots.

Two weeks later, the first COVID cases were reported among those locked on the island jail.[14] Rikers stopped in-person visits and instituted one-hour video visits, installing closely spaced booths in the visiting room.[15]

For Tracy and many others, these video visits became their lifeline. But getting to and from them became another source of trauma. Jail policy requires that incarcerated people be strip-searched before and after each in-person visit. Each search requires that a person remove all of her clothing. Then she must squat facing the officers, turn away and squat again, show them the bottoms of her feet, open her mouth, stick out her tongue, and shake out her hair. Only after this demeaning ritual was complete could she pull on her prison-issued jumpsuit and proceed to the visiting room to see her loved ones. These searches were ostensibly to prevent people from passing or receiving items during their visits.

The policy was not updated when video visits replaced in-person visits. Each of the ten jails implemented its own interpretation, depending on the whims and caprices of the visiting room officer. At the women's jail, officers initially did not require strip searches. In April 2020, Tracy had half a dozen video visits with her children, sister, and mother. No one demanded that she take her clothes off.

At the end of April, however, Tracy heard other women say that a particular officer had returned from vacation and was requiring strip searches before and after each video visit.

On May 1, Tracy had a visit scheduled with her sister. It was nearing the one-year anniversary of their brother's death and the sisters needed to support one another. At the entrance to the visiting room, the officer ordered her to strip. Tracy refused and demanded to see a captain who was higher up in the chain of command. "I'm protesting. You don't need to see my pussy for me to get on the computer," she told them.

The captain arrived and informed Tracy that strip searches were required before visits. If she refused, she would be limited to a non-contact visit. Tracy argued that video visits were already non-contact, but the captain remained unmoved. She issued an ultimatum—Tracy could submit to the strip search or else forgo her visit. Tracy stripped, a humiliation which she likened to being paraded around an antebellum plantation.

The following day, Tracy received a notice that she was being charged with three infractions of jail rules—refusing to obey a direct order, disorderly conduct, and participating in a demonstration—and that her visits for the next forty-five days were canceled.

She appealed the infractions and the cancelation of her visits. She also wrote a grievance, or formal complaint, to the Board of Correction, the city agency tasked with overseeing jail conditions. She even paid extra to have it delivered overnight. But the pandemic had also wreaked havoc on the US Postal Service and, although the address was correct, the letter was returned as undeliverable.

Tracy's indignity continued for months. "I would tell them every single time that it was not right. What contraband can we pass over the computer? What sense does this make?" she recalled. "We should not have to show our vaginas to get on the computer."[16] While she and outside advocates eventually succeeded in forcing the policy's rescission, that first long summer of COVID uncertainty and disconnect was intensified by this additional, utterly unnecessary mortification.

※

Those first months were indicative of the responses that jails and prisons would roll out under the justification of COVID prevention. Like everything in the carceral systems, these policies tended to demean, disempower, and often endanger those inside rather than encourage and empower people to protect themselves.

This was not the first time that carceral facilities dehumanized people because of a virus. Throughout the 1980s and 1990s, jails and prisons frequently isolated people who had HIV. When Jonathan Kirkpatrick was jailed in Washington State in the mid-1990s, he was placed in an isolation pod because of his HIV status. When guards brought his meals, they ordered him to move to the back of his cell, turn around, kneel, and place his hands behind his head. Only then would they open his door and place his tray on the floor. When he had finished eating whatever had not sloshed out, he had to repeat the debasing process before they entered to collect the tray.

Later, guards began wearing plastic face shields, paper gowns, and thick rubber gloves. But their irrational fears of contracting HIV did not prevent them from beating him bloody when he refused to return the plastic utensils with his meal.[17]

In 1985, forty-six of the country's fifty-one state and federal prison systems segregated incarcerated people who had HIV. And this figure does not include the individual facilities, such as the jail where Kirkpatrick was held, that had no such written policy but nonetheless subjected people to these degradations. In 1994, six of those systems were still holding fast to these scientifically unnecessary policies.[18] It was not until 2013 that South Carolina, the last holdout, ended its policy.

The COVID-19 pandemic response promised a replay of these same dynamics, in which stigma and fear, rather than science and empowerment, shaped both policy and practice. But during the height of the AIDS pandemic in prisons, incarcerated people—some of whom were living with HIV or AIDS and others who were not—took on the challenge of battling widespread ignorance, misinformation, discrimination, and even violence around the virus. Both individually and collectively, they educated their peers and encouraged them to take steps to protect themselves. In some systems, they were even able to convince sympathetic administrators to allow them to form officially approved organizations. In New York, that led to the formation of the AIDS Counseling and Education (ACE) program at the Bedford Hills women's prison. Soon after, administrators in the state's men's prisons approved the Prisoners' AIDS Counseling and Education (PACE) program, a similar peer group. Other prisons slowly followed suit, and incarcerated people began combating the misinformation and stigma that ran rampant behind bars.

In 2020 and the years that followed, some of these same people would take on the task of educating their peers about the novel coronavirus and preventive measures. When vaccines became available, they answered questions and dispelled the fears propagated by media, celebrities, and anti-vaccine staff members. But all of that was to come later. During those early months, they, like everyone else, were locked in their cells with the terrifying, unanswerable question, "Am I going to die in here?"

Chapter 2

# Dire Predictions for a Prison Nation

The United States has long had the world's highest incarceration rate. The US population accounts for only 5 percent of the world's population, but its incarcerated population accounts for 25 percent of the globe's prison population[1]. In 2020, 629 of every 100,000 US residents were imprisoned, making jails, prisons, and other sites of confinement prime corridors for contagion.

Author and abolitionist Beth Richie coined the term *prison nation*. The term refers to both the gargantuan numbers of people behind bars as well as the ideological and public policy shifts that respond to social problems with criminalization and punishment. The latter includes not only more aggressive policing for a widening range of behaviors, but also policing by other agencies, including child welfare, schools, and medical institutions. The prison nation encompasses these overlapping forces that use the law to control people, especially those who are disadvantaged.[2]

While the term *prison nation* is relatively new, the United States has a long history of weaponizing confinement against marginalized people, starting with the European colonization of the continent.[3] Colonizers made criminalization a key weapon in their conquest.

One of the first buildings the Spanish constructed when they arrived in what would become California was a jail. They used incarceration not only as a response to violence, but also as a way to remove unwanted people—particularly the Indigenous people they were displacing—from public spaces and city limits. Colonists along the east coast did the same.

During the 1830s, California authorities conducted weekly sweeps to arrest Native people who were assumed to be drunk. Those who were arrested could either pay a fine or be forced to work on public work projects. By 1844, arrests broadened to all unemployed Native people, regardless of perceived drunkenness. Authorities also widened the net to allow private (white) citizens to benefit from their labor. During the Gold Rush of the 1850s and 1860s, Native people unlucky enough to be arrested were auctioned to the highest-bidding white employer every Monday morning outside the jail.[4]

Removing unwanted populations through imprisonment became even more apparent after the Civil War. Former slave states enacted Black Codes, or laws criminalizing certain behaviors—but only if the person was Black. These laws penalized Black people for a wide range of acts, such as being outside after a certain hour, gathering in small groups, being absent from work, vagrancy, or possessing a firearm. The laws also changed the severity of an offense. Petty thievery, for example, became a felony after large numbers of newly emancipated Black people were forced to steal in order to survive.

The Black Codes drastically changed the color and nature of Southern imprisonment. Before the abolition of slavery, for instance, 99 percent of Alabama prisoners had been white. Following the Civil War and the state's passage of Black Codes, Black people became the majority of the penitentiary's prisoners.[5] In antebellum Tennessee, less than 5 percent of state prisoners had been Black. In 1866, that number ballooned to 52 percent and, by 1891, to 75 percent.[6] In Mississippi and Georgia, Black imprisonment rates rose 300 percent during the postwar years.[7]

The Black Codes enabled further bondage. While the Thirteenth Amendment abolished slavery and involuntary servitude, it made an exception for those "duly convicted" of a crime. In the American South, a convict lease system developed, in which private

companies rented groups of prisoners from the state prisons to per-
form hard labor, such as plantation work in Mississippi and coal
mining in Alabama.

The Codes also created county convicts, or people convicted
of misdemeanors and sentenced to up to two years of hard labor.
County convicts were responsible for paying their own court costs
and any costs incurred by the sheriff. The latter typically amounted
to fifty dollars, which they worked off by serving additional time at
the rate of thirty cents per day.[8]

There was nothing remotely rehabilitative about sentencing
newly freed Black people to the same types of backbreaking toil
that they had recently escaped. But rehabilitation wasn't the point
of the Black Codes. And, given that white people who engaged in
these behaviors escaped criminalization, these codes were never
intended to promote safety or protect the public. Instead, just as
jailing removed Native people from the new California settlements,
criminalization and incarceration served the dual purpose of removing recently freed Black people from the public and utilizing
them as cheap or free labor.

The United States continued using incarceration to remove
other unwanted populations. Starting in 1892, it targeted, detained, and deported Chinese immigrants who failed to register
with the federal government, and, during the 1920s, it jailed Mexican migrants. Each time a new jail or prison opened, it quickly became overcrowded, leading to demands for more beds.[9] Expanding
incarceration never increased public safety. Instead, it continually
utilized criminalization as a means of social control.

༄

Imprisonment was not originally intended as punishment. Instead,
people were jailed while awaiting judgment and sentence. Those
sentences included vicious physical acts such as flogging, time in
the stocks, indentured servitude, or execution.

In 1773, the United States started using imprisonment as punishment with the creation of Philadelphia's Walnut Street Jail. The jail offered no pretense of rehabilitation. Instead, people were thrown together to serve their sentences in large rooms, where they often had to ward off not only attacks by their jailers but also those incarcerated alongside them. If they survived, they were released once their sentence ended.

The idea of imprisonment as a means of rehabilitation began nearly two decades later in 1790 with the opening of a new cellblock—the Penitentiary House. Meant to induce penitence in the lawbreaker, the Penitentiary House confined people in complete isolation, ostensibly to pray, reflect upon, and repent for their wrongdoings.

In 1829, Pennsylvania opened the nation's first prison—the 250-cell Eastern State Penitentiary, which continued the goal of correction through isolated penitence. People were locked in individual concrete cells where the only light was that filtering in from a small skylight. Each cell opened onto a small exercise yard with a ten-foot wall. Each person was allowed two and a half hours in that small yard. These stretches were timed so that no two people would be outside at the same time. They had no human interaction, not even sound. Twenty inches of masonry separated each cell, and guards even wore wool socks over their shoes to muffle their footsteps.[10]

Large penitentiaries with single-cell isolation units proved costly. Prisons built in later decades tended to follow the less expensive model of New York's Auburn prison. There, men were isolated in their cells at night. During the day, they made commercial items, such as nails, barrels, clothing, furniture, brooms, clocks, and harnesses, which offset the cost of their imprisonment. They labored in the same room, where silence was rigorously enforced. The prison's thirty women were assigned more feminine forms of labor such as picking wool, knitting, and spooling. Silence was not as rigorously enforced for them.

Even as newer prisons turned away from extreme and expensive isolation and toward the Auburn model, they maintained the notion that imprisonment was somehow rehabilitative. It's a myth that persists to this day.

※

In the mid-twentieth century, the United States began its buildup to becoming the world's prison nation.

During the 1960s, politicians conflated crime with the civil rights protests playing out on the nightly news. The specter of crime became a dog whistle as lawmakers utilized policing and imprisonment to simultaneously woo white voters and incapacitate marginalized communities before they could organize.[11]

As in previous decades, incarceration remained the solution for populations that had been made superfluous (or, as geographer Ruth Wilson Gilmore describes them, "surplus") by globalization and capitalism.[12] This time, the targets weren't displaced Native people, formerly enslaved people, or migrant workers; they were people of color and other disadvantaged communities who might organize and challenge the existing social, political, and economic orders.

In 1965, one year after laying out his War on Poverty, President Lyndon B. Johnson introduced a vastly different agenda, one that significantly devastated the same communities that his social safety nets were intended to help. That was his War on Crime. Days after presenting the Voting Rights Act to Congress, he signed the Law Enforcement Assistance Act (LEAA), which allotted $30 million (or $223 million in today's dollars) in federal grants to local and state law enforcement for militarized policing.

The effect was astronomical. Between the end of the Civil War in 1865 and Johnson's 1965 War on Crime, the United States had sent 184,901 people to prison.[13] But between 1965 and 1985 alone, the US sent 251,107 people to state and federal prisons.[14]

His successor, Richard Nixon, rejected Johnson's belief that poverty was a root cause of crime. During his presidential campaign, he told voters, "If the conviction rate were doubled in this country, it would do more to eliminate crime in the future than a quadrupling of the funds for any governmental war on poverty."[15] Under Nixon, lawmakers supported the construction of hundreds of new state and federal prisons. Prisons nationwide went from majority white to majority Black and Latinx.

Nixon launched the LEAA's single largest initiative—the $20 million "High Impact" program. Nixon officials worked with mayors and local police to establish local criminal justice planning agencies that implemented new surveillance and patrol programs. These programs increased contacts between police officers and residents, particularly in low-income neighborhoods of color.[16] Nixon also declared a War on Drugs, which his adviser later admitted was a cloaked approach to criminalizing both Black people and the anti-war left.[17] By 1976, the country had a record number of 250,042 people in jails and prisons.[18] That figure would double by the end of the 1970s.[19]

Nixon's impeachment did not end the race to incarcerate. President Gerald Ford created the Career Criminal program, which, instead of focusing on organized crime, targeted single, unemployed Black men.[20] The federal government invested $330 million in twenty-two cities, but the program failed to decrease violence. Houston, for instance, targeted five hundred people as career criminals, sentencing them to an average of thirty years in prison. Six years into the program, the city's homicide rate peaked at 701 deaths.[21]

In 1982, President Ronald Reagan ramped up the War on Drugs.[22] The administration, and later the media, whipped up fears of the (Black) crack addict who would rob, rape, and murder for a hit of crack—as well as predatory "crack dealers," "crack whores," and "crack babies"—to pass harsher laws and more severe sentences. Over the next decades, these laws would entrap, ensnare, and imprison millions—primarily people of color and low-income people—for lengthy, if not life, sentences.[23]

Throughout the 1990s, both Democratic and Republican politicians at the federal, state, and local level raced to be "toughest on crime." They cemented the United States as a carceral state, slowly stomping out the last vestiges of a liberal welfare state.[24]

In 1994, then-senator Joe Biden coauthored the Violent Crime Control and Law Enforcement Act, popularly known as the 1994 Crime Bill. The act encouraged states to pass more punitive sentencing laws. It earmarked $9.7 billion in federal funding to states to build jails and prisons in exchange for eliminating earned time and rehabilitative opportunities for incarcerated people. Supported by both Democrats and Republicans, the bill was signed into law by President Bill Clinton.

Once the act became law, twenty-eight states and the District of Columbia enacted stricter sentencing laws for violent convictions, including truth-in-sentencing laws that required people to serve at least 85 percent of their sentences regardless of their achievements and personal transformation while imprisoned. By 1995, prison populations nationwide had grown by 88,400 people (an increase of 9 percent) to reach 1.1 million total, the highest number of prisoners per capita worldwide.[25] That record high would be repeatedly eclipsed as prosecutors reached for the most serious charges, and judges became increasingly required to mete out lengthier sentences, including life imprisonment.

The federal government then passed the Antiterrorism and Effective Death Penalty Act of 1996 (AEDPA), which restricted appeals in federal courts involving prosecutorial misconduct, inadequate legal defense, and other problems in state trials.[26] Thus, while crime rates declined, the numbers sentenced to prison rose from 789,610 to 1,252,830—or a 59 percent increase—between 1991 and 1998.[27] By 1999, the rate of incarceration had reached 476 for every 100,000 US residents, or more than 2 million people.[28] Between 2006 and 2009, 1,000 of every 100,000 adults were behind bars.[29]

✳

These federal policies also held out financial incentives for states to follow suit. And state lawmakers jumped at these enticements, swelling existing prison populations and embarking upon their own prison building booms. In 1973, New York governor Nelson Rockefeller established mandatory sentences for drugs. The Rockefeller Drug Laws required prison sentences of fifteen years to life for selling two ounces or possessing four ounces of narcotics. They were no longer able to consider mitigating circumstances or the lack of a prior conviction. Even people who were in the same vehicle were sent to prison for decades, even if the drugs were not theirs. At their height in the late 1990s, the Rockefeller laws were responsible for incarcerating roughly 23,000 of the state's 71,000 prisoners.[30] Two-thirds had never been imprisoned before.[31]

In 1993, Washington State passed the nation's first Three Strikes law, which required anyone convicted of a third felony to be sentenced to life in prison. The following year, fueled by the kidnapping and murder of twelve-year-old Polly Klaas by a man who had been paroled months earlier, California enacted its own Three Strikes law. California's law required judges to double prison sentences for those convicted of a second felony and automatically issue sentences of twenty-five years to life for those convicted of a third felony, regardless of its severity or how long ago their previous felonies occurred. Within the next decade, more than 80,000 Californians were sentenced as "second strikers," and more than 7,500 people as "third strikers."[32] Under Three Strikes, courts could and did enhance acts as minor as stealing pizza, possessing crack, and stealing twenty dollars of coffee from a church kitchen.[33]

By 2000, the number of people serving these types of life sentences had doubled—and that number continued to climb throughout the early 2000s. Confronted with the threat of sentences so long that they might as well be serving life, over 90 percent of those facing criminal charges pled guilty to lesser charges and shorter sentences rather than take their chances at trial.

This web of forces, played out over decades, has led to growing numbers of arrests and longer prison sentences (including life without parole). Between 1980 and 2019, women's incarceration skyrocketed by 700 percent—a rate far surpassing that of men's incarceration year after year.[34] Despite carceral building booms, cellblocks and dormitories became chronically overcrowded in state after state. And this web has disproportionately ensnared people of color.

In 2020, Black people comprised approximately 14 percent of the total US population. But they were imprisoned at a rate nearly five times that of white people, who make up 71 percent of the nation's residents.[35] Black people also spent more time in prison than their white counterparts and were more likely to be denied parole.[36]

Latinx people were imprisoned at twice the rate of their white counterparts. The US Census did not report their share of the country's population, and they have not been included in studies on racial disparities in parole. While Native Americans make up less than 3 percent of the US population, they are four times more likely than whites to be imprisoned.[37] In Oklahoma, where Mary is imprisoned, Native people make up 9.5 percent of the state's population, but 11.5 percent of its state prison population. They are 24 percent more likely to be incarcerated than non-Native residents.[38] Native women, comprise only 6 percent of the state, but they are imprisoned at three times the rate of their white counterparts.[39]

The ballooning, aging, and increasingly expensive US prison populations have spurred moderate criminal justice reforms in recent years. Politicians who had previously touted their tough-on-crime records began introducing bills to slightly decrease prison sentences and populations. Their most widely embraced proposals tied decarceration to measures extending carceral control in other forms, such as electronic monitoring, home confinement, and lengthy probation sentences.[40]

Long before politicians began repudiating their former "lock 'em up" zealousness, people had been organizing to reduce imprisonment. Some organized to reform and repeal laws that have locked up so many people. Others, arguing that prisons, in all their manifestations, can never be reformed to meet people's needs or be humane, advocated eliminating incarceration altogether. Prison abolitionists drew inspiration from the nineteenth-century movement to abolish slavery, the twentieth-century movement to end second-class citizenship for Black people, and the contemporary movement to eliminate the death penalty. Others drew additional inspiration from the resistance against political repression, joining or forming campaigns to free political prisoners and to end racist policing.

Hand in hand with the call to abolish prisons are demands, campaigns, and initiatives to create and expand resources to prevent and address violence and to meet the needs of individuals and communities. Organizers create responses that address harm without the dehumanization of imprisonment, which is more likely to replicate and exacerbate violent behaviors than to solve them.[41]

For many today, the idea of abolishing prisons may seem unattainable, but, as late as the 1850s, so did the notion of ending chattel slavery. In 1856, antebellum southern writers predicted that as many as 100 million Black people would be enslaved within the next century.[42] As Gloria Anzaldúa has rightfully noted, "Nothing happens in the 'real' world unless it first happens in the images in our heads."[43] Centuries ago, abolitionists imagined a world without slavery—and made it happen.

While the end goals of reformers and abolitionists continue to diverge, their demands and organizing frequently dovetailed into campaigns that have both slowed the churn of people into jails, and prison and reversed some of the policies that had sent people to die behind bars.

At the same time, incarcerated people have long mobilized to improve conditions and challenge the growing carceral apparatus. Throughout the 1960s and 1970s, incarcerated people continually resisted and rebelled. In 1971, incarcerated people took over New York's maximum-security Attica State Prison for four days, issuing a series of demands for immediate improvements. At least seventeen other prison uprisings occurred nationwide that year. The following year, forty-eight prisons erupted in rebellions—the most recorded in a single year in US history.[44]

Throughout the 1990s, grassroots campaigns mobilized to stop the construction or expansion of new jails and prisons. Local organizers also connected with imprisoned activists to provide ongoing support and outside scrutiny of conditions—and to lessen the likelihood of retaliation for those who spoke out. They organized campaigns to free people serving draconian sentences for political actions and those sentenced under mandatory minimum laws.

In 1998, thousands of organizers and educators came together for a three-day conference entitled Critical Resistance: Beyond the Prison Industrial Complex. The conference launched a campaign to stop California's twenty-year prison building boom. It also inspired new campaigns and reenergized existing organizing across the country. Attendees returned to their communities to create new organizations, campaigns, and projects. They connected with other groups to close prisons, stop jail construction, and build non-carceral resources, particularly in neighborhoods that had long suffered disinvestment. These groups and coalitions also worked to shift the political framing of incarceration. Instead of viewing incarceration as a result of individualized personal failures, they reframed it in the context of structural racism and the organized abandonment of marginalized communities.

On the state level, organizers succeeded in rolling back some of the draconian laws that had long swelled prisons. In 2004, New York reformed the Rockefeller Drug Laws, reducing sentences for first-time convictions, doubling the amounts of narcotics needed for a conviction, and permitting resentencing for those serving life sentences. In 2009, lawmakers removed the mandatory minimum sentencing requirement altogether.

Three years later, in 2012, California amended its Three Strikes law to apply the third strike only to serious or violent felonies. Some states reduced penalties for certain acts, such as marijuana possession. In Oregon, lawmakers decriminalized all drug possession. Several states passed laws allowing resentencing for certain groups of people, such as those with nonviolent convictions, those who were juveniles at the time of their crime, or those whose convictions stemmed from abuse. These reforms reduced prison populations enough that some states, such as New York and California, closed a few prisons—not as a gesture of humanitarianism but as a cost-cutting measure. They then shuffled people into the remaining prisons, causing more crowding and chaos.

Still, fears of being called "soft on crime" continue to cause most elected officials, even those who have rebranded themselves as "smart on crime," to shy away from releasing people even as those people grow grayer and require bifocals, dentures, walkers, wheelchairs, and palliative care. By the end of 2019, more than 2.2 million people were incarcerated at an annual cost of nearly $85 billion. Hundreds of thousands had been languishing—and aging—during decades-long sentences. Their mobility decreased, their health needs multiplied, and their risk of severe illness or death increased. By 2020, one in seven had been sentenced to age—and die—behind bars, and 15 percent of the nation's prisoners were ages fifty-five or older. When COVID hit the United States, these long-crowded sites of confinement erupted into infernos of exposure.

※

Despite their walls, bars, and razor wire, jails and prisons remain porous places with staff and volunteers entering and leaving each day. Staff are never entirely separate from those whom they are paid to guard. They escort incarcerated people to and from different areas, from a housing unit to the medical clinic or classroom or visiting room. They pass out medications and mail, make regular rounds, and conduct searches that require extremely close contact.

Throughout 2020, the general public was repeatedly reminded to practice social distancing, self-quarantining, and other acts to "flatten the curve," or slow the spread of COVID. All of those measures are impossible behind bars. Instead, jails, prisons, and other places of confinement are what political anthropologist Eric Reinhart dubbed "epidemic engines that multiply and spread sickness and death throughout broader communities."[45] When he and I spoke, he pointed to post-Soviet Russia as a prime example of how incarceration enabled an epidemic to fester behind bars and then spread to the larger community. During the 1990s, Russian incarceration swelled by over 50 percent—largely for petty crimes caused by poverty and the dismantling of the welfare state. The country also experienced tuberculosis outbreaks that quickly spread in its packed jails and prisons. Those who had started treatment while incarcerated had their treatment interrupted upon release, leading to the development of multi-drug-resistant tuberculosis.

Just as viruses don't respect prison walls, they also do not adhere to borders. Multi-drug-resistant tuberculosis exploded throughout Eastern Europe throughout the 1990s and early 2000s. Tuberculosis also spread through US jails and prisons, comprising nearly 4 percent of the nation's cases.[46] Researchers with the Centers for Disease Control and Prevention noted that jails and prisons contain a "greater proportion of persons who are at high risk for tuberculosis but who cannot access standard public health interventions." They also noted the specific risk factors behind bars that increase transmission and outbreaks, such as close living quarters, poor ventilation, and overcrowding. As incarceration soared throughout the

1990s, overcrowding led to the spread of other infectious diseases and infections, including MRSA (methicillin-resistant *Staphylococcus aureus*), HIV, hepatitis C, influenza, and pneumonia.[47]

In 2020, health experts warned that jails and prisons would quickly become hotbeds for COVID transmission and urged drastic decarceration. They recommended police stop arresting and detaining people for low-level crimes and misdemeanors. In New York City, they also called for the release of anyone over age sixty from pretrial detention. Between March and May 2020, physicians working at Rikers Island wrote more than 1,400 letters on behalf of incarcerated patients who were at risk for severe COVID-19.[48] Correctional Health Services, the city agency providing jail medical services, worked with public defender offices to support bail applications in order to shrink the numbers behind bars.

Their Herculean efforts were somewhat successful. Within weeks, 1,500 people had been released. The city's jail system hit its lowest population since the 1940s.[49] But even this dramatic drop did not stop the virus from blazing trails of extreme illness, chaos, and death through the jails. And unlike the buildup of the prison nation, momentum in the direction of decarceration was short-lived. By summer, New York jails were rapidly filling once more.

In other parts of the country, public health officials' warnings remained partially followed or altogether ignored. Some, like Texas governor Greg Abbott, even prohibited early releases.

The apathy toward the millions of people trapped behind bars went beyond indifference. The obstinate refusal to follow recommendations concerning decarceration seemed guided more by the continued zeal to punish people than by any desire to ensure public health or safety. When the pandemic hit, that fanaticism prevented politicians and other policymakers from reversing the country's status as a prison nation, even if it would have stopped a plague.

## Chapter 3

# Deadly Inadequacies Amidst an Uncertain Spring

I n late January 2020, a few days before his fifty-fourth birthday, Malakki called his best friend Pearl. It was their nightly routine after she had finished work for the day.[1] That week, US headlines were dominated by the helicopter crash that killed basketball player Kobe Bryant and his daughter. Malakki had recently been transferred to the prison's special needs unit, the only area with handicap cells that could accommodate his wheelchair and decreasing mobility from multiple sclerosis. He had not yet heard about the novel coronavirus devastating China.

Pearl, however, was a microbiologist, and she had been tracking it. She worried about what would happen not if, but rather when, the highly contagious virus hit the Pennsylvania prison where Malakki was confined. Multiple sclerosis rendered him more vulnerable to severe, and possibly fatal, COVID. But Malakki didn't share her alarm.

"It was so far away—almost another planet away," he recalled thinking. "I thought she brought it up because of her interest in science, discussions at her job, and was just concerned for purely academic reasons."

For Pearl, the virus wasn't simply academic. It was another threat to her best friend, who was already undergoing the slow deterioration from both multiple sclerosis and years of inadequate medical care. For months, Pearl, Malakki's family, and his lawyers had been advocating for the prison to authorize a different medical treatment, and their efforts seemed to be paying off. Malakki had recently been approved for the treatment, though it would be several months before he would receive his first dose.

A few days earlier, he had been in the prison's infirmary. There, staff had administered steroid infusions to temporarily slow his body's deterioration and prevent permanent nerve damage. That evening, he was in less pain and able to move more easily from his bed to his wheelchair and from his wheelchair to the toilet.

Pearl warned that, because multiple sclerosis is an autoimmune disease, Malakki should search for items to fashion into a mask to cover his mouth and nose. Malakki laughed. "It's in China," he responded, staring at the square blue phone as if the two were speaking face-to-face.

The virus was moving quickly and would be in the United States in no time, she warned. From there, it was a matter of time before it made its way into the nation's jails and prisons—where crowded conditions would allow it to rip through captive populations. Malakki was incredulous, snickering at what he thought was excessive worry. It didn't matter that she had a master's degree in microbiology and had worked for a decade as a microbiologist. "How could a sickness in China reach me in a prison in Pennsylvania?" he recalled thinking. It seemed unfathomable.

Prison calls cut off automatically after fifteen minutes. Malakki didn't want to waste those precious minutes arguing, especially about science—a topic on which he knew he couldn't prevail. He assured her that he would find mask-making materials and changed the subject.

Within a week, France announced its first confirmed COVID case. Watching CNN, he followed the virus as it tore through Italy, then blazed through New York. This prompted hospitals to erect tents and morgues, and to rent refrigerated trucks for the overflow of bodies. He realized that she had been right. It wouldn't be long until it reached Pennsylvania—and, from there, scorch through its jails and prisons.

The previous winter, the prison had experienced a bad flu outbreak and medical staff had given him a blue surgical mask. As he watched the news, he dug it out, though he didn't put it on.

One afternoon, Malakki was brought to a neurologist appointment outside the prison. When he returned, he was forced to wait in the transport van for several hours. When he was finally brought inside, an officer told him that his entire unit was on lockdown.

"Was it a bad fight?" Malakki asked, assuming that the lockdown was a response to a fight, stabbing, or slashing.

The officer pointed across the hall to a large body bag. "That guy just came from your block," he said. But the body wasn't the tragic result of an act of violence. "There's a lot of guys sick on your block," the officer warned.

Later, Malakki learned that the man had lived on the upstairs tier, someone whom he had seen but didn't know well. As he was escorted to the medical unit, he saw seven other men from his cellblock. One man, his eyes bloodshot, was holding his mouth and lying down. Others sat shaking their heads, hoping that they had a cold or, at worst, the flu. All had tested positive for COVID.

Days later, staff began handing out masks. Not long after, another man on his unit died. Although not close, the two had spoken every day. More than two years later, Malakki still cried when he remembered that death. "I couldn't imagine what his family was going through," Malakki recalled. "It made me think about what my family would go through if it happened to me." That was when Malakki realized that Pearl's fears were now his reality.

That January, while Malakki was still laughing at Pearl's fears, forty-seven-year-old Mwalimu Shakur had been rendered temporarily blind. He had recently had eye surgery and during recovery, he could not see out of his right eye. Mwalimu was imprisoned across the country from Malakki at the California State Prison at Corcoran. In the 1990s, the prison had been notorious for the brutality of both its staff and the incarcerated men there. Guards had even staged gladiator fights among members of rival prison gangs, summoning other staff to watch and bet on outcomes. They also shot the men who failed to obey the guards' (belated) orders to stop fighting. Over an eight-year period, guards fatally shot seven people and wounded another fifty during these gladiator fights.[2]

While this level of extreme violence had lessened by 2020, physical fights still happened regularly. Being partially blind made Mwalimu vulnerable, but his friends protected him whenever he left his cell. Despite the risks, he was relieved to have had the operation. He had agitated for a year before prison officials approved his surgery. Behind bars, one year is a quick turnaround for any sort of medical authorization. Many wait multiple years as their health declines, sometimes drastically. Some even die from conditions that could have been treated.

But approval was that swift because Mwalimu had filed numerous complaints, known as "602s" in California prisons, charging that staff had damaged his cornea when they had pepper-sprayed him after a fight with his cellmate. Filing a 602 is a multistep process in which the complaint winds its way through the prison's chain of command. First, a sergeant reviews the complaint, deciding whether to accept or reject it. Then it goes to a lieutenant, who conducts an interview. Then the complaint—along with video of the interview—is sent to prison headquarters in Sacramento for a final decision.

Mwalimu was less worried about that final decision than about making sure he completed the required paperwork in case he needed to file a lawsuit. Meanwhile, the all-volunteer advocacy group Prisoner Advocacy Network (PAN) requested, then reviewed, his prison medical records. Armed with that information, Mwalimu's family, friends, and advocates, including a doctor associated with PAN, repeatedly called the prison. These actions all sped along the normally sluggish process. Otherwise, Mwalimu might still have been waiting for eye surgery by the time the coronavirus closed California. When the pandemic hit, his follow-up appointments were canceled.

On March 24, 2020, California governor Gavin Newsom issued Executive Order N-36-20, suspending new arrivals into the state's prisons for thirty days. That halted three thousand new arrivals—and three thousand possible new transmissions. The prison system later extended that suspension until August 24, though it did admit some recently sentenced prisoners in May and June. But it failed to suspend transfers between prisons, which, in a system that has long been over capacity, had explosive consequences. When the pandemic hit in March, California's prison system was operating at over 130 percent capacity. More than a dozen prisons hovered between 140 to 169 percent capacity.

Nonetheless, California's state attorneys asked federal judges not to intervene by ordering prison releases. Prison officials announced that the state was considering releasing up to 3,500 people to prevent the spread of COVID. Thousands had already been approved for release within the next two months; officials were simply expediting those much-anticipated dates. Governor Gavin Newsom issued twenty-one additional commutations to people in prison, allowing their release.

Still, those measures were insufficient. In May, COVID exploded inside the California Institution for Men, three and a half hours south of Corcoran. When they heard the news, Mwalimu and the men around him doubled down on disinfecting every surface—phones, tables, chairs, benches, and even floor fans. But their efforts soon proved futile.

Prison officials ordered 189 men from the California Institution for Men to be handcuffed, shackled, and loaded onto buses to San Quentin and Corcoran. Neither prison had COVID, but the transfers changed that.[3] Despite an earlier directive limiting emergency transfers to no more than nineteen people per bus, officials packed twenty-five men onto each bus.[4] Most were driven more than six hours to San Quentin. Sixty-seven were driven over three hours north to Corcoran. What officials neglected to do was test any of the men before sending them off.

Of the 122 men transferred to San Quentin, 91 later tested positive. California prisons used PCR tests, requiring a wait of more than seven days for results.[5] During that week, the men were quarantined in housing units with metal grates instead of solid doors. Even if they could not freely circulate, their breath and respiratory droplets could—and did. The ventilation system included a fan system that had not been turned on in years and windows that had long been welded shut.[6]

Prison practices then broadened the spread. Staff typically move between several different areas throughout their shifts. Even with the threat of a contagious airborne virus, they frequently wore porous cloth masks or no masks at all. By the end of August, more than 2,200 of San Quentin's 3,300 prisoners and 277 staff members had contracted COVID. Twenty-eight incarcerated men and one staff member died.[7] Corcoran also experienced a small outbreak of ninety-eight cases shortly after these transfers, though officials claimed that only one positive test was directly connected to the move.[8] As high as those numbers were, they remained undercounts. Many hid their symptoms, knowing that a positive test would send them to solitary. Instead, they remained in their cells while others risked their own safety to check on them, bringing them meals and medications they would otherwise miss.[9]

This was not San Quentin's first failure to prevent an outbreak during a global pandemic. Opened in 1852, the prison's architecture proved to be prime corridors of contagion. It has a number of open tiers in which individual cells are separated from one another—and the walkway—by metal grates. These tiers are often stacked on top of one another on adjacent floors with no solid barrier.

In 1903, half a century after San Quentin opened, California legislators passed a law requiring adequate ventilation in all public detention facilities but did not include requirements to retrofit older buildings. It was an omission that proved fatal fifteen years later.[10]

In 1918, a worldwide flu pandemic swept the globe, sickening an estimated 500 million people, or one-third of the world's population, and killing at least 17 million. Then, as now, the flu has no cure. Public health officials ordered street cleanings, distribution of soap and clean water, prohibitions of crowds outside shops, and limits to the number of public transit passengers. But the most effective measure was quarantining those who had symptoms.

The practice of quarantine originated in the Middle Ages as a precaution against the plague. Ships entering Venice were required to wait forty days at sea before being allowed to land. From those forty days, or *quaranta giorni*, came the word *quarantine*.

By the time the flu was decimating the world several centuries later, quarantine had already been enforced in the United States on several occasions. In 1878, the government passed federal quarantine legislation to curb yellow fever. In 1892, it posed even more stringent quarantine regulations after cholera broke out. By 1918, both local and federal governments were accustomed to imposing quarantine restrictions on individuals and even entire neighborhoods during epidemics.[11]

In March 1918, the first outbreak of what would become the influenza pandemic was reported at the military barracks in Fort Riley, Kansas, with one hundred soldiers stricken. Within a week, that number quintupled. In early April, another outbreak was reported at the barracks in Haskell, Kansas.

Prison officials could have prepared—and followed the federal government's existing quarantine regulations. They did not.

That April, a man was transferred from the Los Angeles County Jail to San Quentin. He told staff that multiple men at the jail had been ill and that, before arriving, he himself had been racked with pains and a fever. Staff ignored the possibility that he might be the harbinger of a flu outbreak. They allowed him to remain in general population, where he mingled with the prison's 1,900 other men. On his second day, he was sent to the hospital with a 101-degree fever, chills, and an aching sensation in his back and bones. Soon, other men complained of similar symptoms.

Nonetheless, prison routines continued. Men reported to their jobs, congregated in the yard, and, on Sunday mornings, crammed into a poorly ventilated, partially underground room for the two weekly movie screenings. "Here, at one or the other of the shows, almost all of the 1,900 prisoners attend, and before the morning is over the room is moist, warm and foul with smoke and human odors," described L. L. Stanley, the prison's physician.[12] Within two weeks, approximately half of the prison population had fallen ill. One hundred and one men were hospitalized, and three died.

In early October 1918, another man was transferred from the Los Angeles County Jail. He said that the deputy who had transported him had complained of a cough, restlessness, and thirst.[13] Not having learned their lesson from the previous outbreak, officials failed to quarantine him. He ate with others in the mess hall and talked with the old-timers, who were eager for news of the outside world. The following day, he too became sick enough to require hospitalization. This time, however, the Sunday morning picture show had been replaced with a concert in the yard. The men crowded around the band and cheered loudly, with each shout spreading respiratory droplets and, as it turned out, virus. Not surprisingly, the number of men hospitalized increased the next day.

Two days after the man's arrival, the prison distributed masks made from flour sacks to the incarcerated men, staff, and their families. The physician noted that the majority of incarcerated men masked for several days. Still, those differences seemed to be enough. The October outbreak hit far fewer people—sixty-nine became ill and two died.[14]

In November, four days before Thanksgiving, the prison held its first Sunday movie in more than six weeks. Three days earlier, however, a man had arrived from Colusa County, which had been ravaged by the flu. When he became ill, he did not report to sick call and stayed in a room with a dozen other men. That Sunday morning, he attended the picture show. That evening, he was admitted to the prison hospital with a 102-degree fever and what the prison physician described as "unmistakable signs of influenza." In between the movie and the hospital, he had accidentally sneezed and coughed on one of his cellmates. Later, that man and another cellmate came down with the flu.[15] This time, officials stopped all public assemblies, including picture shows and group sports. Staff isolated newly arrived men for four days and required them to wear masks during visits, though they could otherwise remain unmasked. That measure drastically reduced exposure. The third and last outbreak lasted nine days with fifty-nine cases and no deaths.[16]

Over a century later, as another global pandemic with no vaccine or treatment crashed through the San Quentin gates, little about the architecture—or pandemic prevention measures—had changed. That failure, coupled with the already poor prison medical care, led to dire—and sometimes deadly—consequences.

In the United States, health care is not a guaranteed right. Even before the pandemic, one in ten adults incurred significant medical debt, and tens of thousands of people died each year due to lack of insurance.[17] The only US residents with a constitutional right to medical treatment, surprisingly, are those behind bars. In 1976, the US Supreme Court ruled, in *Estelle v. Gamble*, that jails and prisons that demonstrated a "deliberate indifference" to people's serious medical needs violated the Eighth Amendment protection against cruel and unusual punishment. However, the court issued no specifications about the quality of care necessary. What resulted was a hodgepodge of systems, with some jail and prison systems managing their own services and others contracting with for-profit corporations.

People behind bars are more likely to enter with or develop serious health conditions than those who have never been incarcerated.[18] They are three times more likely to have at least one disability.[19] Furthermore, conditions of confinement—including poor nutrition and an ongoing atmosphere of violence, deprivation, and uncertainty—negatively affect their bodies.[20] And, as Mwalimu learned, staff can deliberately inflict injuries that necessitate emergency or ongoing care. None of these issues are addressed by the *Estelle* ruling.

The Supreme Court decision also failed to address another barrier to basic care: as late as 2020, forty state prison systems required a person to cough up a co-pay if they needed to see a nurse or doctor.[21] Co-pays typically ranged between two to five dollars, but could be as high as eight dollars per visit. For people behind bars, who earn pennies per hour, if they have paying jobs at all, even those few dollars can put medical attention out of reach.

For decades, people in prison have sued repeatedly to ameliorate these inadequacies. In 1990, incarcerated Californians filed *Coleman v. Wilson*, a class-action lawsuit charging that the lack of mental health care amounted to cruel and unusual punishment. In 2001, a different group of Californians filed *Plata v. Brown*, a class-action lawsuit alleging the same about prison medical services. In 2002, to settle *Plata v. Brown*, the state agreed to provide adequate services in its prisons by 2008. Three years later, in 2005, a court-appointed panel of medical experts visited San Quentin. They found that the prison remained "antiquated, dirty, poorly staffed, poorly maintained with inadequate medical space and equipment and overcrowded."[22] Ten people had died over the past several years. In each instance, the experts found "serious problems" with each person's treatment, concluding that most of these deaths had been preventable. Doctors and nurses misdiagnosed patients, gave them incorrect medications, neglected patients with chronic illnesses for months, and sometimes years, and delayed sending them to outside hospitals until their illnesses became fatal.

In 2006, a federal judge appointed former hospital administrator Robert Sillen to solve the many problems plaguing the health services provided in the state's thirty-three prisons and to bring it into compliance with constitutional standards. On his second day, Sillen toured San Quentin, where he found a shortage of qualified doctors and nurses, a lack of space to provide services, unsanitary conditions, a medical records system in shambles, and turf wars between medical and custody staff, the latter of whom often resented and undermined providers' care.[23] He began overhauling the worst of these conditions, raising pay to attract more qualified medical staff, securing adequate space for clinic use and supplies, and creating a new records protocol. Still, those fixes weren't enough to overhaul a prison with century-old architecture, failing infrastructure, and long-standing institutional indifference to the lives of those locked inside.

That same year, the plaintiffs in both *Coleman* and *Plata* filed motions to limit California's ballooning prison population. Three years later, a panel of three federal judges ordered the state to reduce its prison population by approximately forty thousand people. That didn't happen. Instead, the state appealed to the US Supreme Court.

By 2011, California's prisons, which had been designed to hold fewer than 80,000 people, were packed with nearly twice that many (156,000 prisoners). Many were growing older—and needed greater medical services. In 1997, the state had 3,924 elderly people behind bars. By 2010, that number had more than tripled to 13,577.[24] In May of the following year, the Supreme Court ruled that California's prison overcrowding violated the constitution by preventing the delivery of medical and mental health care, resulting in "needless suffering and death."[25] The court ordered the state to reduce its prison population to a maximum of 137 percent capacity, or release at least forty-six thousand people, within two years.[26]

Three years later, in 2014, California's prisons remained above that benchmark. The same three-judge panel ordered the state to implement further measures. This included an elderly parole program in which Californians aged sixty and older and who had served at least twenty-five years of their sentence would immediately become eligible for their first parole hearing. (Elderly parole did not extend to those sentenced to death or life without parole.) That summer, more than 4,400 incarcerated people worked as firefighters against the hundreds of wildfires raging across the state. Although their labor saved the state over $1 billion, they were paid less than two dollars per day. But they were rewarded with "good time" credits, which shortened their sentences and qualified them for an earlier release.[27] The three-judge panel ordered that these credits be extended to those who were not working as firefighters. But the state's attorneys resisted this order, arguing that offering these credits would result in more early releases—and possibly fewer incarcerated workers to pick up trash, cook meals, and clean the prisons.[28]

On March 11, 2020, when California canceled all prison visits for the foreseeable future, over 117,000 people were in its state prisons.[29] But even with thousands of fewer people behind bars, delays, inadequacies, dismissal of patients' complaints, and other shortfalls persisted—and worsened—during the pandemic.

In Pennsylvania, Malakki had been struggling with multiple sclerosis for over a decade. Until his arrest in his late twenties, he walked two or three miles each day, navigating the hills of Pittsburgh with ease. He had briefly enlisted in the military and, after choosing not to reenlist, DJed and performed poetry. He had survived mental health crises and threats at gunpoint. When he entered prison, he was still in good physical health.

When he turned forty, however, his body began changing—dramatically. He started experiencing incontinence, which he chalked up to the stress of imprisonment. The following year, he began dropping things and tripping over his own feet. His "walkie," a friend with whom he walked around the yard, noticed the growing lack of coordination, and urged him to see the doctor.

Malakki's one and only adult experience with medical care happened shortly before his arrest. He had sought mental health care from a local hospital, where providers prescribed an antipsychotic medication. His memories of those medicated months are elliptical. It felt like he was always waking up in the middle of something, whether he was eating, in the bathroom, at his mother's house, or in the middle of a conversation with Pearl. What happened before and after each of these moments remain blank spaces, even today. Family members later told him that he spent at least twenty hours asleep every day. He stopped the medications, but the experience left him with a deep distrust of the medical system, which discouraged him from seeking help when his mental health tanked and, later, while in prison.

In addition to the unexplained clumsiness, Malakki's vision narrowed to 20 percent in one eye and 40 percent in the other. That was when his walkie decided that he was done asking. "I'm taking him to medical," he told the officer on duty—and dragged Malakki to the prison's clinic. There, an optometrist told him that his optic nerve was inflamed and authorized an MRI. That MRI led to the diagnosis of multiple sclerosis. At first, Malakki didn't understand what that meant. The doctor's explanations didn't make sense. He searched for court cases involving multiple sclerosis in the prison's law library. He read descriptions of the condition and its effects. Once he thought he understood what he was facing, he broke the news to his mother.

That was when he learned that his great-grandmother had had multiple sclerosis. Throughout Malakki's childhood, relatives had simply told him that the old woman had been "bedridden." Now, he began to understand what she had been going through.

For years, agonizing tingling in his shoulders, legs, and side woke Malakki several times every night. The tingling subsided after he spent an hour stretching and moving his legs. He could only sleep on his right side; rolling onto his left caused more pain. The constant interruptions left him sluggish and fighting to stay awake the following day.

Then he began losing his ability to speak—slurring his words and sometimes struggling to find those that he needed. Malakki had been a poet and spoken word artist before his arrest and, even behind bars, continued to write poems, essays, and stories. His loss of vocabulary was an even greater gut punch than the physical pain. And that physical pain was seemingly inescapable.

Jails and prisons, no matter when they were built, were designed for healthy young men. Prisons are often spread across multiple buildings, requiring people to leave one building and traverse walkways to another—a housing unit to a mess hall, classroom, or visiting room.

Malakki went from walking with a cane to requiring a wheelchair. At times, he could not muster the strength to push his wheelchair to his destination. "The condition of the wheelchairs is not great," Malakki explained. The condition of the walkways was even worse, riddled with potholes and bumps. Sometimes, he wheeled himself backward, using his right leg to push himself along. Sometimes, another man would ask the officer on duty if he could push Malakki into the yard, so that the older man could see the sky, feel the sun, enjoy the breeze on his skin, and watch the pickup basketball games.

At times, the friend pushing his wheelchair failed to avoid a pothole or bump and Malakki toppled out of his chair. Had they had not gotten permission from the officer on duty, his friend might have been blamed for the accident. He could have faced a disciplinary ticket, leading to a loss of privileges. He also might have been required to pay for any medical costs incurred by the accident, and also lose his job and, with it, whatever paltry wage that allowed him to buy soap, food, or other necessities that the prison did not provide.

By 2019, Malakki's body started retaining water and his left leg swelled. Medical records from that year noted increased spasms, twitching, buckling, and weakness. He had trouble finding words, his fingers were losing dexterity, his grip was weakening, and his body would jerk as his brain attempted to process movements.

Malakki was approved for a drug treatment, but he continued to feel fatigued. His speech remained slow and sometimes slurred. An MRI revealed that his multiple sclerosis was progressing. The neurologist recommended that he be switched to a different treatment.

Even before the pandemic, medical orders rarely moved quickly in a carceral setting. Months passed as Malakki waited for officials to approve the neurologist's recommendations. Meanwhile, providers noted his increased difficulty in speaking and moving, including getting out of his wheelchair.

"During flare-ups, time and space are different," he told me when I pressed him for a more precise timeline of these delays. "It's like I'm in a different dimension, like trying to move from this to this. First, it's just telling my body to move from here to here. Then it's getting the gumption to go through the pain to move my body. Then it's going through the mental process to make my mind get the gumption . . . you understand what I'm saying? I find myself stuck sometimes and trying to think about how much time happened and I don't know. Maybe it's quick? I'm just going through and trying to encourage myself to think because my brain sometimes stops."

In April 2020, the authorization for his new treatment finally came. But before Malakki could receive it, he was quarantined for two weeks because, although the prison had yet to record a positive COVID case, outside providers wanted to foreclose any possibility that the virus might hitch a ride to their clinic. Then two guards drove him to the clinic, where he spent six hours hooked to an IV. While the guards noodled on their cellphones, he watched movies on demand on the room's television, the first time he ever had the ability to do so, and tried to eat crackers and drink soda while wearing a mask.

Malakki had been skeptical that the new treatment would work as quickly as the neurologist had claimed. But that first day, he noticed an immediate improvement. The pain lessened dramatically. He could speak faster.

When he returned to the prison, Malakki was quarantined for another two weeks to ensure that he had not contracted COVID. Staff failed to place him in a handicap cell with a bar next to the toilet. Instead, he needed to position his wheelchair near the toilet as a makeshift handicap bar, typically a laborious process. After a few days, the routine became easier. It took him less time to get dressed, tie his shoes, or accomplish other basic tasks. The agonizing tingling no longer woke him at night. For the first time in years, he felt refreshed in the morning. He no longer felt weak, sluggish, and fighting to stay awake.

When he was returned to his usual cell, the entire prison had been quarantined. When he called Pearl or his mother, Malakki could hear the worry in their voices. He tried to keep his tone upbeat, assuring them that he was locked in his cell more than twenty-three hours each day and that he wore his mask during his twenty minutes out. He even covered the phone receiver with a clean sock before bringing it to his face.

Malakki was fortunate that the pandemic had not further postponed his new treatment. When the time for his next infusion neared, he wasn't as lucky. That fall, prison staff told him that it had been rescheduled. They offered no explanation, which is typical in many jails and prisons. His medical records stated that his missed therapy was "due to COVID," though Malakki had never contracted or tested positive for the virus. No new appointment was scheduled.

Instead, through the window of his cell door, Malakki watched officers place paper "plus" signs on the doors of those who had tested positive, each one closer to his own door.

Later, in a halfhearted effort to ensure confidentiality, staff replaced the plus signs with signs bearing the word "MEDICAL," but in his mind's eye, Malakki still saw rows of plus signs creeping nearer.

Left untreated, Malakki's condition rapidly deteriorated. The pain returned, badly enough to bring tears to his eyes. Sometimes he was in too much discomfort to use the shower. His mobility and speech worsened once again. "There were times when I might have four or five days in a row where my speech mobility was impacted and I could hardly use the phone," he said. Calling loved ones had allowed him to feel connected to the outside world. Deprived of those conversations and being trapped in a cell all day made him feel like he was moving closer and closer to the grave.

In spring 2021, six months after that canceled follow-up and one year after his initial treatment, his appointment was approved and he received his next infusion. Still, that experience of utter helplessness left him shaken. "I'm still recovering from being in a situation where I could hardly move and watched this [pandemic] happen at the same time," he told me over a year later.

Just as the pandemic led to staffing shortages in the outside world, prisons and jails also experienced staffing shortages. When I interviewed him in spring 2022, Homer Venters, a court-appointed federal monitor, had visited over forty jails and prisons to inspect their COVID protocols. He had also conducted another fifteen inspections of medical care behind bars unrelated to COVID. "Staffing has never been as bad as it's been right now," Venters said. "I routinely go to places where half of the CO [correctional officer, or guard] positions are unfilled."

Although they are not medical staff, guards are nonetheless essential to incarcerated peoples' access to health care. They collect requests for sick call. They issue passes or escort people to the clinic. In some facilities, they dispense daily medications. When people are locked in their cells, they must flag the attention of guards during a crisis. Even in facilities that retained robust staffing, such as Rikers Island, guards often do not monitor people in their cells, frequently fail to bring them to medical appointments, and ignore their calls for help, sometimes with fatal outcomes.[30]

In facilities with fewer guards overseeing many more people, people locked in their cells have even less hope of signaling for help during critical moments, leading to preventable deaths. When a person like Malakki requires outside care, he must be escorted by at least two officers. If two are unavailable, he cannot go. These chronic staffing shortages have led to thousands of canceled appointments.

At the start of June 2022, more than two years after the pandemic hit the United States, the Pennsylvania Department of Corrections had more than 560 overdue outside specialist appointments.[31] That backlog impacted one in every sixty-four people in that prison system, and, as Malakki's experience demonstrates, delays in specialty treatment can have dire consequences.

Pennsylvania's carceral system was not the only one where health care, already inadequate and sometimes deadly, worsened during the pandemic. In 2022, California prison officials admitted that the pandemic had caused a severe backlog of essential visits, including more than ten thousand overdue specialty appointments, approximately six thousand overdue primary care appointments, and nearly one thousand overdue ultrasound exams for end-stage and advanced liver disease.[32]

Rikers Island confined an average of 5,842 people during the first three months of 2022. But between January and April 2022, detained people missed nearly forty thousand medical appointments (or an average of 7.7 appointments per person).[33] A state supreme court judge had previously held the city in contempt for failing to comply with her earlier order to provide access to the jail's clinics at least five days a week. In August 2022, she ordered the city to pay $100 to detained people for each appointment missed between December 11, 2021 through January 2022, for an estimated total of $200,000.[34]

California, New York, and Pennsylvania are not outliers, but these life-threatening inadequacies are known in their systems because of ongoing litigation and court oversight. Other states and jurisdictions have no mandate to collect or publicly report data about medical services—or the lack thereof—leaving family members, advocates, and taxpayers in the dark.

The pandemic pushed state and federal prison systems to report the numbers of active COVID cases, but this new data transparency failed to extend to other aspects of life behind bars. National prison statistics are still released up to two years after the fact, while jail data are reported separately. Both classify only the numbers of people held inside prisons or jails. Neither examine the conditions under which these hundreds of thousands of people are held.

No one knows the full extent of how the pandemic affected the already appalling provision of health care behind bars. "There's no doubt that there's systemic neglect," physician Eric Reinhart stated. "But we don't have the capacity to measure the extent. And if you can't measure it, you can't report it."

Litigation can lead to oversight. A lawsuit can cause a court to order federal monitors or other outside experts to assess the needs of those confined in a jail or prison, and how well (or not) the facility is meeting their needs, as well as assess new risks to their well-being and improvements needed.[35]

But while lawsuits can force some improvements, a 1996 federal law has made it much more difficult for incarcerated people to turn to the courts. The Prison Litigation Reform Act requires that a person exhaust the jail or prison's internal grievance process before filing a lawsuit. That's why Mwalimu made sure he followed each and every step of the grievance process even though he held little hope he would prevail.

In addition, the act prohibits incarcerated people from suing for mental or emotional injury if they cannot also demonstrate physical injury. As the Supreme Court's decisions in *Estelle v. Gamble* and *Plata v. Brown* show, court rulings may still not result in substantially tangible benefits.

Eric Reinhart reminded me that, even before the pandemic, tens of thousands of people died of preventable deaths annually because they could not afford medical care.[36] That number increased exponentially during the pandemic—with one study counting more than 338,000 preventable deaths between 2020 and 2022.[37] "The pandemic should have been a wake-up call to the United States," he told me.

But it wasn't. Instead, it exacerbated not only existing dysfunctions, but also all the conditions that worsen a person's health and increase their vulnerability to premature and preventable illnesses, debilitation, and death.

## Chapter 4

# Long Hot Summer in Lockdown

"It's really somewhat comforting that everyone is living like me now," Kwaneta reflected from her cell as spring turned to summer. If she stuck her arm through her cell's small window, she could feel the sunlight heating her skin, but its beams never reached her face. She smelled the freshly cut grass from the lawn below and heard the songbirds, who woke her before the sun and temperatures rose. She saw feral cats who had learned that the bored women would feed them scraps from their trays through the windows. That month, yellow flowers bloomed in front of the building across from theirs, but she only knew about them from Jack, who yelled descriptions through their shared air vent. Inside her cell, the long-legged nurse could take three steps from her bed before she reached her steel door. Another three steps brought her back to the bed.

"This is like slowly being buried alive," she told me. "Every day adds a shovel full of dirt."

Texas holds more than three thousand people in administrative segregation or restrictive housing, the state's terms for solitary confinement. More than five hundred of those people have been isolated for over a decade. Kwaneta had been in segregation for four years when COVID hit the United States.

The pandemic further shrunk her already-tiny world. Kwaneta and Jack stayed in their cells for months. To avoid the close contact of strip searches and escorts by barefaced guards, they refused the hour of recreation in an outdoor cage offered three times a week. They bathed in their sinks. But when Kwaneta reflected on that time, she realized that she had already become accustomed to staying in her cell for weeks, sometimes months. Officials frequently placed units on lockdown for a variety of reasons—security, lack of staffing, or even an incident as minor as a person on the telephone at an unauthorized time. Sometimes these lockdowns happened back-to-back, with officials not even allowing one day of what might pass for normalcy in the prison within a prison.

She hoped that the national lockdown experience—and most people's inability to cope with enforced isolation—would lead to widespread demands to end solitary confinement.

Meanwhile, she attempted to keep busy, writing letters and reading the many books that her family and friends had sent. Whenever she paused, her neurons filled the mental silence with recriminations and rebukes. "When you are in a concrete box, you're forced to deal with your mind," Kwaneta explained. "And your mind will conjure thoughts that scare you." Her brain replayed every bad decision, every bad relationship, every regret. Drowning in the sea of guilt-laden reminisces pushed her from depression to anger. "Either you blame others and these mental silences transform to revenge fantasies or you internalize the blame, and those mental silences become self-harm fantasies," she told me. Several times a day, she felt as if she were teetering on the edge. "Change the channel," she told herself out loud, forcing her mind into a more distracting direction.

Kwaneta has seen what happens when people are unable to change the channel—from sheets fashioned into nooses to pools of blood on cell floors and walls. Guards nearly always respond with pepper spray. Then they handcuff the coughing and wheezing person before pushing them down the corridor to the unit's medical clinic. There, they are stripped of their uniform, stained orange from the spray, issued a paper gown but no undergarments, and thrust into a cage where a guard watches their every movement. If they need toilet paper, they must ask the guard. If they are menstruating, the guard will give them a pad, but not underwear, forcing them to clench their thighs to prevent blood from trickling down their legs. To get a new pad, they must trade in the soiled one.

During her four years in segregation, Kwaneta counted seven women who succeeded in ending their lives.

Adding to her anxieties was the constant arrival of ambulances, each heralding yet another medical emergency that no one would explain. The ambulances reminded her that, locked away and unable to call home, she had no idea how her family was coping. She wrote letters, but worried that she might inadvertently transmit the virus from the prison to her aging, disabled mother, who was caring for her two daughters. She instructed her mother to put the letters in the icebox before opening them.

When letters arrived from home, she learned that her cousin, also a nurse, had contracted and nearly died from COVID. The two had been close, sometimes working together before Kwaneta's imprisonment. The family's early brush with pandemic mortality sent her into a spiral of dread. "My biggest fear isn't my own death, but my loved ones," she told me. "I had daymares about losing my mother." She played out the scenario. A letter would come. She would beg for an emergency call home, hoping a sympathetic guard would be on duty. And who would take care of her youngest daughter?

The extended lockdown also led to smaller food portions. "I've never been so hungry in my life," she recalled. "I had hunger pains for days." That gnawing hunger made her realize her vulnerability inside prison. Her family had always ensured that she had enough money on her account to buy food at the commissary. She never had to rely solely on the meager prison meals. She had never had to barter sexual acts for food from a guard willing to take advantage of those who lacked outside support. But when the pandemic hit and the commissary closed, she realized that officials could starve them. It was a terrifying revelation.

Texas prisons began distributing masks in early April. The beige masks were sewn at the neighboring Hilltop women's prison with cotton usually used for T-shirts and strings as stiff as shoelaces. Later, the prison would distribute blue surgical masks, which guards sometimes confiscated as contraband, either mistakenly telling women that they were not allowed to have them or demanding that they not wear the same blue masks as the guards themselves.[1] But the preventive measure brought a trade-off, particularly for those in segregation who could only see a few feet past their cell door window and already had to strain to hear announcements through their solid metal doors and the surrounding commotion. To communicate, women had to yell through their doors and across the corridors, competing with the people with severe mental illnesses screaming incoherently, the din of cups or mirrors hitting the steel doors, and others bellowing their own conversations. Guards and other staff had to yell to be heard above the clamor—and they were not always successful.

During the brief period that guards wore masks—and occasionally face shields—hearing and understanding them became nearly impossible. If those in segregation were unable to hear staff, they missed whatever was on offer. "When the pill lady comes to our pod, she or the officer yells, 'Pill line!'" Kwaneta explained. "You must be at the door waiting when she walks by. They don't go backwards, meaning they will not return if you grab your water off the table and miss them." Similarly, if a person was not fully dressed and at their door when meals were announced, guards would not give them a food tray.

By mid-April, some three hundred thousand people in prisons across the country were in some form of lockdown. Depending on the prison, they might be allowed outside for one or two hours. Otherwise, they were left to idle in their cells, feeling punished rather than protected. The number on lockdown encompassed only people in state or federal prisons who were confined to a cell. It did not count those who had been ordered to sit on their beds in dormitories or the hundreds of thousands in local jails, immigrant detention, or youth prisons.[2]

When summer rolled around, many prisons had been on lockdown for weeks, if not months. In some prisons, administrators even used solitary units to quarantine and isolate those who might be sick. In Arkansas, the prisons' director instructed the wardens of the state's twenty prisons to "prepare a portion/area of your punitive isolation areas to house inmates effected [sic] by the corona virus."[3] But, noted Jennifer James, an assistant professor at the University of California San Francisco Institute for Health and Aging, "lockdowns are not designed to do public health work, they're designed to punish. That's really debilitating for incarcerated people."[4]

Years before the coronavirus catapulted the term *lockdown* into the public vocabulary, critics, including psychiatric and public health experts, had condemned solitary confinement as torture. In 2011, their criticisms were bolstered by United Nations special rapporteur Juan Mendez, who stated that solitary confinement exceeding fifteen days constitutes torture.

Despite the growing awareness about the harms of extreme isolation, the practice grew. In 2012, more than 89,000 people were isolated in jails and prisons on any given day.[5] By 2019, 122,840 people, or over 6 percent of the country's jail and prison populations, were locked in their cells for twenty-two or more hours each day.

☀

The nation has a long history of solitary confinement—stretching back to the establishment of the penitentiary. While the penitentiary's extreme solitude proved to be both ineffective at inspiring rehabilitation and costly to local governments, the practice did not end. Instead, it became a tool for punishment and, during the prison building boom of the 1980s, a means of controlling the skyrocketing numbers of people behind bars. States even built entire prisons designed for indefinite isolation.

In 1989, California cut into a forest near the Oregon border to construct the nation's first supermax prison.[6] The 275-acre Pelican

Bay State Prison was built near towering redwoods and the Pacific coastline.[7] But those locked inside could see none of this beauty. Instead, they spent twenty-three hours each day in windowless seven-by-eleven-foot cells inside the Security Housing Unit.[8] Authorities called it the prison for the "worst of the worst"—people who were classified as gang members or affiliates. These classifications—or "validations," in prison parlance—frequently relied on evidence that could be as circumstantial as having drawings of Chicano or Aztec art, exercising with others who had been labeled gang associates, or signing a group petition. Sometimes validations were based on confidential information and confidential informants, leaving the accused clueless about the reasons for their validation and indefinite isolation.

For decades, there were only three paths out of the SHU—"parole, debrief, or die." Debriefing entails both renouncing gang membership and informing on other gang associates. Those named in a debriefing are then validated and sent to the SHU.

In 1998, four years after he first entered prison on a drug-dealing conviction, Mwalimu was sent to the SHU at Pelican Bay. Authorities charged him with inciting a riot, although he insists that he had not. They also validated him as a member of the Black Guerrilla Family.[9] Mwalimu never learned the reason for his validation, but believed it was his participation in African American study groups. His guess wasn't baseless: other Black people who studied Black history and culture had also been validated and sent to the SHU.

Mwalimu remained in the SHU for two years. When he was paroled, the validation remained in his file. For the next three years, each time he returned to prison—for a parole violation or a new charge—officials placed him in the SHU even though he had not broken any prison rules.

Todd Ashker, one of Pelican Bay's first prisoners, had spent even longer in the SHU. Todd was first sent to the SHU at Folsom State Prison after he fatally stabbed another man during a fight in

1988.[10] Officials classified him as a member of the Aryan Brother-hood, an affiliation that Todd has continually denied.[11] Two years later, he was sent to the recently opened Pelican Bay, where he would spend the next twenty-seven years—and eventually mobi-lize to end the practice of indefinite isolation.

Between 2008 and 2009, Todd read *Nothing but an Unfin-ished Song*, a biography of Irish political prisoner Bobby Sands. Sands had embarked upon a sixty-six-day hunger strike to protest prison conditions in Northern Ireland. He died with his goals un-fulfilled, but the idea of a collective hunger strike inspired Todd. Throughout the next year, he and other men shouted through the windows of their cell doors, discussing the possibility of a protest. Based on their conversations, often shouted from person to person down the corridor like the children's game of Telephone, Todd drafted a written complaint, which he sent to legislators and prison officials. "The prison's response was, 'File a grievance if you haven't already,'" he later told me.[12]

In 2009, Todd and Danny Troxell, who had spent twenty years in the Pelican Bay SHU, filed a federal lawsuit charging that prolonged solitary violated the Eighth Amendment prohibition against cruel and unusual punishment. They also charged that the lack of meaningful review of their continued isolation violated their right to due process. Both men became part of the Short Cor-ridor Collective, named after the short hallway of their unit. They shouted potential strategies up and down that corridor before de-ciding on a mass hunger strike to demand an end to both indefinite solitary and the gang-affiliation policies that placed—and kept—them there.

In July 2011, they launched the first of three hunger strikes. That first strike encompassed 1,035 of the 1,111 people in Pelican Bay's SHU. They issued five core demands: an end to group punish-ments for one person's rule-breaking; an end to the debriefing pol-icy and changes to gang classifications; adequate food; constructive programs; and an end to long-term solitary.

The three-week strike spread to thirteen other state prisons and, at its height, involved 6,600 men and women incarcerated throughout California. In September, they launched a second hunger strike. This time, twelve thousand people participated over three weeks. Mwalimu joined both, meditating and reading about Jesus's forty days of fasting to ward off his own hunger pangs.

In 2012, lawyers with the Center for Constitutional Rights (CCR) joined the legal fight and filed an amended complaint. The following year, CCR lawyers asked the court to certify the lawsuit as a class action, which meant the outcome would affect hundreds languishing in the SHU under the state's opaque gang-classification system.

Then, in July 2013, more than thirty thousand prisoners went on hunger strike issuing the same five demands. Mwalimu refused food for forty-five days until he passed out. He vaguely remembered others yelling, "Man down! Man down!" then being rushed to the hospital ward, where doctors inserted an intravenous feeding tube.

Todd and nearly a hundred others continued refusing food for another fifteen days. The sixty-day hunger strike attracted nationwide attention to not only Pelican Bay, but also the wider issue of solitary, reframing the practice as torture rather than an administrative tool to prevent individuals from sowing bedlam and violence throughout the prisons. The remaining hunger strikers resumed eating after state lawmakers announced plans for a hearing to examine the state's SHU policies.[13] Still, they remained in the SHU and their options remained to debrief, parole, or die.

Two years later, in September 2015, attorneys and family members announced a "landmark settlement" with the state prison system. Under the settlement, people who had spent ten or more years in the SHU would be placed in general population or in a new unit. They would still be subject to intense supervision, but could have face-to-face interactions with others, participate in group programs, and have contact visits with loved ones. The settlement also limited placement in Pelican Bay's notorious SHU to no more than five years and changed criteria for SHU placement. No longer could a person be placed in isolation simply on the word of confidential informants and circumstantial evidence. Instead, isolation could only be used when a person had committed a serious infraction of prison rules.[14] For the first time in years—and, for several, the first time in multiple decades—hundreds were allowed to see other people.

Despite the settlement—and the increasing outrage around the practice—solitary confinement continued in California and nationwide under a variety of names: the special housing unit, the security housing unit, administrative segregation, protective custody, restrictive housing, and the closed custody unit. In 2019, California isolated nearly 4,742 (or 4 percent) of its state prisoners.

※

In 2020, prison and jail administrators turned to solitary as their primary means of prevention. At first glance, the practice might make sense. After all, cities, states, and nations had shuttered schools, workplaces, and businesses in an effort to encourage people to stay away from one another. But unlike people sheltering at home, those behind bars could not escape human contact or deadly respiratory particles.

For some, lockdown increased their dangers. In January, "Nancy," a trans woman in a federal men's prison, was moved into a new cell.[15] Initially, she wasn't worried. She already knew her cellmate, who had never hassled her. Once they were in the same cell, however, he repeatedly pressured her for sex. She dodged him by staying off the unit—attending her work assignment and programs. The COVID lockdown cut off those escape routes. During the next several weeks, he raped her multiple times. Nancy never reported these attacks. Although the 2003 Prison Rape Elimination Act mandated that prison officials investigate all sexual harassment and assault allegations, these complaints were rarely addressed. If she lodged a complaint, staff would place her in solitary and she would face further danger from her attacker and his friends.

The rapes ended when he was moved to another unit for a work assignment. But Nancy's respite lasted less than a day. Her next cellmate, enraged at being housed with a trans woman and boiling with resentment from his own six years in prison, turned her into his personal punching bag. The beatings stopped after he was placed in quarantine just before his release. Nancy remained in prison and hoped that her next roommate would be less abusive.

*

In all prisons, including those in which people are locked down supposedly for their own protection, staff remained a constant threat of transmission. Even when prison administrators attempted to stave off this possibility, other agencies undermined their efforts. In April 2020, Arkansas prisons mass-tested both staff and incarcerated people. But the state's health department issued a memo instructing asymptomatic staff who had tested positive to continue reporting to work. Four days later, 826 incarcerated people and thirty-three staff tested positive.[16] Later, the Arkansas prison system, which incarcerated roughly sixteen thousand people, had the nation's tenth-largest outbreak. Similarly, Texas prison officials had initially ordered staff to report to work, even if they had been exposed or tested positive, so long as they were asymptomatic.

From the start of the pandemic, health experts stressed that medical isolation should not mirror punitive solitary.[17] They warned that isolating people would deter them from reporting symptoms, cause additional stress, prevent identifying those who had COVID, and ultimately worsen the crisis. Health professionals urged instead that quarantine and isolation be overseen by medical staff and that the patient be allowed their belongings and daily access to medical and mental health staff. Jails and prisons that could not follow these recommendations needed to decarcerate to prevent COVID outbreaks. The experts especially urged California officials to reduce San Quentin's population—then at 3,547 people—by 50 percent.[18]

Their recommendations were largely ignored. Instead, lockdowns became normalized as the primary response. Conditions mirrored those in punitive solitary. By mid-April, people under some form of lockdown increased 500 percent from sixty thousand to over three hundred thousand within a matter of weeks.[19] And those lockdowns failed to stem the spread, particularly in the prisons already identified as potential hot spots. By June 2020, San Quentin had more than 1,400 active cases, becoming a nightmarish landscape of disease and death.[20]

During the day, nurses went from cell to cell to check vital signs, ask if patients were experiencing symptoms, and call for emergency responses. They repeatedly heard complaints about weakness, pain, difficulty breathing, dizziness, and collapse. Each night, cries of "Man down!" were repeated from cell to cell, alerting the guard on duty to call for medical help.

"Ambulances stationed outside the prison gates awaited fallen COVID-19 victims day and night," recalled prison journalist David Ditto. "A tent city was set up on the recreation yard to temporarily house about 100 infected residents. Incarcerated people were moved into the gymnasium. Four chapels were converted into temporary housing. A factory was converted into an Alternative Care Site and a supplemental medical team was contracted to house and care for over 200 of San Quentin's sickest patients."[21]

That same month, the prison began using its Death Row—which bore the Orwellian name of the "Adjustment Center"—for quarantine and isolation. Known as a "prison within a prison," the Adjustment Center was used also to isolate people whom officials considered a threat to prison security.[22] "No warning shots are fired in this unit or in the exercise yards," cautioned the first page of the orientation manual.[23]

Inside the Adjustment Center, men spent nearly twenty-four hours a day in six-by-eight-foot cells. Their sole windows were two slivers in hollow steel doors facing the corridor; there was no daylight or air flow.[24] At waist height sat a small slot, locked from the outside and unlocked only to deliver food or to handcuff a person before bringing them out of the cell. Mental health visits were also conducted through that slot. A nurse stood outside the cell with a laptop opened so that the men could have telehealth visits with a doctor. While people in other units could use headphones to ensure that the doctor's remarks remained private, the headphones did not fit through the slots in the Adjustment Center doors, allowing everyone within earshot to hear the entire appointment.[25]

Even for those who avoided both COVID and the onerous quarantine conditions, lockdowns felt like further punishment. In Corcoran, Mwalimu felt as if he were back in the SHU. This time, he also had to grapple with the ever-present threat of death. The corridor reeked of disinfectant and chemical sprays. Nurses, blanketed in protective gear, went from cell door to cell door. Some men could barely walk to their door for the temperature check. Others had temperatures so high that they were immediately wheeled from their cells to the prison's medical unit.

"It felt like death was all around us, but you didn't know who was next," he recalled. He wasn't wrong. Later, he learned that some of the men who had been wheeled off had died.

Death wasn't limited to prison walls. When the virus exploded behind bars, each departure carried the probability that staff would bring it home to their families and neighbors. The Prison Policy Initiative, a nonprofit research organization, estimated that, during the summer of 2020, prisons and jails contributed to more than half a million additional COVID-19 cases nationwide—roughly 13 percent of all cases during that stretch of time.[26] Had policymakers heeded the admonitions of public health officials and allowed large-scale releases, they could have averted both outbreaks behind bars and hundreds of thousands of cases in the surrounding areas.

᠁

"Solitary confinement has significant medical consequences," noted Eric Reinhart, the political anthropologist who has studied COVID outbreaks in jails and prisons. People locked in cells frequently cannot flag the attention of the officer on duty. Many people told me that the cell's emergency call button, if one existed, had long been broken. Their only way to call for help was to bang on the door and shout. Sometimes others in neighboring cells would join in, hoping to create a cacophony that could not be ignored. But, like so much about the goings-on behind bars, there is no data about acute incidents in solitary that go unaddressed.

Even when call buttons work, assistance might not arrive in time. Even when staff do respond, they may not actually help. For several years before the pandemic, I had been corresponding with Heather, a trans woman incarcerated at a federal men's prison. Heather had been physically and sexually assaulted by prior cellmates and had been pressing, unsuccessfully, to be transferred to a women's prison. When the prison was locked down—first as a COVID prevention measure and then in response to the Black Lives Matter protests sweeping the nation—she told me that she considered herself lucky that her cellmate treated her with respect. She turned her energies from transferring to a women's prison to preparing for her anticipated release date, peppering me weekly with questions about housing options for formerly incarcerated trans women in New York City.

In October, I stopped hearing from her. Wondering if she had been transferred, I looked her up on the federal prison database. I was stunned to find her listed as deceased. No cause was given. Shortly after, I began receiving e-messages from her cellmate, who told me that Heather had been in increasing pain all month.

"Whenever Heather tried to get medical's attention, they wouldn't even look through the door," he told me. He assumed that she had had a stroke, but the few times they were able to cajole a nurse into examining her, the nurse ignored anything he said.

On the day that Heather died, he told me, a nurse had made rounds in the housing unit offering flu vaccines. Both he and Heather attempted to tell him about her chest pains, but the nurse did nothing. Later that afternoon, when Heather's chest pain worsened, her cellmate hit the emergency call button. It worked—and brought the officer on duty to their cell. The officer took Heather's plight seriously and called for medical help. That brought a nurse, who took her blood pressure and pronounced her fine. One hour later, Heather began throwing up blood and bile. Medical staff gave her acetaminophen and a shot of Maalox, but did not bring her to the medical unit for further examination. Several hours later, Heather collapsed and died.[27]

Another man at that prison wrote me later. His cellmate had witnessed medical staff stopping at Heather's cell throughout the day, then leaving without having done anything. He himself had noticed the deadly hour-long lapse between hearing the alarm from her cell and emergency services arriving.[28]

As far as I know, Heather did not have a next of kin who could press to learn the cause of her death, let alone attempt to hold the federal prison system—including its medical staff—accountable for its inaction. Instead, Heather became another statistic among the 505 deaths in federal prisons that year.[29]

Even when not deadly, prolonged isolation can cause ongoing medical and mental health issues. In the 1990s, psychiatrist Craig Haney began documenting the effects of prolonged solitary on a group of men isolated in Pelican Bay. None had been in solitary for more than four years at that point, but more than 80 percent had already developed overwhelming anxiety and nervousness, regular headaches, severe insomnia, and chronic lethargy. Over half of the men complained about persistent nightmares and heart palpitations. They also grappled with obsessive ruminations, confused thought processes, irrational anger, oversensitivity to stimuli, and increasing fears of interacting with others. Many feared having a nervous breakdown.[30]

Further studies have confirmed the physiological and psychological consequences. A 2019 California study found that hypertension was nearly three times higher among those in solitary than for those in general population. Even relatively short amounts of time in isolation can increase anxiety and disordered thinking; worsen mental health problems; cause hallucinations, paranoia, depression, and post-traumatic stress disorder; and heighten the risk of suicide. It can also cause cardiovascular and gastrointestinal complications, migraines, deteriorating eyesight, fatigue, and muscle pain.[31]

Mary, the Creek grandmother in Oklahoma, can attest to the emotional and mental distress caused by even a short time locked away with just her thoughts. She once spent sixty days in solitary after a fight with her roommate. She was allowed one book, shower supplies, paper, envelopes, stamps, one pair of pajamas, and three bras and three pairs each of panties and socks. The rest of her belongings, including her television and the cheesecake she had purchased from commissary, were placed in the property room. She was left alone with her thoughts. "You don't want to go digging around in there and review all the terrible things people have done to you," she later told me. Her mind replayed the many times she was bullied when she first entered prison—and of the times she fought back. ("I had been in many fights. Growing up with seven brothers I guess has its advantages," she reflected.)

Three times a week, guards cuffed her hands and feet, then escorted her down the hall to the shower. Otherwise, she remained inside the cold cell, attempting to throw spitballs at the ceiling vent

to block out the constant currents of cold air. She was less successful at blocking the constant stream of painful memories.

Even as little as one week in solitary can significantly change
the brain's electrical activity, affecting the hippocampus, which affects learning, memory, spatial awareness, and the body's response
to stress. Isolation also causes a surge of activity in the amygdala,
the region of the brain responsible for mediating fear and anxiety.
People held in isolation frequently report high levels of both.

"There's something about being isolated in a room with one-
self and not having anything productive or meaningful to do that
causes an exacerbation of every form of mental illness," said Terry
Kupers, a psychiatrist who has interviewed more than five hundred
people in solitary. But clinicians are more likely to label repeated
self-injuries as malingering or manipulative behavior rather than as
signs of serious mental illness or suicidality, even though 50 percent
of all prison suicides occur among those in solitary.[32]

These effects haunt people long after they are allowed to re-
join the outside world. Throughout my years of reporting on prisons, I've interviewed dozens of people who have been in solitary.
Many told me that, even years after leaving prison, they suffered
continual headaches, migraines, vertigo, and claustrophobia. They
were leery of crowds and found it draining to connect with others, even their sorely missed loved ones, preferring to stay alone
in their rooms.

Prolonged isolation even augments the risk of premature
death. One of the most tragic examples is Kalief Browder, who, at
age sixteen, was jailed at Rikers for allegedly stealing a backpack.
He maintained his innocence and refused to plead guilty to a crime
he had not committed, even when pleading guilty might have meant
his immediate release. He spent three years awaiting trial. Two of
those years were in solitary confinement.

In 2013, the district attorney withdrew the charges. Kalief
was released. Even as he attempted to rebuild his life, finishing high
school and enrolling in college, he frequently shut himself in his

bedroom and shunned large groups of people. Two years later, he died by suicide. He was twenty-two years old.[33]

Kalief's experience is not unusual. A study of nearly 230,000 people released from incarceration in North Carolina found that people who spent any time in solitary were 24 percent more likely to die in the first year after release, especially from suicide (78 percent more likely) and homicide (54 percent more likely). They were also 127 percent more likely to die of an opioid overdose within the first two weeks of their release.[34]

In 2020, that solitary experience was replicated in cell after cell and dorm after dorm. And this time, the forced inactivity brought both an onslaught of upsetting recollections, recriminations, doubts, fear, and an abject terror of the lethal virus tearing through prisons—and possibly the homes of the loved ones they had left behind.

※

At the start of the pandemic, advocates across the country, including formerly incarcerated people and family members frightened for their imprisoned loved ones, demanded that policymakers respond to the crisis with decarceration. In some states, public pressure pushed lawmakers to heed health experts' advice—at least to a limited extent. In New York, where then governor Andrew Cuomo had been hailed as a hero of the pandemic, advocates and family members held vigils and rallies outside his office and mansion, drawing attention to the population he had been neglecting and demanding that he grant clemencies, or sentence reductions, to lessen the numbers of people in prison. They also organized rallies outside prisons to call attention to the governor's failure to protect his thirty-three thousand imprisoned constituents.

In late March, Cuomo announced that he would release 1,100 people who were in county jails for parole violations. Two weeks later, he lifted warrants for 737 people who had been jailed.

Many confined in the state's prisons for parole violations, however, remained incarcerated. Many of these prisons would soon become hotbeds of exposure.[35]

In California, Governor Gavin Newsom announced the release of some 3,500 people who were already within two months of their release dates. That same week, California prisons held 122,265 people, or 130 percent of their design capacity.[36] Between the two coasts, policymakers and legislators also issued a number of releases to stem the potential spread behind bars. In Arkansas, prisons issued early releases of 658 people who were within six months of release for nonviolent, nonsexual convictions.[37] Kentucky governor Andy Beshear commuted, or shortened, the sentences of roughly one thousand people in the state's prisons. Washington governor Jay Inslee combined commutations with an emergency proclamation, releasing 1,016 people from prisons.[38] New Jersey legislators passed the Public Health Emergency Credit law, allowing people with one year left on their sentence to be released up to eight months earlier. On the first day that the law took effect, 2,258 people were released.

In other places, lawsuits forced early releases. In North Carolina, where the 1994 elimination of parole had caused more crowding, the NAACP, Disability Rights North Carolina, and other civil rights organizations filed suit against the state's prison system, winning the early release of some 3,500 people. These expedited releases applied only to those who were already within six months of their release date; they did not extend to those still facing one or more years behind bars.[39]

Altogether, state and federal prisons released 549,600 people in 2020. Of those, 80,658 people were released under some measure related to the 2020 pandemic response.[40] Those numbers might seem adequate until compared with the previous non-pandemic year. In 2019, 608,026 people were released after finishing their sentences or being granted parole.[41] The number of pre-pandemic releases was 10 percent higher than the combined total of emergency pandemic and regularly scheduled releases.

These releases did not prevent chaos and death once COVID made its way inside. In mid-December 2020, six months after the much-publicized early pandemic releases, a team of public health experts visited California's Corcoran State Prison. By then, although the prison had spent most of the year on lockdown, over 3,000 prisoners (nearly 70 percent of Corcoran's population) and one-third of staff had tested positive.[42] The prison also remained over capacity, incarcerating 4,314 people in a facility designed for 3,424 men. Nearly every housing unit had positive cases.

Unlike San Quentin, Corcoran had solid walls and solid doors separating cells, but virus-laden air still circulated through the vents connecting the cells.[43] In mid-October, outbreaks had occurred predominantly in these cellblocks. Although those outbreaks slowed, people continued testing positive. By July 2023, over 70 percent of Corcoran's 3,732 prisoners had tested positive. Across the state, over 97 percent of California's total prison population had been struck by COVID and 260 individuals (or 3 percent of state prisoners) had died. In comparison, the state's COVID death rate was 23.2 for every 100,000 Californians (or 0.023 percent).[44]

Policymakers—whether lawmakers or prison officials—could have followed the guidance of public health experts and released sufficient numbers of people to adequately reduce the risk of pandemic morbidity. Decarceration also would have been a significant step in addressing the ongoing crisis of mass incarceration and the destruction it has wreaked on millions. Instead, they transformed the tactics recommended to people on the outside—especially isolating at home—into another means of punishment.

## Chapter 5

# The Twin Pandemics

The coronavirus starkly illustrated the racial and economic disparities of US social structures. By late May 2020, the first wave of stimulus checks had arrived and been spent, leaving low-income people once again struggling to stay afloat in an economy that had tanked. COVID disproportionately killed Black people, underlining the systemic racism within both the economic and health care systems. At the same time, Black people continued to be disproportionately policed and punished, with the pandemic as the latest justification. Black and Indigenous people of color were two and a half times more likely than their white counterparts to be policed and punished for violating local COVID policies. Black people were also four and a half times more likely to experience police enforcement of public health orders and were more likely to be arrested as part of that enforcement.[1]

Two years earlier, in 2018, the American Public Health Association had adopted a resolution recognizing police violence as a threat to public health. The association also demanded a public health approach to addressing the social health determinants and inequities that create criminalized behaviors. That approach included increasing access to housing, educational and employment opportunities, medical and mental health care, and substance use treatment.[2]

In the criminal legal system, the racial gap behind bars slowly began to dwindle during the seven years before the coronavirus upended the world. In March 2013, Black people comprised nearly 42 percent of state prison populations. By March 2020, they made up less than 39 percent of state prisoners. The disparity was still staggering, given that Black people made up 13.4 percent of the nation's residents. But the decline indicated that some reforms had started to narrow the gap.

That stopped with the pandemic. During the first eight months, the nation's prison population decreased by 17 percent (or nearly twenty-eight thousand people) as courts closed, fewer people were sentenced to prisons, and prisons continued to release people as scheduled (and, in some cases, via early releases). But these measures were not implemented equitably across racial lines. During those months, the percentage of Black people behind bars rose nearly 1 percent. "People look at the [percentage] increase and can say it's not a big deal but we know that 1 percent is tens of thousands of Black individuals that are affected by this," explained Elizabeth Hinton, a Yale professor and lead author of the study that uncovered these racial disparities.[3]

At the same time, systemic racism continues to shorten lives. Between 1999 and 2020, the nation had 1.63 million more deaths among Black people than their white counterparts. Their deaths totaled more than 80 million lost years.[4] Researchers found that these higher mortality rates were caused not by genetics, but by the cumulative effects of the United States' long history of racism, which has long undermined educational, housing, and job opportunities for generations of Black people. Dr. Arline T. Geronimus, a health behavior professor at the University of Michigan, uses the term *weathering* as a framework to describe the corrosive effects of systemic oppression on marginalized people's bodies. Groups that experience systemic cultural oppression, long-term material hardship, exploitation, stigma, and political marginalization experience biological aging before they have actually aged.[5]

These racial disparities have become so entrenched that higher mortality rates persist across education and class lines. Black women with college degrees are still more likely to die from pregnancy complications than white women without high school diplomas. Black Americans who complete college are at higher risk for heart disease than white Americans who have not graduated from college. Middle-age Mexican immigrants are more likely to suffer stress-related chronic diseases if they've lived in the United States for more than a decade even as their incomes rise. The toxic stress of racism causes increased heart rate, blood pressure, and stress hormones. Continual toxic stress—and continual increases in these reactions—accelerates the aging process.[6]

Accumulated weathering and toxic stress meant COVID impacted marginalized people worse than their more privileged counterparts. Black people were 1.6 times more likely to die from COVID, while Native Americans were twice as likely to die and 2.5 times more likely to be hospitalized with severe COVID than their white counterparts.[7] The twin pandemics of structural racism and the new contagious virus proved to be a debilitating, and often deadly, combination.

This all came to a boil on May 25, 2020. That Memorial Day afternoon, Derek Chauvin, a white Minneapolis police officer with a lengthy history of brutalizing people, killed forty-six-year-old George Floyd. In front of a crowd of horrified onlookers, he knelt on Floyd's neck for eight minutes and forty-six seconds as Floyd repeatedly gasped that he could not breathe. Seventeen-year-old Darnella Frazier captured those deadly minutes on her cell phone. She posted the video to Facebook, where it quickly went viral, sparking international outrage.

Floyd's murder came on the heels of several well-publicized killings of other Black people—the February murder of jogger Ahmaud Arbery by two white men in Georgia and the March murder of Breonna Taylor by Kentucky police who fatally shot her during a no-knock raid at the wrong house. Two days after Floyd's death, Florida police fatally shot Tony McDade, a trans man.

Between 15 and 26 million people donned masks and took to the streets nationwide in protest, many under the banner of Black

Lives Matter. Many demanded the arrest and prosecution of Chauvin. And across the country, many also issued another demand of their city officials as they were finalizing the following year's budgets—to defund the police, or decrease the police budget and redirect those funds to perpetually underfunded resources, such as low-income or affordable housing, health care, and education. That demand became a rallying cry echoed in cities—and smaller towns—across the nation.

Hundreds of protests, which the New York Times described as the largest movement in US history, and the brutal police response, drew widespread public attention to the other, often overlooked pandemic in the United States—institutional racism.[8] In the second half of 2020, The Lancet and, later, the New England Journal of Medicine, two of the world's oldest medical journals, would identify racism in the United States as a public health crisis.[9]

Many locked within the country's jails and prisons were already well familiar with the country's institutional racism. In 2020, Black people in the United States were incarcerated in state or federal prisons at five times the rate of their white counterparts.[10] They made up 33 percent of the US prison population, despite only comprising 14 percent of the nation's population.[11]

※

Memorial Day 2020 was a typical day in segregation at Texas's Lane Murray Unit. One woman, hearing about Floyd's murder on the local radio, yelled through her door, "106, y'all. Somebody shot another one!" But by the time Kwaneta tuned into the rap station, the news was over. She turned to NPR, which said nothing about it. She fiddled with the radio dial until she landed on a conservative talk station whose hosts said that the Minneapolis district attorney would not press charges.

Later, she and Jack shouted through the air vents about the latest killing. They wondered what justification police and prosecutors would use to not investigate or prosecute. Would they say Floyd had been resisting arrest? Failing to comply? Then Kwaneta began hearing about the protests in hundreds of cities, many with majority-white populations. She recalled high school lessons about white activists working alongside Black civil rights organizers during the 1960s. But before 2020, she had never heard about white protesters physically putting themselves between police and Black people.

As she followed the protests on NPR, Kwaneta wondered whether the movements to defund the police and seek greater police accountability would extend to more restrictions on prison staff violence against those they guarded. "Will the banning of chokeholds apply in prison?" she wondered. As the news spread, Black women at Murray wrote "Black Lives Matter" on their masks. Some white women wrote "All Lives Matter" on theirs. The guards, many of them white, seemed more on edge. They accused the Black women of attempting to incite a riot, sending five to segregation. Whenever a woman said, "Black lives matter," guards responded, "All lives matter."

As a mother, Kwaneta always worried about her three children who, by that point, had spent most of their lives without her. As a Black mother, she was plagued by the additional fear that they could become statistics of police violence. When she heard about Floyd's murder, she wrote to Antonio and Alana, who were both old enough to drive. She urged them to be careful. She reminded them that, if they were pulled over by the police, their goal was to get home alive.

Kwaneta had never been to a protest. She did not worry that Antonio, then in his twenties and largely focused on his career, would take to the streets and risk arrest. Alana, too, had shown little interest in protests. "Funny, I didn't talk too much to my youngest about it," Kwaneta recalled. Later, Kwaneta's mother told her that "Autumn," then in her early teens, had protested with her father and his family.[12]

"Mom said she turned on the TV and she was in the background [of a protest]!" Kwaneta recalled. While Autumn never answered her mother's questions about protesting, or how she felt about being on the streets, Kwaneta remembered receiving a letter in which Autumn said that her mother's generation had failed hers. In her response, Kwaneta apologized. That was the extent of their conversation about protests and the issues that had sparked them.

Kwaneta later explained to me that she had spent her adult life preoccupied with working, raising her three children, and surviving. Surviving included living through—and leaving—several abusive relationships. The one time she had attempted to go to a protest was before her children were born. She and her then husband lived on a military base in California. He had prohibited her from attending a protest, fearful that his white colleagues would disapprove. When she tried to go, military personnel refused to allow her off base.

Even so, Kwaneta wasn't unfamiliar with police militarization. She had grown up in Detroit where, every October 30, hundreds of buildings were set ablaze in a terrifying tradition that became known as "Devil's Night." The sounds of fire engine sirens were accompanied by gunshots as homeowners fired into the air to warn away would-be arsonists.

Police militarization intensified in the mid-1980s as city officials attempted to douse the yearly destruction. That included police tanks rumbling down the streets, thousands of patrolling volunteers, and a citywide curfew for anyone under age seventeen.

When she was seventeen, Kwaneta's boyfriend visited her at her grandparents' house that evening. Fearing that police would arrest him simply for being a young Black man on that particular night, Kwaneta's grandparents allowed him to stay over—although the boy slept in their den and Kwaneta remained in her room. Kwaneta still remembers standing on her grandparents' porch and seeing a police tank on the corner. But years of these coordinated policing efforts had already extinguished the worst of the conflagrations. No fires occurred on their block that night. No stench of smoke wafted over from the surrounding blocks.

Kwaneta recalled thinking that the night hardly seemed to warrant her grandfather's—or the city's—extreme reactions.[13]

Reading about the heavily militarized police presence at the protests made her remember not only the fires that, once upon a time, had set her home city ablaze, but also the extreme police responses that continued long after the tradition had been snuffed out.

※

In the cell directly below Kwaneta's, Jack had been working on a drawing about his own experience with police brutality when NPR first broadcast news of Floyd's death. His parents had warned him at a very early age not to disrespect or antagonize police if he encountered them. But being respectful didn't protect him from police harassment. Once, after his cousin's ex-girlfriend claimed that he had run her over, police pulled Jack and his cousin out of their car at gunpoint and ordered them face down onto the sidewalk. They remained there, terrified, until another officer confirmed that the woman had not been injured. The police left, offering no apology.

When he had been homeless, police continually harassed him for panhandling or sleeping outside. Sometimes they issued violations, which quickly turned into warrants and a night in jail. Other times, they destroyed the encampment where he was staying.

Police violence toward Black people seemed so commonplace, however, that Jack registered, but didn't dwell on, Floyd's death. Like Kwaneta, Jack also had a subscription to USA Today, courtesy of an outside friend. Shortly after that NPR broadcast, he began reading about the demands to defund the police. Yet, aside from a frustrating conversation shouted through the vent to an older white woman in an adjoining cell, who believed that Floyd's death was an isolated incident blown out of proportion, Jack didn't discuss the events unfolding across the nation. In November, he was scheduled to go before the prison's classification committee, which would decide whether he should remain in segregation or be moved to a less restrictive unit after more than six years in isolation. Jack knew that a write-up for violating any prison rule, even a bogus ticket from a guard who disagreed with his political views, would count against him. He would take no chances.

"Had I been in the free world, I would have been part of the multitude of protesters taking to the streets," he explained. "But being inside is a game of survival and I unfortunately had to put my best interest ahead of where my heart was telling me I belonged."[14]

In Oklahoma, two women on Mary's unit staged a short-lived protest—tacking up handwritten signs with the names of people killed by police on cell doors. Mary had never participated in a protest—either in or out of prison, but she allowed one of the women to post a sign on her door.

In prison, people are not allowed to post items on their doors—not photos, drawings, and especially not protest signs. Officers quickly quashed the demonstration, ordering women to remove the signs. By then, the cafeteria had reopened and women were allowed to walk there, retrieve their meal trays, and bring them to their pods. Shortly after Floyd's murder, Mary tried to crack a joke after waiting in line for ten minutes. "They ran out of burgers and now we're getting bologna!" she exclaimed. "We'll have none of that," the officer in charge sharply scolded her.

That officer was not one known for punishing or even chastising women. She and Mary had always been on good terms. Her reprimand made Mary realize how nervous the guards were. "I could tell the officers are ready for a riot, and I understood, even joking, I could be taken to lock [solitary confinement]. I could even be maced," she told me, referring to the officers' practice of using pepper spray against those in custody.

It wasn't an unreasonable fear. Even during non-pandemic times, being pepper-sprayed causes a burning and stinging sensation in a person's eyes, nose, mouth, and throat. Some have described feeling as if they are being asphyxiated or drowning. In jails and prisons, where a person is often handcuffed and thrown into solitary immediately after being sprayed—and denied the opportunity to wash their face—the pain can last several hours, if not multiple days. It has also caused deaths.

Mwalimu has been sprayed while in prison. It felt like his skin was on fire. Although prison policy dictates that guards place a person into the shower to wash the contaminant off, they instead placed him in a holding cage where he had just enough room to stand up. There was no sink. He remained there for three hours. That was what had triggered the need for surgery.

The pain isn't limited to those who are sprayed. Though he has never been sprayed while imprisoned, Jack has been nearby when guards have sprayed someone else. The residual gas caused his eyes to burn and his mucus membranes to go into overdrive. For the next twenty minutes, mucus poured over his mouth and chin while tears streamed from eyes that became too painful to open.

During the pandemic, however, the excruciating pain came with the added risk of increasing susceptibility to viruses, including the coronavirus. A 2014 study by the US Army had already found that recruits who were exposed to tear gas as part of a training exercise were more likely to develop respiratory illnesses, such as the common cold and the flu. "We have a lot of antiviral defenses that can inactivate viruses and prevent them from entering cells," stated Sven Eric Jordt, a researcher at Duke University's School of Medicine who studies the effects of tear gas. But, he cautioned as the summer protests—and police reprisals—heated up, tear gas both depletes and compromises these defenses.[15]

His warnings were echoed by Dr. John Balmes, a pulmonologist at the University of California, San Francisco, and an expert with the American Thoracic Society. "I actually think we could be promoting COVID-19 by tear-gassing protesters," Balmes cautioned. "It causes injury and inflammation to the lining of the airways."[16] The inflammation impedes the body's defenses, increasing the likelihood that someone who is COVID-positive but asymptomatic will become sick. Dr. Amesh Adalja, a spokesperson for the Infectious Diseases Society of America and a senior scholar at the Johns Hopkins Center for Health Security, agreed, stating that the choking and coughing caused by tear gas increases respiratory—and thus viral—spread.[17]

Law enforcement ignored these admonitions. On the streets, police responded to protests by unleashing pepper spray in crowds. And, in jails and prisons across the country, guards continued to spray people heedless of the additional—and potentially deadly—risks.

In the 2000s, Mwalimu went from prison brawls to studying Black history and Black freedom struggles. He read books by and about Marx, Engels, Mao, Che Guevara, and Robert Williams. He also read about racial capitalism, a phrase originated by Black Marxist Cedric Robinson to examine the ways in which capitalism depended on deriving social and economic value from the racial identity of other people. He read about the Black Panther Party. He also studied the words of people who became politicized while in prison, including Malcolm X and George Jackson, who had also been influenced by the Panthers. These readings reshaped his worldview.

In 2017, Mwalimu was released from the SHU. He and others in his housing unit formed study groups. He also participated in reading groups with outside activists. They sent him the books they were studying. Then he called in to their meetings and, via speaker phone, voiced his thoughts and reflections.

Surprisingly, he and his study cohort did not discuss the protests, the demands to defund the police, or what their communities might look like with more resources from divested police budgets. Instead, their readings and conversations remained focused on the conditions they confronted on a daily basis—and challenging every infringement upon the few rights they had.

That summer, as Black Lives Matter protests swept the nation, he and others filed grievances over the prolonged pause on programs and against officers who targeted Black men, ransacking their cells and confiscating their reading materials. They filed writs of habeas corpus, petitioning the courts to release them from COVID-filled prisons. "We felt like it's good that they're organizing out there and challenging injustices, but we're still doing likewise in here," Mwalimu replied when I asked about their seeming disinterest. "Prison lives matter too."

Pennsylvania prisons were still on lockdown when Floyd was killed. By then, Malakki had become accustomed to spending most of his day alone in his cell. He had enrolled in correspondence courses toward a degree in social work. He was working on his homework when the television aired footage of protesters holding signs demanding that police be defunded. The concept was not new to Malakki. "I first heard and talked about defunding the police in the early '90s," he told me, referring to pre-prison days when he and others had DJed dance parties and performed spoken word in and around Pittsburgh. During the late 1980s and early 1990s, he had watched television footage of armored personnel carriers demolishing homes in Los Angeles's poor communities of color during police drug raids. He and his circle of spoken word artists incorporated analyses of this blatant state violence into their poems and pieces. In between performances, they also held lively discussions with one another.

In the mid-1990s, Malakki was sentenced to death for fatally shooting a man during a robbery. Shortly before he arrived at

Death Row, six men had dug a forty-foot-long tunnel and escaped from another Pennsylvania prison.[18] In response, officials locked down all prisons. They also issued new regulations drastically limiting what people were—and were not—allowed to do, particularly on Death Row. Staff confiscated radio antennae, rendering the devices useless. All belongings had to fit inside one box. Whatever didn't fit would either be shipped home, at the incarcerated person's expense, or destroyed.[19]

These new regulations were implemented as Malakki shuffled off the transport bus. For those facing execution, being unable to readily access their legal work—boxes accumulated over years of court challenges and motions—could literally mean the difference between life and death.

The men on Death Row launched a rolling hunger strike. Each day, a certain number of men refused their food trays. Waging a rolling hunger strike allowed them to rotate on and off, lessening the chance of serious health consequences within a system that had repeatedly proven unconcerned about their well-being. Because Malakki was new, they assigned him the role of second-string, or backup, hunger striker. He stepped in to relieve men who had refused food for four or five days. He doesn't know how many people stopped eating, but some of the older men, who later became his mentors, estimated that at least seventy people participated in the month-long strike.

Members of the nearby Bruderhof community, a politically progressive Christian movement opposed to the death penalty, rallied outside the prison. Their protests made the demands visible and attracted media attention. The combined actions forced authorities to rescind their restrictions. Men were allowed to keep their belongings, and those who had already mailed out their possessions were reimbursed for the hefty postage costs.

It was Malakki's first protest. The victory felt empowering.

Decades later, Malakki participated in the prison's first Inside-Out program, in which outside college students and incarcerated men took a course together. They learned about restorative justice, an approach in which the focus is not on meting out the harshest punishment to the wrongdoer, but instead on centering and meeting the needs of the person(s) injured or harmed. In prison, Malakki and the other Inside-Out students were pushed to reflect on the damages they had wrought—not just to their immediate victims, but also to their victims' and their own loved ones. They examined their own past histories of trauma, explored the idea that "hurt people hurt people," and brainstormed ways to stop the cycles of violence and harm.

From there, Malakki and other incarcerated students started a think tank to share these concepts with their peers. When he was transferred, Malakki tried to start a think tank at the next prison, but COVID stymied his efforts.

In the summer of 2020, the prison remained on lockdown. Even if they had been so inclined, no one could gather to discuss the police killings, the mass protests, or their implications. Each day, staff opened four cells at a time for twenty-minute periods. During those scant minutes, those four men raced to the phones or showers, hoping to hear a loved one's voice or wash the grit off their bodies. They had no time for chatter, let alone a conversation, about the politics and protests unfolding in the world outside. Instead, their focus was on surviving inside.

By June, the mood at Mabel Bassett had quieted. No one talked about police violence, George Floyd, or protests. Instead, the women were looking forward to an upcoming talent show. The unit manager, ordinarily a stickler for the rules and the officer most likely to confiscate even their prison-approved belongings, had organized a talent show for Juneteenth. "Several of the ladies had family members who had succumbed to the COVID disease," Mary explained. The show was an effort to lift their spirits and establish "a semblance of normalcy to our disrupted lives."

Juneteenth commemorates the 1865 day in which two thousand federal troops rode into Texas and announced that slavery had ended. Two years earlier, Lincoln had issued the Emancipation Proclamation, ending chattel slavery in states that had seceded during the Civil War, but enforcement had been sparse in the Lone Star State. Juneteenth had long been celebrated in Black communities, particularly Southern Black communities, as the end of chattel slavery in the United States. But despite its name and timing, the Juneteenth talent show had no connection to that historic day. Instead, the unit manager envisioned it as an apolitical celebration of life, divorced from the country's current or past racial reckonings.

That afternoon in the yard, the mood was jovial. On the basketball court, women lip-synched, sang, and danced. A prison band of two guitarists, a drummer, and keyboardist played Bruno Mars's song "24K Magic" while women line danced. The unit manager handed out frozen pops of assorted colors to the waiting performers. This included Mary, who nervously rehearsed her four jokes while the sun scorched her skin. But, overcome by the heat, half of the women had pulled their masks to their chins or removed them completely. The warden, monitoring through the yard's surveillance cameras, saw the lack of compliance and ordered the show stopped.

Women grumbled as they were herded back inside, complaining about being expected to mask while sweltering under the sun. Mary returned to her cell and griped to her bunkie, "Just my luck! The talent show got shut down before I could tell my awesome jokes."

While the people with whom I had been corresponding were either physically unable to protest Floyd's killing or wary of reprisals, others were vocal about both expressing their outrage and tying his death to the injustices they faced behind bars.

In April, more than two hundred people detained at the Mesa Verde immigration detention center in Bakersfield, California, went on hunger strike to demand that Immigration and Customs Enforcement (ICE) stop transferring new people from jails and prisons. This had been a long-standing demand by immigrant rights advocates, but it took on greater urgency as each new arrival brought the threat of an outbreak. The detention center, operated by private prison contractor GEO Group, confined four hundred people split between four 100-bed dorms, making social distancing impossible.[20] Hunger strikers also demanded that staff wear masks and gloves, that detained people be given adequate hygiene and cleaning supplies, and that they be tested when experiencing COVID symptoms.[21]

Although fourteen women were abruptly released from Mesa Verde in early May, conditions still hadn't improved much by the time Floyd's murder rolled across their television sets. The week before, seventy-four-year-old Choung Woohn Ahn had died by suicide while in medical isolation.[22]

As they watched the footage of Floyd's death, then of police brutalizing protesters, the men at Mesa Verde embarked upon another hunger strike. This time, their actions were not only to protest the deplorable conditions but also to express solidarity with the Black Lives Matter movement outside. On June 4, Asif Qazi, a father who had been detained since February, handed a piece of paper announcing the strike to a guard.[23] "We, the detained people of dormitories A, B, and C at Mesa Verde ICE Detention Facility, are protesting and on hunger strike in solidarity with the detained people at Otay Mesa Detention Center," he had written. "We begin our protest in memory of our comrades George Floyd, Breonna Taylor, Oscar Grant, and Tony McDade. Almost all of us have also suffered through our country's corrupt and racist criminal justice system before being pushed into the hands of ICE."

Nearly every person in Qazi's seventy-person dorm joined in the strike. That weekend, they used the prison's video-visiting equipment to record a statement to the outside world. "We stand with the Black Lives Movement, and against the system that took the life of George Floyd, Breonna Taylor, Tony McDade, and so many Black people," one man read from a prepared statement. He called on ICE to release people from detention, where social distancing remained impossible, and demanded that the governor and state attorney general investigate conditions inside. As he read, other men, clad in bright orange jumpsuits, briefly walked to the screen, holding up signs and white cloth masks on which they had written, in English and Spanish, "Stop the discrimination," "BLM," "Stop racism," and "We are human."[24]

Their strike lasted four days. The next month, after a nurse had tested positive, seventy people embarked on another hunger strike. Once again, they demanded that ICE make the environment safer, enacting COVID prevention methods and providing food that was not spoiled or moldy. If the agency could not ensure their safety, the hunger strikers demanded, it should release them. They also announced that their strike was in solidarity with another hunger strike at San Quentin, where more than one-third of the imprisoned population had tested positive.[25]

That same month, at the federal prison in Danbury, Connecticut, Esther Arias made a video call to her son and asked him to stream it on Facebook Live. One month earlier, then attorney general William Barr had ordered federal prison officials to release more people to home confinement. While they would still technically be incarcerated, they would at least be in their homes rather than dormitories crammed with hundreds of others. But, Esther told her son, although all of the women there were classified as low risk and should qualify, Danbury officials were selecting women whose release dates were within a few months. She and hundreds of others remained trapped in potential hot spots simply because of their release dates. Staff were also cavalier about the safety of those left behind: one woman in Esther's housing unit had tested positive three times, yet staff refused to move her from the dorm that confined 160 others.

Esther made two other video calls that month. Both times she asked her son to stream them on Facebook Live, hoping to reach a wider audience. She reported on the prison staff's continued refusal to move the woman who had tested positive. Two weeks later, when her bunkmate became sick, the lieutenant on duty refused to call for medical help. Only after another person on the unit, fifty-eight-year-old Marius Mason, called his attorney was the woman taken to the hospital.

In her video calls, Esther repeatedly asked viewers to contact the attorney general's office and demand more releases. Inside the prison, she urged others to tell their families to do the same. Esther faced consequences for speaking out. When she tested positive later that month, she spent two weeks in the visiting room, which had become the makeshift quarantine unit. When she tested negative, officials moved her to solitary, where she remained over three weeks until her release date. "They said I was the reason they were getting so much attention," she told me when I interviewed her later that year.[26]

Even those who were not actively engaging in protests or collective organizing faced repercussions.

On July 20, 2020, at the Correctional Training Facility in Soledad, California, approximately two and a half hours north of Corcoran, prison officials launched Operation Akili (the Swahili word for "intelligence"). At 3 a.m., guards from Soledad and neighboring prisons, clad in full riot gear, pulled approximately two hundred Black people from both their slumber and their cells, forced them to strip, then herded them into the cafeteria. Some slammed the handcuffed men against the wall or to the ground, placed them in chokeholds or headlocks, pushed them down the stairs, punched, and kicked them. Officers lobbed the N-word and other racial slurs at them. One man recalled that guards shouted, "By the time this ordeal is over, you n—— will have COVID-19!" Another said officers burst into his cell yelling, "Black Lives Don't Matter!"[27]

The men remained handcuffed and held close together in the cafeteria for hours while guards tore apart their cells searching for evidence of gang-related activity. Many were in their underwear, and none had had time to put on masks. Other staff interrogated them about their views about Black Lives Matter. "How do you feel about what happened to George Floyd?" one officer asked.[28] Staff also questioned them about the Black Guerrilla Family, which California prison authorities classified as a "security threat group." Officials have used possession of books and literature about Black history and the Black Power movement, as well as photos of Black political leaders, as evidence of a person's affiliation. Until 2015, any alleged affiliation was justification for isolating a person in the SHU. (This had happened to Mwalimu.)

With the 2015 settlement agreement, validation no longer resulted in immediate and indefinite isolation. But the label still subjects the person to increased surveillance and harassment, including more frequent cell searches.[29]

Hours later, the men returned to their ransacked cells. Many were missing letters, writing supplies, photos, books, and the phone numbers and addresses of family members. In the weeks that followed, authorities validated fifty to seventy people as suspects, associates, or members of the Black Guerrilla Family.

Within days, the prison, which had had no cases, reported its first three COVID cases. Two had been victims of Operation Akili. The third was the cellmate of a person who had been searched.[30] But that was just the start. Confirmed cases began to rise exponentially, doubling and sometimes tripling each month. One month after the raid, the prison had 70 confirmed cases. By November, that number had skyrocketed to 248, and by early December to 660.[31]

The following year, the men who had been brutalized filed two separate lawsuits. The first, *Adams et al. v. Koenig et al.*, accuses prison officials of racist violations, assault, battery, the weaponization of disease, and the intentional infliction of emotional distress. The second, *Williams v. CDCR*, was filed as a class-action lawsuit challenging the state prison system's validation policies regarding security threat groups.[32] As of 2023, both were winding their way through the court process.

These raids—and the threat of additional punishments—have not stopped organizing among incarcerated people, either in solidarity with other movements or to improve their immediate conditions. Repression also has not halted efforts by incarcerated people to educate and support one another, whether through formal groups or by informally lending each other reading materials or sharing new concepts. Shouting through the door of her solitary cell in Texas, Kwaneta continued to teach younger people in neighboring cells about ideas like consent. She debunked commonly held misconceptions, including the idea that miscarriages and HIV were punishments from God. In Oklahoma, Mary, who had never had the chance to complete high school or attend college before her incarceration, shared what she learned from her college textbooks, explaining concepts like postpartum depression and alcoholism. "Women like me never hear these words," she explained. Although they didn't know the words, these unspoken realities had shaped their lives, and she wanted to be sure that they understood these forces.

These organizing and mutual aid efforts continued even as summer temperatures soared and the ongoing dangers posed by COVID continued to shrink their already restricted worlds.

## Chapter 6

# Pandemic Summer: Outbreaks, Overheating, and Organizing

The state of California reopened for business as usual in May 2020. Unsurprisingly, new outbreaks soon erupted. By July 7, the state had a daily record high of 9,500 new cases and a total of nearly 285,000 cases. The virus—and fatalities—also reached into the state's thirty-four prisons. By July, the entire prison system reported a total of 7,687 cases among incarcerated people, or 4.8 percent of all state prisoners. It was a rate that prison physician Joshua Connor explained as the "equivalent to about 1.8 million Californians testing positive for the coronavirus, compared with [the actual number of] 284,000 confirmed cases."[1] Forty-seven people died.

People inside mobilized. They filed grievances. When those failed, they turned to the courts.[2] They also publicized their plight, drawing on connections they had made with organizations and advocates through years of agitating for both decarceration and improved conditions.

Inside San Quentin, those locked in cellblocks where the virus had exploded managed to pass messages to those who still had phone access. These men called family members and outside advocacy groups, both individually and during online organizing meetings. They gave firsthand accounts of the intensifying crisis that would otherwise have remained out of sight.

San Quentin had an existing media program producing podcasts and visual documentaries. Participants had formed working relationships with outside media, advocates, and even some progressive politicians. They utilized these connections to broadcast what was happening behind the walls. They called in to news programs, describing the terror of being locked in prison during an airborne pandemic. They held press conferences from dayroom phones, passing the receiver to one another so that each could share their experiences—and their fears of not making it home. Since media was not allowed into the prisons to speak with them, incarcerated activists and outside advocates launched Empowerment Avenue, an organization that placed incarcerated writers' stories in outside publications. At least half of their first twenty articles depicted the rapidly unfolding disaster at San Quentin.[3]

Concerned families and advocates held protests outside San Quentin, other state prisons, and the privately run Otay Mesa immigration detention center. Their efforts soon coalesced into the Stop San Quentin Outbreak Coalition. The coalition demanded that the state issue more large-scale releases, halve its overall prison population, and stop transfers between prisons and to ICE detention. They called for ongoing COVID testing, free personal protective equipment, and free phone calls, e-messages, and video visits while in-person visits were suspended. They also demanded that prisons provide opportunities for good-time credits, or time off a person's sentence, through correspondence courses and other distance learning programs.[4]

These efforts had moderate success. On June 30, the state announced its plan to release people who had fewer than 180 days remaining on their prison sentence, but only those with nonviolent convictions. People with violent convictions, even if they met the time criteria, would remain behind bars—and pray that they survived those final six months. That month, more than 1,300 people incarcerated at San Quentin contracted COVID. Six died.[5]

On July 9, advocates again rallied outside San Quentin, urging the governor to release aging and medically vulnerable people. They invited him to visit the prison to see conditions firsthand.[6] The following day, officials announced an expansion of early-release eligibility to those with one year or less on their sentence—an estimated 8,000 additional people. During the next month, the state granted early release to 4,500 people. Once again, however, people with violent convictions remained ineligible.

Many of those excluded were older, had already spent decades behind bars, and were more vulnerable to severe or lethal COVID. But despite their age—and the growing body of research showing that older people imprisoned for serious violent convictions in their younger years are the least likely to end up back in prison—they were still barred from consideration.

Organizers continued to urge officials to grant those with violent convictions the same opportunity. In July, organizers chained themselves to the fence outside the governor's home.[7] In August, they held a vigil outside the Sacramento home of prison director Ralph Diaz. They rallied outside the Central California Women's Facility, the state's largest women's prison, where a few months later over five hundred women and trans people (or a quarter of its population) would test positive within a two-week period.

Between July and November, the state allowed nearly 7,600 people to go home early. Only sixty-two of those people (or less than 1 percent) were released because of serious medical conditions, even though the federal receiver overseeing health care improvements had identified nearly seventeen thousand people as high risk for severe COVID.[8] The vast majority of those released—nearly seven thousand—were within 180 days of release.[9]

Even with these releases, nineteen prisons remained over capacity—twelve prisons were between 120 or 149 percent capacity at that time—and five hovered at nearly full capacity.[10] But while the overall prison population decreased, the proportion of people aged fifty to sixty-nine increased. So did the proportion of incarcerated people who were Black or Hispanic.[11]

※

In 1918, the women at San Quentin escaped the flu. In 2020, those in California's two women's prisons were not as fortunate.

Throughout March and April, women at the California Institution for Women (CIW) sewed masks for prisons and other state agencies. They worked in the prison factory ten hours a day for eighty cents an hour, a sum enabling them to buy hygiene items, food, and credits for calls and electronic messages.

The fabric that they used came from the nearby California Institution for Men. The factory boss and several supervising staff shuttled between the two prisons.

Staff warned women that they could lose their jobs for missing a day of work. They also threatened them with disciplinary tickets for refusing to work, tickets that could jeopardize their chances of parole. Fears of a write-up outweighed fears of the virus. Women continued to report to work.[12]

In mid-April, the prison reported one positive case. That number doubled, tripled, quadrupled, then exploded. By mid-May, forty women had tested positive.[13] When women in the factory began testing positive, the prison closed the factory. But it came too late to stop the outbreak.

In early May, a fellow incarcerated woman found Robbie Hall, one of the factory workers, sprawled across the floor in her cell, gasping for breath and unable to talk. She flailed her hands trying to signal that it was an emergency. Paramedics rushed Robbie to a community hospital where she spent weeks in and out of consciousness with COVID-related pneumonia. She returned to the prison with an oxygen tank, walker, and painful case of shingles.[14]

Her collapse triggered a lockdown. No one knew how long they would be locked in their cells with as many as seven other people. "The stress got worse and worse for me to the point that I was crying, I was upset, I couldn't get out of the room," one woman described. She already suffered from high blood pressure, but the additional anxiety and feelings of helplessness caused it to spike.[15]

By 2020, April Harris had been imprisoned for decades at CIW and had long been organizing with the California Coalition for Women Prisoners, an advocacy group challenging abuses behind bars. April also tested positive in May and was moved to quarantine. She resolved to document everything, using her prison-issued tablet to send daily messages to Colby Lenz, another longtime coalition volunteer and legal advocate.

April spent her first twelve hours in quarantine without toilet paper, sanitary supplies, or a mattress. Some women went four or five days without showers or time at the kiosk, where they could sync their tablets to receive and send messages. The extreme isolation exacerbated the sense of despondency, especially among those already struggling with suicidal ideation. One person, a trans man quarantined across the hall, made four formal requests to be seen by mental health staff. He verbally repeated his request each time staff took his temperature. Falling deeper into despair, he refused food, medicine, and the twice-daily temperature checks. Those refusals should have triggered a response, but staff did nothing. He tried to cut his wrists, but his blade kept breaking.

Finally, he set the stuffing from his mattress on fire.[16] When April saw the flames, she repeatedly shouted, "Their room is on fire!" Other women took up her cry, banging on their doors and screaming, "Fire!"

Black smoke poured from the cell when guards finally opened the door. One guard doused the blaze with a fire extinguisher. The other opened each cell individually instead of pressing the button that would open all cells simultaneously.[17]

That was not the only medical emergency during those two months. In her daily messages, April chronicled repeated seizures, other suicide attempts, and the guards' glacially slow response. She also described women repeatedly banding together. Sometimes it was to call for help during the many medical emergencies. Other times, they refused to reenter their cells, once even staging a sit-in in the hallway to protest the lack of showers.[18]

Through their connections with the California Coalition for Women Prisoners, April and others alerted media. Outside organizers highlighted their experiences through press releases, rallies, and social media campaigns. They also connected those inside the prison with journalists, circumventing a 1996 policy which prohibited scheduling media interviews with incarcerated individuals.[19]

Coalition organizers also protested outside the prison. In early May, nearly a hundred advocates, including formerly incarcerated people and relatives of those still confined, drove to both CIW and the neighboring California Institution for Men. Many hung signs on their car windows or painted messages across their hoods exhorting prisons to release people. Their rally not only spurred local media to cover the mounting COVID numbers, but also alerted those in quarantine (and others throughout the prison) that the public was taking notice and taking action.

April could not see the protest from her cell, but knowing about the rally—and hearing the excited shouts of those who did see it—buoyed her spirits. That encouragement lasted beyond those few hours. When another medical emergency occurred that afternoon, more women recorded the details.

The next day, guards began escorting women to the showers and kiosk. "Somebody somewhere is doing something. I am so grateful to everyone who has been calling up here trying to make our voices heard," April wrote that day.[20]

※

These actions built upon the decades-long history of inside-outside organizing established in California's prisons.

In 1995, women at the Central California Women's Facility filed *Shumate v. Wilson*, a class-action lawsuit challenging ongoing medical negligence. Charisse "Happy" Shumate and other women serving lengthy and life sentences started by documenting medical abuses. They asked their peers whether nurses and doctors took their complaints seriously, explained their findings, or offered treatment besides Tylenol. Armed with these facts, they went to court.

They also reached out to outside advocates, who formed the California Coalition for Women Prisoners. Even after the suit ended, coalition members continued to organize with people inside to improve conditions and increase opportunities for release.

*Shumate v. Wilson* not only compelled the state to improve health care, but also inspired others in the prison to become more proactive about advocating for and documenting their own medical care. For many, it was their first foray into political organizing. And for many, it was not their last. Even after they went home, many continued to engage in efforts to improve conditions for those that they had left behind and to demand more releases.

That same inside-out organizing extended to CIW, where suicides and suicide attempts reached a crisis level several years before the pandemic. Between 2013 and 2015, the prison had sixty-five suicide attempts and five suicides. A suicide prevention expert audited CIW in 2013 and again in 2015, calling the prison "a problematic institution that exhibited numerous poor practices in the area of suicide prevention."[21] These poor practices included low completion of suicide risk evaluations, inadequate treatment planning, and low compliance rates for annual suicide prevention training, factors likely contributing to the prison reporting multiple suicides during one year. By 2016, CIW's suicide rate was eight times the national rate for women's prisons and more than five times the rate for all California prisons. The prison was at 135 percent capacity, with 1,886 people confined in a facility designed for 1,398.[22]

Those who survived their attempts were placed on suicide watch, where they were stripped naked, given a rubber smock, and placed in an empty cell where they were continually observed by a nurse for any signs of suicidal behavior. "You are not allowed anything for the first week," one woman, who had attempted suicide, told me. "Then you can 'earn' a book. And maybe a muumuu gown if you are calm and cooperative. You aren't even allowed a roll of toilet paper. When you need to use the toilet, they hand you a tiny bit and watch you use it."[23] None of this lessened her desire to die.

With the high rate of suicides and suicide attempts, that unit was frequently full. Staff placed others into what they called the "overflow unit" in the SHU, ignoring the fact that isolation can cause anxiety, panic, depression, agoraphobia, paranoia, aggression, and neurological damage, even in people who are not feeling suicidal or struggling with mental health issues.

As they would again in 2020, organizers held vigils and protests outside the prison. They linked grieving family members to media outlets. They connected journalists to people inside the prison, who exposed the conditions that had led to such widespread despair. These inside-outside efforts thrust the ongoing disaster into public view and led to improved conditions on suicide watch, increased oversight, and the forced retirement of the warden, who had done nothing to address this crisis for three years.[24]

The sustained advocacy also triggered state audits of suicides at both women's prisons and at two men's prisons. But these changes proved inadequate once COVID—and the accompanying lockdowns, widespread fear, lack of information, and seeming indifference from those charged with their well-being—hit California's prisons.

Lockdowns often disrupt support systems. The scant minutes out of one's cell are often not enough for them to call loved ones. Time limits also prevent many from using the handful of kiosks to read or write e-messages. Lockdowns impede people from leaning on their internal support systems as well. While incarcerated, people often form deep relationships and care for each other when they are sad, ill, grieving, or otherwise in need of support. These relationships often extend across cells or housing units. But under lockdowns, people could no longer talk, share food, or simply sit in companionable silence. Instead, each person was locked away with their private jumble of fears.

The lockdowns also exacerbated the mental health crisis in California prisons. Non-emergency mental health visits were limited to consultations shouted through locked doors, making it harder for clinicians to identify those needing additional assistance. The complete lack of privacy deterred people from asking for help. "We are not going to yell through the door what's really going on with us for everybody to hear," explained the woman with high blood pressure. The lockdown triggered her anxiety, but she did not want to alert the whole unit. Instead, she waved away the clinicians who approached her door.[25]

California prisons reported a decrease in mental health referrals during the pandemic. One study, which interviewed ten health care professionals working in the state's prisons or jails during the pandemic, found increased obstacles to meeting mental health needs. Fewer providers were available to speak with people, and they spent less time with each patient. Shouting through steel doors discouraged people from revealing their mental health struggles. Group therapy and one-to-one consultations were paused, leaving many flailing with no support other than a few coloring pages or puzzles.[26]

Even with these disruptions, the inside-outside organizing at San Quentin, CIW, and other prisons over the preceding years had established lines of communication and built trusted relationships with people outside. Without that groundwork, those inside could not have immediately alerted those outside about pandemic mismanagement—and those outsiders might not have mobilized as quickly when crises hit.

※

California wasn't the only state to resume prison admissions and transfers. In Oklahoma, state officials did that while instituting cost-cutting measures that fueled a summer of outbreaks.

In June, the state announced the closure of two prisons—the Cimarron Correctional Center, a private men's prison, and the Kate Barnard Correctional Center, a women's minimum-security prison.

The 1,452 men at Cimarron were transferred to various male prisons. The two hundred women at Kate Barnard were crammed into the remaining two women's prisons—the Mabel Bassett Correctional Center and the Eddie Warrior Correctional Center. While Mabel Bassett has both individual cells and group dormitories, Eddie Warrior consists entirely of dormitories, except for its solitary unit.

Since April, officials at Eddie Warrior had ordered its 860 women to remain on their bunk beds. The order was not to punish them, the warden explained, but to protect them from COVID. But it still felt like punishment. For two months, adult women had to request permission to leave their beds and use the bathrooms. They were allowed one shower and one phone call each day. Each day, fifteen women at a time were allowed onto the outdoor patio for fifteen minutes. That time was later increased to one hour. Otherwise, they sat on their beds.

The prison issued masks, ordering women to wear them whenever they left their beds. But with bunk beds a mere three feet apart, the precaution proved futile. Even worse were the dorms with cubicles. The cubicles, each with two sets of bunk beds, are separated only by a thin piece of particle board that failed to reach the ceiling. "Any cough [or] sneeze cloud just wafts right on over," Geneva Phillips told me.

Officials converted the gym into its quarantine sick bay. The giant room lacked both air conditioning and showers—and few wanted to be sent there as temperatures rose.

In June, restrictions loosened. Women could leave their beds. They could walk to the cafeteria, though they had to eat their meals in the dorm. They could resume working their jobs. They could receive visits, although they weren't allowed to touch. No hugs, no hand-holding, no contact whatsoever.

The women remained depressed and frustrated. "The truth is, none of it matters," Geneva wrote me that month. "There is no COVID here and it can only come in from the outside. We're safe as can be until it comes in and then, when or if it does, it will devastate this tightly packed dormitory-style facility."

In August, weeks after the transfer from the shuttered Kate Barnard, Geneva's prediction came true. At first, forty-seven women at Eddie Warrior tested positive. Officials labeled the prison a "COVID hot spot."[27] Then they caused those numbers to skyrocket.

Late one Saturday night, around 2 a.m., staff woke women and ordered them to pack their belongings and move so that the COVID-negative women could be confined in one dormitory. Hundreds of bleary-eyed women shuffled down the corridors carrying armload upon armload of blankets, pillows, letters, photos, and other possessions. Each and every one of the 860 women had to crisscross the prison several times, each time lugging as many items as her two arms could carry. Each trek down the hall required passing hundreds of her peers.

After they had managed to bring their possessions to their newly assigned dorms, they were confined for another few weeks.

By jostling each other in the hallways, hundreds were exposed to and later contracted COVID. This included thirty-two-year-old Kayla Absher. After the move, she noticed a dry cough. Then came the migraines followed by body aches and the loss of both taste and smell. It felt like a five-hundred-pound sledgehammer pressed down on her chest. "I was freezing but sweating, my chest and back were hurting, and I had a headache that wouldn't go away," she told me.

Although other women who experienced similar symptoms remained quiet, Kayla asked to be tested. But, because her temperature was 99.5, she was not tested until weeks later, when the state health department tested every person in the prison. By then, she had largely recovered. The positive test simply confirmed that her "feeling like death" had been COVID.

Ultimately, 781 women, or 91 percent of the incarcerated population, tested positive.

Kayla's cough lingered for three months. "I'll start coughing and it'll continue for a few minutes or even all day," she described, adding that this cough had been so ubiquitous that women nicknamed it the "COVID tickle."

One year later, she still felt depleted, unable to walk for long without feeling short of breath or dizzy. "It'd feel like maybe I'd just ran a marathon. My legs didn't feel like I had the strength to walk the distance, so I'd have to stop to take a break," she told me. But the cafeteria, classrooms, chapel, and commissary are spread across different buildings, making it impossible to avoid walking. Her throat still felt scratchy and she could no longer laugh without coughing. Like many who have had COVID, she began having problems remembering certain things. She told me that she used to have an impeccable memory, but now found herself struggling to remember a name, word, or even her mother's phone number, which had remained unchanged for the past four years.

"I'll be mid-sentence and I'll just forget what I was going to say," she told me. "Are you going to finish?" her friends asked whenever she trailed off. "Well sure, I would if I could, but I have no clue what I was going to say," remained her regular response.

Despite these lasting effects, Kayla still viewed herself as a survivor. She survived prison, a decade-long separation from her children based on bogus charges, and COVID.

Others, however, did not survive. Two women died shortly after the middle-of-the-night move. Deanna Thomas, a fifty-eight-year-old with six months left on her prison sentence, died in early September. Less than two weeks later, seventy-year-old Vernita Watts died.

The transfers also sparked an outbreak at Mabel Bassett. By August 27, 201 women had tested positive.[28] The prison instituted another lockdown. While officials gradually allowed women to go to work or the cafeteria, they did not implement universal testing. Only those who were transferred to another housing unit or soon to be released were tested, leaving many uncertain about the causes of their illnesses. This included Mary who, when finally able to muster the energy to write a letter, described spending July with "a bad cold like I never had before." Trying to get medical attention would have taken weeks, so she didn't bother. Instead, she doubled up on vitamin C and multivitamins bought from commissary. Then she wrapped herself in blankets to sweat out the fever.

Staff only tested incarcerated people if they displayed COVID-like symptoms or were part of a targeted test of vulnerable populations.[29] Mary was in her late sixties, yet officials did not consider her vulnerable enough for testing.

The outbreaks weren't limited to prison. That summer, cases in communities surrounding prisons rose, adding half a million more cases to the national count. In Oklahoma, 1,589 confirmed cases (or forty new cases for every 100,000 residents) were linked to mass incarceration.[30]

In mid-September, seventy-five advocates rallied outside Eddie Warrior Correctional Center. Protesters included formerly incarcerated women, concerned relatives, residents, and local politicians who feared that a prison outbreak would decimate the neighboring town of Taft, whose population of 250 had already suffered one COVID fatality.

"So now we have 249—pretty soon, all we're going to have is some pigs, cows and dogs, if we wait on the government," said Tiffany Walton, the Taft nurse who had organized the protest.

Inside the prison, women hung signs from their windows that said, "Failure to Protect," "Free the Sick," and "Our Lives Matter."[31] Their exhortations went largely unheeded. Unlike California, where continual public pressure and organizing pushed the state to expand early-release criteria and ultimately release over seven thousand people, Oklahoma, which lacked similar prolonged advocacy, granted far fewer releases. Governor Kevin Stitt announced that he had commuted the sentences of 404 people, who would be released by mid-April, but only 111 people were ultimately released.[32]

※

The summer outbreaks and lockdowns were made even more unbearable by the rising temperatures.

Both Eddie Warrior and Mabel Bassett, built in 1988, have air conditioning, enabling Mary, Geneva, Kayla, and thousands of Oklahomans to escape 90-degree days in concrete cellblocks. But they were among the fortunate few.

Approximately 350 miles south in Texas, Kwaneta and over a thousand others grappled with not only surviving the ongoing pandemic, but also the blistering sensation of feeling cooked in their cement cells. It was a double threat faced by those imprisoned in the forty-four states that provided no air conditioning or other ways to cool off.[33]

By mid-July, temperatures throughout Texas had reached triple digits. At Murray, women in general population were supposed to have continual access to ice water and cold showers. They could seek respite in the air-conditioned chapel. Those locked in segregation were also supposed to be given ice water every two hours and cold showers upon request. But the unit's ice machine remained broken, and the short staffing meant guards were not available to search and escort women from their cells to the showers. The women were also supposed to have access to an air-conditioned respite area, but no staff or administrator seemed to know where that was.

These increasing and unmitigated signs of global warming were experienced by hundreds of thousands incarcerated throughout the country, particularly in the nation's hottest regions. Eight of the ten warmest years on record were between 2012 and 2022 and climate change promised to intensify extreme temperatures even further.[34]

Prolonged exposure to extreme heat can cause dehydration and heat stroke, both of which can be lethal. Even when not fatal, prolonged heat can affect the kidneys, liver, heart, brain, and lungs, leading to renal failure, heart attacks, and strokes. Prisons are filled with people who have entered with or developed health conditions, including diabetes, heart disease, and high blood pressure. All of these make them especially vulnerable to heat-related illnesses. Furthermore, approximately 40 percent of the prison population takes psychotropic or blood pressure medications, putting those individuals at greater risk during months of unabated extreme heat.[35]

It's also no coincidence that as climate change made summers more severe, the number of infectious diseases increased. During the heat wave of 2022, COVID cases more than doubled in heat-struck regions worldwide. New cases in parts of Africa climbed by nearly 300 percent. Researchers found that over 69 percent of COVID cases during the sizzling summer of 2022 could have been avoided had there not been heat waves. As temperatures rose, people sought respite in air-conditioned indoor public spaces, reducing their ability to socially distance. And, as the canceled talent show at Mabel Bassett demonstrated, high temperatures also made people more inclined to shed their masks. But unlike colds and flus, COVID is not killed by extreme heat and, with the relaxation of precautions, the virus spread.[36]

That certainly proved true in Texas that first pandemic summer. By July 14, temperatures were already above 100 degrees, and more than twelve thousand state prisoners and 2,100 staff had tested positive. Ninety-four incarcerated people had died, which, at the time, was the highest number of COVID deaths in any state prison system. One week later, temperatures had dropped to 90 degrees (which Jack sarcastically dubbed "a cold front"), but the spread continued. That week, Texas recorded a total of 13,408 confirmed cases among incarcerated people and ninety-four deaths. At Lane Murray, fifty women had been placed on medical restriction. Three miles away, at the Mountain View Unit where Jack would later be transferred and contract COVID, another 103 women were medically restricted.

By the time temperatures dipped in October, Texas prisons counted 190 COVID deaths among its incarcerated population.

In 2014, men in the state's Wallace Pack Unit filed a lawsuit charging that confining them in temperatures that regularly rose above 100 degrees constituted cruel and unusual punishment. The court sided with them, ruling that the prison system had been deliberately indifferent to the potential harm of excessive heat. Texas fought the lawsuit—spending over $7 million in legal fees—before settling in 2018. The cost of installing air conditioning at the Pack Unit was less than $4 million.[37]

That settlement did not extend to other Texas prisons. Years later, Kwaneta, Jack, and dozens of others were still sweating in cells that felt more like cauldrons. Despite the extreme heat, guards at Lane Murray were ordered to resume cell searches every three days. Some guards skipped the requirement, not wanting to enter oven-like cells weighed down with their newly required stab-proof vest, safety goggles, mask, and gloves. Other guards entered each cell, frisked and removed its occupant, then searched for contraband. Once again, each search brought the threat of COVID along with the degradation and frustration of watching strangers paw through one's belongings.

Each time, guards searched Kwaneta. In April, administrators had charged her with fraud after a journalist made a mistake while registering for her phone list. After unsuccessfully attempting to correct what she assumed to be a misunderstanding, the journalist wrote a magazine article that named the warden and quoted her refusal to drop the charge against Kwaneta.[38] The guards rifled through Kwaneta's cell weekly, sometimes as often as five times during a two-week period. These constant intrusions—especially compared with the lack of searches for the other women—seemed like clear retaliation, but, as with many outrages in prison, Kwaneta could do nothing about them.

Women could open their windows and hope for a breeze, but their windows lacked screens, allowing mosquitoes inside. Some used mesh bags as makeshift screens, but, if caught, guards would confiscate the bags, leaving the women with no way to carry items to the shower or back from commissary. Periodically, the power went out, and with it, the slight breeze provided by their commissary-bought fans. In mid-July, the water was turned off for several hours with no warning. When the taps started flowing again, the water was hot.

Sunset did not cool their cells. Temperatures finally dipped around two or three in the morning, but that respite was all too brief. At 6 a.m., the sun rose and, with it, the temperatures.

Meanwhile, COVID continued spreading. In mid-June, staff placed a woman who had tested positive in the cell next to Kwaneta. Guards reassured Kwaneta that the woman was not technically under quarantine because fourteen days had elapsed since her positive test. But Kwaneta was not reassured, noting that Texas prisons never test a person a second time before placing them near others. The two women shared a vent, allowing noise—and respiratory droplets—to freely move between their cells.

In August, Kwaneta fainted. It could have been the heat, but she believes she somehow contracted COVID. She felt weak for days. Her memory worsened. But she was never tested.

⁂

In mid-May, unbeknownst to Kwaneta, Jack, and many others melting in their cells, dozens of advocates had gathered, masked and socially distanced, outside the governor's mansion calling upon Abbott to release people. "Let them live out on parole rather than in a body bag," said rally organizer Lovinah Igbani.[39]

Family advocacy organizations met weekly with prison officials about COVID numbers. At these meetings, they repeatedly voiced their concerns about the inedible sack lunches, ongoing medical neglect, and potentially lethal heat. Still, in Texas and across the country, officials failed to implement meaningful improvements.

As the long, hot summer progressed, the California Institution for Women demonstrated that decision-makers had not learned from the first outbreak. "This is a controlled environment. The only way we get anything is through staff. Checking their temperatures did not stop them from infecting us. Taking my temperature allowed me to walk around clueless that I was infected and possibly affecting others," April reflected.

"I think that there will definitely be a second wave here. Worse than the first one," she predicted in late May.[40] She was right. In July, another woman called to tell me that at least three of the prison's six housing units were in quarantine and on lockdown. "We are all fearful that soon it will be the whole institution," she said.[41]

That month alone, COVID cases more than doubled from 164 to 325. By mid-August, more than 350 people had tested positive, and the prison had its first COVID death.[42]

CIW is in Southern California, where July temperatures reach the low 90s. The prison utilizes swamp coolers, which cool the air by adding water, rather than centralized air conditioning. But these swamp coolers struggle to provide relief in more humid climates, including those near the ocean. Women at CIW, less than 40 miles from the Pacific Ocean, have repeatedly told me that these coolers fail to reduce temperatures. The prison's population includes many of the state's aging incarcerated women, who are at higher risk for heat-related illnesses and fatalities.

In August, the state was ravaged by the fourth largest wildfire in its history. Smoke plumes darkened every county for at least forty-six days.[43] If they were allowed out of their sweltering cells, people faced the choice between virus-laden particles in the dayroom or smoke particles in the yard.

The California prison system's plan for extreme heat, or days in which temperatures exceed 90 degrees, includes several options, such as increasing access to water stations, fans, showers, and ice. But it does not require staff to implement any of them. At Corcoran, twice a day, staff distributed cups of ice only to people who were on psychotropic medications, leaving others with no relief. But Mwalimu's unit had long been engaged in what he called "practicing socialism," and what people on the outside called mutual aid. Those who received ice shared with others around them, allowing everyone a few blissful minutes of frosty respite.

That wasn't the only way they practiced socialism. California commissaries sell electric fans for anywhere from eight to seventeen dollars. Mwalimu paid twelve dollars for his, but many could not afford to do the same. When summer temperatures soared, men shared their fans. If two cellmates both had fans of their own, they lent one to a cell that had none.

Women in Texas did the same—and much more. In 2011, five years before she would be thrown in solitary, Kwaneta was incarcerated at the Hobby Unit in Central Texas. That summer, statewide temperatures reached over 100 degrees for seventy-one days. Waco, the nearest city, had triple-digit temperatures for seventy-two days that summer, while Austin, a hundred miles south, baked at over 100 degrees for ninety days.

During that scorching summer, women broke rule after rule to ensure their peers' survival. The Hobby Unit not only lacked air conditioning, but its windows had also been nailed shut, turning cells into broilers. Prison rules dictate that women must be fully dressed to go to the dayroom, where large industrial fans circulate the warm air. Women who had financial support could buy T-shirts, shorts, and Crocs from commissary. But many others lacked assistance to buy the lighter garments. They had to wear the thick white prison uniform, thick gray socks, and canvas shoes.

Women donated their old summer clothing to their poorer peers. But sharing is prohibited behind bars, making even the simple act of giving away a T-shirt a laborious task. A person's name and prison number must be written in magic marker on all belongings, including clothing. Before she could give her old clothes away, a woman had to repeatedly rub sunscreen over the name and number until they faded, then label the clothes with the new owner's information. The new owner might be in an ill-fitting T-shirt, shorts, or Crocs, but they could at least escape the searing heat of their cell for the less stifling heat of the dayroom.

Women also shared other items, including powdered electrolyte packages and ear plugs. The latter, Kwaneta explained, were crucial. Many slept on the floor instead of the plastic mattress that radiated the day's heat. Earplugs kept the prison's many insects from crawling into their ears.

Other women, who were more heat intolerant because of age, medical conditions, or medications, stayed in their cells in what's known as a "prison bikini" (or bra and panties). But staying in meant missing the ice water periodically distributed in the dayroom, where guards allowed women only one cup at a time. Waiting in line often took an hour. Some women did so multiple times to fill an additional cup for a peer who stayed in her cell. Then they would stand outside the other woman's closed cell door and carefully pour the water into a cup on the other side. Each time, they risked a disciplinary ticket for being "out of place."

Younger women also climbed bunk beds and blocked the cell windows with notebook covers to keep the sun from roasting older women. In doing this, they risked one or more disciplinary tickets: being in another woman's cell and covering windows were both violations of prison rules.

"It's literally survival. You don't, they die," Kwaneta reflected. "The state will let us die and have our bed filled before our body cools."

Mwalimu contextualized these acts of mutual aid as "praxis," or practicing the world we want to live in. "It's important for people to care for each other because it's with love of humanity that our community is shaped," he told me. "Once people start to realize we're all we have, we can be the change we want in society."

## Chapter 7

# Winter, Dashed Hopes, and a Deadly Second Wave

As the leaves turned crimson and yellow, some welcome news belatedly made its way into Oklahoma prisons. In July, the US Supreme Court had issued two landmark opinions. Both held the promise of allowing Native Americans imprisoned in Oklahoma to challenge their convictions. Native Americans make up less than 10 percent of the state's population but 11.5 percent of its prison population. Native women, who comprise 9 percent of Oklahomans, make up 12 percent of the state's prisoners, and are imprisoned at three times the rate of their white counterparts.[1]

In *McGirt v. Oklahoma*, the court ruled that much of eastern Oklahoma, including Tulsa, remains tribal land and that crimes on those lands are subject to federal jurisdiction under the 1885 Major Crimes Act. Those convicted in state courts could apply to have their sentences vacated. In *Sharp v. Murphy*, the court ruled that the United States had never disestablished the Muscogee (Creek) Nation reservation when Oklahoma became a state. The ruling removed the state's authority to prosecute Native Americans in the northeastern Creek territories. Instead, prosecution fell under the jurisdiction of Native authorities except for cases of serious violent offenses such as murder, manslaughter, serious injury, and sexual assault. Those were now prosecuted only by the federal government.

While rumors spread like oil fires within prisons, actual news is often slower to trickle in. Thus, Mary and other Native women at Mabel Bassett didn't learn about these summer decisions for months. But Mary also had personal connections to the case. Patrick Murphy had gone to school with her older siblings, and George Jacobs, Murphy's victim, had been Mary's first high school boyfriend. She met him each Saturday night at the weekly stomp dances. While Mary's father led the dances, the pair would sneak off to make out in the older man's green Ford.

In 1999, the year that Murphy killed Jacobs, Mary had finished a three-year prison sentence for shoplifting and was desperately trying to regain custody of her sons. She gave little thought to the tragic fate of her teenage flame.

In 2020, when they heard about the Supreme Court decisions, the women scrambled to learn if they had been arrested in Creek territory. The pandemic still restricted access to the law library, making their task more onerous. Instead of poring over legal documents with the help of library clerks, Mary had to submit a "kite," or paper request, with specific questions and wait for a response. At times, the clerks couldn't locate what she needed, like the treaties for the Kickapoo and the Potawatomi Nations. Mary instead had to leaf through her own small cache of books.[2] Other times, she asked me to help figure out boundary demarcations. In October, she filed her appeal and helped several others file theirs. Then they waited.

"Hope. I been trying to get out of prison for nearly twenty years now," she wrote in her journal on the day that she filed.

For years, Mary had dreamed of building a transitional home for formerly incarcerated women on her land in Creek territory. She had ordered catalogs of log cabins and spent hours poring over the many possibilities. She had even persuaded her oldest son, who built houses, to construct it once she herself came home. With the Supreme Court decisions, that dream seemed within reach.

In November, just as that possible avenue for early release was opening for Mary and other Native people's early release, Oklahoma sealed off a different one. Previously, the state deducted fifteen days for each month in which a person received no tickets for rule breaking. Every year of good behavior meant 180 fewer days in prison.

Prisons have long lists of rules that can easily be broken. People must be in specific places at specific times. They must stand by their beds or outside their cells during count. They cannot cover a window to prevent the summer sun from blasting in. They cannot hang a sheet for privacy while on the toilet. They are not allowed in another person's cell. They cannot hold hands, touch each other, or share items. Any of these could lead to a misconduct ticket, and guards in women's prisons are more likely to issue tickets for these minor infractions than those in men's prisons.[3]

Between steering clear of tickets and completing numerous programs, Mary had already earned 540 days off her remaining eight-and-a-half-year sentence. Through her tribe, she had even enrolled in college classes toward her bachelor's degree, an opportunity that had been cut off for many by the 1994 ban on Pell grants for college-in-prison classes.

But in November, the new attorney general announced that simply being misconduct-free did not meet the requirements for earned credit. Instead, the state viewed staying out of trouble each month as the equivalent of completing the same program multiple times.[4] Those who consistently followed each and every rule, even the pettiest ones, could no longer look forward to a shortened sentence. The state estimated that the change would increase its prison population by 3.6 percent.

The change meant that the women at Mabel Bassett—and prisons across Oklahoma—could only look forward to more crowding, longer lines for food, and increased tensions, regardless of how many fights or other rule violations they engaged in or avoided.

❋

Every winter, Mary feels a growing sense of wretchedness settle upon her shoulders as she marks another holiday separated from her children and grandchildren. The pandemic made the season even more dreary. "I miss my AA meetings. I need them," said Mary. By then, she had abstained from all drugs and alcohol for nineteen years and nine months, even though both homemade alcohol and drugs, dropped into the yard by drones or smuggled in by staff, were readily available. But with the pandemic still raging—and recent outbreaks locking down Mabel Bassett—Alcoholics Anonymous and all other programs remained on pause. Prisons prohibit internet access, so, unlike support groups outside, there was no shift to online meetings. Mary struggled to stay sober on her own even as those around her drank and smoked incessantly.

Mary's letters that December described mounting tensions and increasing annoyance with the daily interactions that characterize prison life. By then, she had been moved from her cell to another dormitory filled with noise, drugs, fights, and pandemonium. Several mornings, she was awakened by women pummeling each other, usually over some minor disagreement.

That month, a second wave of COVID spread. Outbreaks exploded in prisons that had previously been spared. Despite having had months to prepare, many prisons remained woefully unprepared. Some prisons even failed to move those who tested positive from cells shared between two and fourteen people.

Shortly before New Year's, Mary learned that her oldest son, a wrestling coach who had refused to wear a mask or adhere to social distancing precautions, had contracted COVID. Terrified, she repeatedly tried to call. No one picked up, leaving her imagination to run wild. Later, she learned that her son had passed the virus to his wife and teenage son. All had been laid up in bed, too exhausted to answer the phone. They recovered. Two of Mary's dorm mates were not as lucky—their relatives died after contracting the coronavirus.

※

In November, Jack was woken at 6 a.m. by a startling announcement. After six years and two months in solitary, and eleven denials by the State Classification Committee, he had assumed that his 2020 hearing would simply be another grueling set of questions followed by a denial, so he decided not to attend. But that morning, a guard ordered him to pack up. After he had stuffed all his worldly belongings—clothes, books, papers, and photos—into seven red bags, he was handcuffed, shackled, then bundled onto a bus to be driven fifteen minutes to the Mountain View Unit. There, he was placed in the G-5 unit, one of several transition units between solitary and general population. He was allowed to bring the bag containing his shower shoes, fan, writing materials, clothing, hygiene items, and a radio. The other six bags arrived two weeks later. He was neither tested nor quarantined upon arrival.

In theory, the G-5 unit should have offered a greater number of opportunities to interact with others and participate in programming, bringing him one step closer to general population. But Jack found few opportunities to relieve his stultifying boredom. "I can't check out any books from the library [or] participate in any educational or vocational classes," he told me. And he knew that officials would hold his lack of participation against him during his first parole hearing.

In G-5, two people are assigned to a cell. After nearly seven years alone, Jack found himself learning to live with a rotating cast of cellmates. He got along with some but had to tiptoe around others to avoid a fight. Some seemed high-strung or struggled with anger issues, but none were transphobic. That was exceedingly important given that, even in this supposedly less-restrictive unit, he and his cellmate still spent most of the day locked in together.

Each day, Jack was allowed a ten-minute shower. Even though he was no longer in segregation, guards still strip-searched and handcuffed him before letting him walk down the corridor. He was allowed out of his cell to eat in the dayroom with others. That was the only time he spent with anyone other than his cellmate.

Everything else was brought to his cell—mail, medications, and commissary purchases. The noise was as loud as the ad seg unit he had just left—except that in isolation he at least could shout about current events and books with Kwaneta. At Mountain View, no one shared similar interests. Women argued over pills or relationships. They banged on the gates, hurled insults at one another, challenged each other to fights, and threatened both each other and guards.

Although less than one mile from Lane Murray, Mountain View did not pick up National Public Radio, leaving him feeling even more disconnected. "Can you tell me what's going on with Trump? And COVID?" he asked in mid-November 2020.

Despite the facility's name, the cell window at Mountain View offered no view whatsoever, having been painted over. "I can no longer look outside, feel the sunshine, nor feed the birds and cats since the window doesn't open," he complained. "What is it they are stopping us from seeing?"

In early December, his head started pounding. He began coughing. He felt as if he had a fever, but without a thermometer he had no way to know for sure. He reported his symptoms to the guard that afternoon, but it was another twelve hours before a nurse took his temperature.

As a child, Jack had caught some combination of cold, flu, bronchitis, and pneumonia every winter. His father would treat him with a home concoction of hot tea mixed with Robitussin, lemon, honey, orange juice, and Jack Daniels, rub his back and chest with Vicks, bundle him in thermals, and place him near a vaporizer. Jack did his best to mimic that childhood remedy, crushing cough drops and mint candy to mix with a lime sports drink bought from commissary and the juice of an orange from his lunch tray. It wasn't the same as his father's cures, but it relieved his symptoms enough to sleep.

He was woken at 1 a.m. by the nurse, who had finally arrived to take his temperature. By then, he had sweated out his fever and his temperature registered 97.7. He was not tested for COVID.

❊

Incarceration has always frayed—and frequently ruptured—family ties. Kwaneta was still breastfeeding her youngest child when she was arrested. That nursing baby, Autumn, is now in high school.

Kwaneta's family lives in Detroit. The distance—and the fact that people in solitary are restricted to non-contact visits behind glass—has meant that she has not seen any of her three children since 2015.

During her first years in prison, Kwaneta called home three times a day. She was lucky—her family could afford the cost of the calls. She and her children talked about everything—school, friends, hopes, dreams. Her son Antonio, who had already graduated from college, told her about his job and coworkers. Though they couldn't see one another, the calls kept them connected. Then came the 2016 accusation of forgery, which sent her to segregation.

During her first year in isolation, she was allowed no calls. The next year, she was allowed two. In 2019, she was only allowed one. Each call lasted five minutes. To make up for her abrupt silence, she wrote her children letters each week. Shouting through her vents, she asked the younger women about pop culture topics to include in her letters. But her three children, then ages eight, fourteen, and twenty-two, assumed that the sudden lack of calls indicated that she no longer loved them. They rarely responded to her letters. She could feel their connection, already so tenuous, unraveling further.

By 2020, she supposedly was to be allowed one 5-minute call every three months. Surprisingly, staff allowed her more calls—seven in all—during that first pandemic year. But before each call, guards strip-searched her. They handcuffed her and, each gripping an arm, escorted her to the telephone room. They dialed her mother's number and put the phone on speaker so that they could monitor every word—and ensure that she spoke only to those on her approved phone list. If a visiting uncle or cousin shouted hello in the background, the listening guard would abruptly end the call. If Kwaneta's mother did not answer, the guards would not call again or try to call a different relative. Instead, Kwaneta would have to wait until her next scheduled phone time.

If her mother did answer, they rushed through those fleeting five minutes as guards held up their fingers to count down the minutes. There was no time for conversations with her children. Kwaneta remained handcuffed the entire time.

At least she knew where they were. Jack, on the other hand, had not seen his four children in over ten years. He had spent much of their childhoods getting high, getting arrested, or being imprisoned. Then, in 1990, he was kidnapped, raped, and beaten. Traumatized and unable to care for himself, let alone four young children, he signed over legal custody to his parents. For his children, the act felt like abandonment. "They felt like I loved prison and drugs more than them," he recalled ruefully. He was arrested and imprisoned several times throughout the next decade.

In 2013, shortly after his release from federal prison, he was arrested and sentenced to twenty years in Texas state prison. By then, his children had grown into adults and dropped out of touch. In 2018, his youngest daughter sent him money and a photo for his birthday. That was the last communication he received from any of them.

Even before the pandemic, Mary's sons, who live fewer than a hundred miles from prison, rarely visited. She blames the disconnect not only on her lengthy sentence, but also the fact that she spent much of the boys' childhoods in and out of prison. In 2017, her eldest son visited, the first time they saw each other in thirteen years. He has not visited since.

She has not seen her second son since 1982. That year, Mary was arrested after stabbing a man who tried to rape her. While she was in jail, the boy's father married her best friend, and the pair convinced Mary to sign over her parental rights. "It was a heart-wrenching decision, but I knew Barbara did not drink or smoke and he would be better off with them," Mary recalled. That was the last time she saw that son.

Her two youngest sons were born a decade after that heartbreaking decision. When they were three and four, she was imprisoned for shoplifting.

Mary resented the fact that, although she had stopped using drugs, her boyfriend, the boys' father, continued to do so. That year, the legislature created the option of home arrest paired with electronic monitoring for people with nonviolent convictions.[5] Mary could have served her sentence at home with her family, but that home needed a telephone. For her boyfriend, however, drugs took precedence over installing a phone. Mary was sentenced to prison instead.

One year before her release, Mary learned that her boyfriend and his ex-wife had gotten together, gotten high, and left the boys in a Taco Bell parking lot. After her boyfriend overdosed in the bathroom, someone called the fire department. Firefighters arrived to find the boys wandering through the parking lot. They were whisked away by child protective services.

The children shuttled through eleven foster homes while Mary made call after call to keep them from falling through the child welfare cracks. Every month, guards awakened her at 4 a.m., placed her in handcuffs and leg irons, then drove her nearly two hours for family court hearings in a tribal court building that, ironically, her father and brother had helped build. Frequently, she arrived only to learn that her hearing had been postponed without explanation. Then she would be handcuffed, shackled, and driven the two hours back to prison.

After many frantic calls, Mary managed to contact the Creek Nation's child welfare agency and arranged to place her sons with a ministry until her release.

Once out of prison, Mary was allowed only supervised visits while she attempted to meet a long list of requirements, including drug testing, employment, and home inspections. Her family hearings were continually postponed or rescheduled. After a year and a half, the court granted her unsupervised visits. By then, her oldest son—who had recently turned thirty—had been granted custody of his younger brothers. While she was relieved that they were with family, the seemingly endless process to get them back wore her down. She fell into what she now calls "stinking thinking" and began using drugs again. From there, her life spiraled back toward prison and two separate sentences that ran consecutively.

In 1997, Oklahoma passed its truth-in-sentencing act, which required people to serve 85 percent of their prison sentence. Mary's first crime, an assault and battery charge, for which she was sentenced to forty years, occurred before the act took effect. By participating in prison programs and college classes, and keeping out of trouble, she whittled that first four-decade sentence down to fifteen years. But her second sentence (for a fight) occurred after the act took effect, requiring her to serve over seven years of that eight-and-a-half-year sentence. Every day, that additional sentence grates upon her.

Even more grating is that these last prison sentences resulted in the loss of another son. In 1997, the same year that Oklahoma passed its truth-in-sentencing law, Congress passed the federal Adoption and Safe Families Act. The act ordered that the state begin proceedings to terminate parental rights if a child had spent fifteen of the past twenty-two months in foster care. When Mary entered prison again in 2002, her youngest son was placed with a foster family. She signed over custody, thinking the couple would adopt him and give him a more stable life.

Nearly two decades later, that same son surprised her with a visit, the only time she has seen him. Her other sons now have their own children, ranging from ages three to twenty-four. She has never met those grandchildren. Instead, she does her best to be the doting grandmother from prison. She sews them quilts and, for the younger ones, pays other women to crochet brightly colored Hello Kitty dolls, Teenage Mutant Ninja Turtles, and slightly terrifying clown dolls. Through the prison's Mommy and Me program, she records videos of herself reading children's books and then sends the video, along with the book, to them.

The prospect of getting out—and getting to be a grandmother—used to get Mary through each day and each week. But as the pandemic dragged on the court remained silent concerning her petition, and her other options for early release dwindled—even that was not enough to sustain her.

※

In January 2020, just before the pandemic upended the world, Mary learned that another possible door for early release had slammed shut. The state's pardon and parole board had denied her application for clemency. In the criminal legal system, clemency can take three forms. The first is a reprieve, or a temporary postponement of a court-imposed sentence. The second, a pardon, erases the consequences of having a criminal conviction and is typically issued after a person has served their sentence. The third, for which Mary had applied, is a commutation, which shortens a prison sentence.

The clemency process varies from state to state. Some states delegate decisions to a pardon board. Others have deciding panels. In a few states, governors have unilateral powers. Whatever the process, commutations are notoriously difficult to obtain.

Mary had applied for clemency in 2019, the same year that Oklahoma had made headlines for the largest single-day commutation. That year, the board had recommended commutations for 527 people, who had been imprisoned for nonviolent drug convictions that had since been reclassified as less serious offenses. Oklahoma's governor must approve all clemency recommendations and, in this instance, he did.[6]

Oklahoma's parole and pardon board does not meet with applicants. Instead, commissioners base their decisions solely on the paperwork in front of them. No prison official bothered to tell Mary that her name had been on the board's list for consideration. Had she known, she would have asked her family members, prison faith leaders, and others for letters attesting to her rehabilitated character. She also would have written a personal letter to convince them that she had sobered up, turned her life around, and deserved a second chance. She had secured a promise of free assistance from a pardon attorney whom she had met at a prison workshop. He told her to have her family call him once her name appeared on the docket. But the only way to know when her name appeared was to regularly check the pardon board website, and no one had done so.

With that 2020 denial, she faced another four years in prison before becoming eligible for parole. Her parole application would be decided by the same board that denied her commutation application.

In Pennsylvania, Malakki had successfully appealed his death sentence and, in 2000, was sentenced to life without parole. In 2018, he applied for commutation. Pennsylvania clemency applications are submitted to the state's pardon board. First, the board of probation and parole conducts an investigation. Then two members of the five-person pardon board must approve a hearing. For crimes involving violence or for people serving life sentences, like Malakki, three members must approve. Without those approvals, the application process ends there. That's what happened with Malakki's application.

Had three members approved his application, he would have proceeded to the next step—the public hearing where, in fifteen minutes, he would have to persuade the board to offer him a second chance. His friends, family members, and other supporters would have the opportunity to speak on his behalf. That same opportunity would also be given to the loved ones of his victims. If the majority of the board voted in his favor, his application would be forwarded to the governor, who makes the ultimate decision. If fewer than three members voted in his favor, Malakki would need to wait another twelve months before applying again.[7]

But Malakki's application never made it to the public hearing stage, leaving him behind bars as the pandemic erupted around him.

Texas's clemency process is similar to Oklahoma's. A majority of the state's board of pardons and parole must approve a person's clemency application. Only then does the application move to the governor, who makes the final decision. But Texas lawmakers typically campaign on being tough on crime, causing few people to hold any hope for a Christmas miracle of compassion. In 2018, the board and Governor Greg Abbott granted commutation to Thomas Bartlett Whitaker, changing his death sentence to life without parole. That same year, Texas executed thirteen other people. Between 2021 and 2022, Abbott and the board granted pardons to ten people, restoring some of their civil rights, including their rights to serve on a jury, hold public office, or act as an executor of an estate. None had ever been sentenced to prison; all had received probation and/or a fine after being convicted.

The paltry number of clemencies—and the fact that nearly none were to people serving extensive prison sentences—discouraged Jack from applying. He's not the only one. He has never met a single person who has applied for clemency during his three different state prison sentences.

Even when clemency appears within reach, it often leaves thousands crushed. New York's state constitution grants the governor the unbridled authority to grant clemency—either as pardons or commutations. New York governor Hugh Carey granted 155 commutations between 1975 and 1982. His successors used their power more sparingly. Carey's successor, Mario Cuomo, granted thirty-seven commutations. The next governor, Republican George Pataki, who ran on a tough-on-crime platform, commuted thirty-two sentences.

In 2015, five years before the pandemic would decimate the state and catapult him into fame, then-governor Andrew Cuomo (and son of previous governor Mario Cuomo) announced the creation of an Executive Clemency Bureau to streamline clemency applications and to pair applicants with pro bono lawyers. His announcement sparked optimism among thousands. Those hopes flickered again and again as each year passed with only a handful of attorney pairings and even fewer commutations.

By the time Cuomo resigned in disgrace in 2021, the Executive Clemency Bureau had received more than ten thousand applications. Cuomo granted commutation to only forty-one people. Those few were ecstatic. Those thousands whose applications had been denied—or were still pending when he left office—were crushed.

# Chapter 8

# Vaccination and Insurrection

On January 6, 2021, millions were stunned when mobs of Trump supporters stormed the Capitol building, attacked a handful of police officers, and hunted for Democratic lawmakers.

Kwaneta, however, was not surprised when NPR broadcast the news. Ever since the 2020 election results had been announced, staff had been grousing. "What is Trump gonna do?" they asked as they dispensed tiny paper cups of liquid and pill medications. "We can't let them get away with it. I'm not gonna live in socialism."

For weeks, guards had been excitedly talking about the upcoming trip to the nation's capital. Everyone seemed to know someone who was going, even if they themselves could not make the trek north. Still, she wasn't prepared for the reaction of the guard on duty that afternoon. When he heard the news crackling from her radio, he threw his fist in the air and cheered. "We're gonna take our country back!"

"Why is everyone acting so surprised?" she asked me the following week. She pointed out that both the Department of Homeland Security and the FBI had previously issued reports about white nationalists' infiltration of both law enforcement and prison staff.[1]

But behind bars, even the insurrection of white supremacists was secondary to the anxious wait for IRS stimulus checks. In 2020, the Trump administration announced a one-time stimulus check of $1,200 under the CARES Act. A California court ruled that incarcerated people were also eligible for payment. Because incarcerated people do not file tax returns, each had to send a 1040 tax return form to the IRS. Not surprisingly, many prisons did not provide these forms. None were available in the law library or any counselor's office. In Oklahoma, Mary repeatedly asked me to send a blank form. Once I did, she asked a woman who worked in the law library to make copies, then helped others with the paperwork. They mailed their forms and waited.

Many other prisons, including Lane Murray, initially refused to allow forms to be mailed from outside. They also refused to provide them.

Kwaneta's mother was single-handedly raising Kwaneta's two daughters on her retirement income. An additional untaxed $1,200 would ease the financial burdens. But Kwaneta was not allowed to receive the forms that I repeatedly mailed. Neither were other women. Some asked relatives to apply for them online despite staff warnings that they would be charged with attempting to establish a business or third-party contact, both of which are prohibited in prison.

Even if Kwaneta had decided to ask her mother to apply online for her, the older woman was not tech-savvy. Kwaneta briefly considered asking Autumn, her teenage daughter, but then rationalized that the IRS must have prepared a way for incarcerated people to claim their checks. When staff finally distributed the forms, Kwaneta helped others fill them out, shouting directions through her vent as they asked what answers to write in which boxes. Several younger women encountered another stumbling block: they had grown up in foster care before being sent to juvenile prisons and, later, to adult prison. No staff or administrator would tell them their Social Security numbers, even though those nine digits were in their prison files. Many had no family to ask. It was another reminder of the ways in which those who had the least financial or family support were also the most vulnerable to repeated criminalization and incarceration.

In January 2021, federal prisons offered COVID vaccines to staff. When many refused, they offered them to incarcerated people. Despite widespread fears of COVID and their firsthand experiences with it, only a minority of incarcerated people agreed to be vaccinated. Those who refused did so for a variety of reasons. Some said that they had been given no information about the vaccine and, given the prison's inadequate response to COVID and typically terrible medical care, were wary of anything else offered. Others worried that the shot would actually give them COVID. Still others believed that vaccines were government conspiracies to implant chips under their skin or cause infertility.

In February 2021, Corcoran began vaccinating incarcerated people. With the vaccinations came an increase in activity. Programs returned although attendance, which had previously been twenty to forty people, was capped at six. Jobs and classes resumed. Men could congregate in the dayroom to watch television, play games, and talk. "They're not letting us out of prison yet, but it looks like the virus is over here at Corcoran," Mwalimu wrote optimistically after his first shot in February.

In Oklahoma, Mary had not fully regained her sense of smell by the time she received her first dose in mid-March. She could taste the gravy and biscuit served at breakfast and the Cheez-Its and chips bought at commissary, but not much more.

The next month, Mabel Bassett administered the second vaccine dose. Minutes before she was called for her shot, she had pulled her daily medications out of the bubble pack. But before she could find water to swallow them with, she was called to the clinic. She stuffed the pills into her pocket. Outside of prison, such a minor act would be no big deal, but inside prison, it was a serious violation of prison rules.

While walking back, Mary dropped her pills. A guard, who was notorious for screaming at the women, wrote her a misconduct ticket for possession of contraband. The ticket limited her commissary purchases to basic hygiene items. Although she had finally received her stimulus check, Mary could not treat herself to extra rolls of toilet paper, coffee, or snacks to make up for the shrinking meals. The punishment placed even more restrictions on top of the already-onerous pandemic restrictions.

In Texas, Jack did not receive his first shot until May. "My arm hurt like hell the next day," he recalled. He moaned about the pain, rubbing the spot, until his roommate mocked him as a wimpy man for complaining.

The following month, he received his second shot. It left him with a headache for two weeks, but also with the hope that he would survive the next outbreak. While some other states, like Pennsylvania, separated vaccinated and unvaccinated people, Texas made no such distinction. Jack was thankful that his roommate, however cruel, had also chosen to be vaccinated. He knew that he might not be as lucky with the next assigned cellmate.

Malakki doesn't recall what month he finally received the Johnson & Johnson vaccine, but he does remember that the prison was still partially locked down. Malakki's yearly flu shot had never bothered him, so he assumed that the COVID vaccine would be, at most, a minor irritant. But the combination of the vaccine and multiple sclerosis wreaked havoc on him within a few hours. That night, he had problems getting to the toilet. By the next morning, he could not move. His aide, another incarcerated man assigned to help him, arrived and had to fetch two other men to move him from his bed to the toilet. Then they took him to the infirmary where he lay in bed, unable to move, for the next few days.

Malakki doesn't remember much from those days. Whenever his condition flares, his mind goes into what seems like another dimension. But when he was lucid enough to think, he reminded himself, "If the shot does this, imagine what COVID will do."

When he returned to the housing unit, a younger man who sometimes pushed his wheelchair told him that he, too, had gotten vaccinated. "I wasn't gonna get it," the man admitted, "but if I'm gonna push you, I gotta get the shot." Even after they had largely discarded their masks, men on his unit continued to mask around him—and exhorted others to do the same. It wasn't uncommon for him to hear, "Hey, man, pull your mask all the way up. You're with Brother Malakki."

※

Kwaneta did not receive her first dose of the Moderna vaccine until mid-June. By then, she had already gotten sick with what seemed like COVID—a sore throat, headache, diarrhea, and body aches. But the prison does not test for COVID antibodies and only irregularly tests for active cases, so she was never able to confirm whether she had contracted the virus.

Being vaccinated was an arduous—and demeaning—process, including a strip search, handcuffs, and leg irons. Before she could leave her cell, the guards cleared the area of the women assigned to clean the halls. "That means all the janitors who work down here from [general] population must get as far away from us and they must face a wall until we pass," Kwaneta explained. Once the hall was cleared and the incarcerated janitors unable to make eye contact with Kwaneta, two guards marched her down the corridor.

Typically, when Kwaneta hobbled past, women would shout encouraging messages. "We love you, Mama Detroit!" they would yell. "Keep your head up! God bless you! Don't let them break you!" But when she was escorted to be vaccinated, no one was in the hall to shout reaffirming words. Instead, as they walked, guards asked why she was listening to "Sleepy Joe," warning that the shot would implant a microchip under her skin.

Once at their destination, the guards cuffed each hand to opposite ends of a desk. Her ankles remained shackled so tightly that, one month later, she still bore a scab where the metal had dug into her Achilles tendon. Kwaneta, who is right-handed, requested the shot in her left arm. The nurse puffed and gasped as if the additional three steps to reach the other arm were a marathon. Kwaneta waited the required fifteen minutes before guards unchained her, cuffed her hands together again, and marched her back to her cell.

The second dose of the COVID vaccine should have been administered twenty-one days after the first shot. But, nearly two months later, when she asked about the second dose, medical staff told her they hadn't yet ordered it. By then, only 31.3 percent (or 23,600 residents) of the neighboring county had received one dose and an even lower number (26.94 percent) had been fully vaccinated, making her worry about contracting COVID from the staff who came in and out each day. In late July, Texas had reported a surge of over ten thousand new COVID cases; five were among Lane Murray's staff.

The return to normalcy also meant a return to mass numbers of incarceration. In the summer of 2021, jails and prisons across the country began climbing back to pre-pandemic levels of crowding and overcrowding. By then, the United States had approved three different COVID vaccines. But the introduction of vaccines and boosters has done little to protect those incarcerated or employed in Texas's ninety-seven prisons. Vaccine hesitancy—among both those incarcerated and employed in US jails and prisons—continued to fuel outbreaks.

Just as it does on the outside, misinformation runs rampant in prisons. But behind bars, incarcerated people have little to no ability to check facts and dispel rumors. "We become a petri dish for conspiracy theories," Kwaneta said. Furthermore, people's life experiences left them with a deep distrust of government.

Their fears were not entirely unfounded. One woman cited the Tuskegee experiment. Between 1932 and 1972, public health officials, under the watch of a succession of US surgeons general, experimented on 600 Black men, 399 of whom had syphilis. Patients were not informed that they had syphilis. Instead, doctors told them that they were being treated for "bad blood." They received free meals, medical exams, and burial insurance. Even after penicillin became the "treatment of choice" in the early 1940s, Tuskegee patients were not given this life-saving medication.[2]

Tuskegee is the most well-known medical experiment, but others, conducted behind prison walls, have recently come to public attention. From the 1950s to the 1970s, University of Pennsylvania dermatologist Albert Kligman conducted scores of experiments, dousing the skin of men at Philadelphia's Holmesburg Prison with toothpaste, deodorant, eye drops, foot powders, and even mind-altering drugs, radioactive isotopes, and dioxins. He paid his imprisoned subjects anywhere between ten to three hundred dollars, depending on the nature of the experiment. Kligman went on to become a wealthy man and famous name in dermatology. "Informed consent was unheard of. No one asked me what I was doing. It was a wonderful time," Kligman stated in 1986.[3]

Two of Kligman's students became researchers at the University of California in San Francisco. During the 1970s, they experimented on at least 2,600 people at a state medical prison. They applied and injected them with pesticides and herbicides, then placed small cages filled with mosquitoes close to or even on their skin. They paid their incarcerated subjects thirty dollars each month, an irresistible incentive in a prison with 2,800 prisoners competing for three hundred jobs, which paid ten dollars each month.[4]

Ironically, some of this historical information was provided by Texas prison guards, predominantly white Trump supporters. They fanned the flames of fear with theories about microchips and government experimentation on imprisoned people. "What can one say when our history of Tuskegee and CoIntelpro are used to persuade us not to get the vaccine by insurrection supporters?" Kwaneta wrote in exasperation.

Medical experimentation behind bars is not a relic of the past. In 2021, an Arkansas sheriff gave Ivermectin, an anti-parasitic drug, to men in the county jail. Federal health authorities and leading medical experts have explicitly warned that Ivermectin should not be used to treat COVID. Nonetheless, jail medical staff administered the drug to men who had tested positive, telling them that the pills were vitamins, antibiotics, or steroids. They did not warn them about potential side effects. After receiving anywhere from two to ten pills daily, the unwitting subjects experienced vision problems, diarrhea, bloody stools, and stomach cramps.[5] In 2023, the court ruled that experimenting on incarcerated people without their knowledge was a violation of their due rights.[6]

Others' reluctance to be vaccinated stemmed not from history, but their own acceptance of conspiracy theories. One woman told Kwaneta that she believed the government created COVID as a means of population control while another, in her twenties, thought that the virus was caused by the Illuminati.

Kwaneta's family pays for a subscription to the *New Yorker* magazine, allowing her to keep up with current events. She read a 2022 article about Johnson & Johnson's past experiments on imprisoned people and its attempts to evade lawsuits over its alleged use of asbestos, widely claimed to be in its baby powder. In one, the company blistered Black men in Holmesburg with chemicals, then dusted their wounds three times a day with talc. In another, Johnson & Johnson paid a different group of incarcerated men three dollars a day to have shampoo dripped into their eyes regularly to perfect the formula for its No More Tears baby shampoo.[7]

Not surprisingly, this history of offering incentives to unwitting subjects of unethical experiments fed people's skepticism. "We all got a novelty ice cream sandwich if we would get the vaccine," Kwaneta said. Other prison systems, such as Pennsylvania's, offered money deposited into a commissary account, while still others rewarded people with slices of pizza, burgers, fries, and other foods normally unavailable. "Paying people to get vaccinated in prison only fueled suspicions. The state won't even allow us to have ice in water during triple-digit temperatures. But they giving away something? I can see the hesitancy."

Science journalist Laura Spinney has noted that distrust can lead to a result opposite to the placebo effect. In the placebo effect, a patient's belief in a treatment results in an improvement, even when the treatment is physically and medically ineffective. But, Spinney wrote in her historical analysis of the 1918 flu pandemic, "if a patient loses confidence in his doctor, or if he perceives that the doctor has lost respect for him, the beneficial effects of the placebo shrink—and that shrinkage doesn't necessarily stop at zero. It can enter negative space, giving rise to a harmful, or 'nocebo' effect."[8] That same holds true in jails and prisons across the country today.

In the summer of 2021, Texas announced that state prisons that reached a 70 percent vaccination rate could roll back protective measures, including regular testing and the mask mandates that few had bothered to follow. But no public health agency had even suggested a 70 percent vaccination rate as the target metric for when prisons could return to pre-pandemic measures. That year, researchers at Emory University, the University of Michigan, and Yale University estimated that, to achieve herd immunity, at least 85 percent of the population would need to be vaccinated.[9]

That June, the Texas Department of Criminal Justice stated that nearly 55 percent of its incarcerated population had been vaccinated.[10] Although it also touted that more than thirteen thousand employees had been vaccinated, staff vaccination remained below 50 percent. The vaccination rate for all Texans hovered at 62 percent, slightly below the 64 percent national average.[11] In September 2021, as the Delta variant overwhelmed hospitals, ravaged neighborhoods and, once again, spread behind bars, thirteen Texas prison staff died from COVID.[12]

Still, staff remained vocally opposed to vaccination. "They will have to shoot me in the head first," one guard told Kwaneta that summer. Another announced that he would have to be tied down first.

At Oklahoma's Mabel Bassett, three-quarters of the women and trans people were vaccinated by April. They were allowed to walk to the cafeteria, where staff had taped Xs to the floor in an effort to keep women six feet apart. They still had to wear masks, even while seated, lowering them only to eat.

Mary huffed and puffed if she tried to walk quickly to the cafeteria, a difficulty she had never before experienced. But if she slowed, the kitchen, still ill equipped to feed such a large number, would run out of certain foods, like burgers or bananas, and she risked an even skimpier meal.

Crowded in dorms and cells, many smoked marijuana and K2, a synthetic form of marijuana, to escape the pandemic blues. Mary stopped using all drugs, but she remained agitated and distraught. The only calm she found was when she sewed baby quilts for her new granddaughters, and even then, the constant strain of prolonged imprisonment—and COVID brain fog—sometimes caused series of mis-stitches that took weeks to correct.

As both leaves and the temperatures fell in late October, Mary worried about the emerging variants, especially given her age, ongoing medical problems, and the crowded conditions. She washed her hands frequently, scrubbed the common areas, and hoped that these measures would allow her to live long enough to walk out of prison. She ate oatmeal, drank water, exercised, and showered every day. These were the only factors she could control in an environment where so much remained out of her control. The prison population, which never decreased to a level making social distancing possible, was once again climbing. The gray bunk beds, which had initially been temporary fixtures in the dayrooms, had become permanent additions.

One year later, in an article for the *New Yorker*, Dr. Dhruv Khullar, a physician, journalist, and assistant professor at Weill Cornell Medical College lamented the recurrence of COVID outbreaks in the general public, and the continued defiance of those who refused to get vaccinated, to mask, or to take basic precautions. By then, the United States had already surpassed 1 million COVID-related deaths, but this tragic milestone went largely unrecognized by government actors and agencies intent on foisting a sense of normality on a pandemic-weary public.

Behind bars, the conditions that cultivated COVID outbreaks had long been considered normal—and even acceptable. Now, it seemed that the new normal would include repeated exposure to a debilitating virus and any lingering effects, no matter how incapacitating. "How many times will we have to sit through quarantines and ride out symptoms, worrying how bad this one might be? How many more surprises could the coronavirus have in store?" Khullar asked.[13]

Even before the 1 million death mark, that was a question asked again and again by people behind bars, whose already restricted realities were made even smaller with each quarantine and outbreak.

# Chapter 9

# What Has (Not) Been Learned

"The pandemic is over," President Joe Biden announced in September 2022. But, he also admitted, "we still have a problem with COVID." Waving his hand at the crowds thronging the Detroit Auto Show, he added, "If you notice, no one's wearing masks. Everybody seems to be in pretty good shape. So, I think it's changing."[1]

Indeed, the United States seemed on the mend. Nearly nine months earlier, on January 14, it had reached a record high with 933,326 new cases and 3,980 deaths in a single day. By September, the daily average had dropped below 807,000 cases and a daily death average of 3,323.[2]

But Biden's optimism was premature. That month, the Johns Hopkins Coronavirus Resource Center listed more than 2 million COVID cases nationally within the previous twenty-eight days. Hundreds were still dying each day.

By then, the federal government had ended funding for vaccines, treatments, and tests, leaving the uninsured and underinsured on their own.[3]

The numbers inside jails, prisons, and other forms of confinement remained impossible to realistically gauge. Even during the height of the pandemic, many jail and prison systems did not report how many people were tested or what circumstances prompted testing. The Federal Bureau of Prisons even artificially deflated its totals by removing cases upon a person's release.[4]

By summer 2022, seventeen states and the District of Columbia had stopped reporting COVID prison numbers altogether. Ten of those states also stopped reporting active COVID cases, while six stopped reporting COVID deaths.[5]

Other prison systems, including California and Texas, continued to report active cases, but not testing numbers, making it impossible to know if their numbers reflected low transmission rates or fewer tests.

In several states, incarcerated people told me that they shunned testing, even when they felt COVID-like symptoms. During the summer of 2020, the Bureau of Prisons listed fewer than one dozen active COVID cases at its prison in Aliceville, Alabama, but women inside painted a different picture.

One of these women, "Alice," told me, "We . . . have a new wave of BA.5 COVID racing through . . . and everyone is ill. I've had it for the last four days and it's a bad one—I was basically unable to get out of bed." But, she continued, "because they send you to the SHU if you test positive, no one is going to health services." Instead of seeking medical help, women drank tea and honey and turned to Vicks, Tylenol, and ibuprofen.[6]

That's what Elena House-Hay, an incarcerated artist in Pennsylvania, decided to do. In 2020, she tested positive. She was ordered to pack her belongings, including her mattress, pillow, and half a dozen bags and boxes, then carry them down the stairs and through the snow-filled yard to the quarantine unit. She had to make several trips, struggling through body aches, fatigue, coughing, and tightness in her chest.

Quarantine was a dormitory with thirty-two cubicles, each with two bunk beds that rose above the cubicle partitions. People on the top bunks lay mere feet away from one another. They were allotted two 30-minute intervals out of those cubicles each day.

After that experience, whenever she felt COVID-like symptoms, Elena did not ask for a test. She wasn't the only one. Many others kept quiet when they felt sick. No one wanted to be moved or cause yet another lockdown. Their numbers were never added to the official COVID tally because, by then, Pennsylvania prisons only tested people who were symptomatic or close contacts of those who had tested positive. With so few people reporting, that prison documented between two to twenty COVID cases on any given day.

Not having an accurate COVID count had ramifications not only for those locked inside jails and prisons, but also for those in the larger community. "We know that people are still getting quite sick. We know that people are still dying from COVID in the community and in prisons," Bennett Stein, then project director of UCLA Law School's COVID Behind Bars Data Project, told me in the summer of 2022. "When there are outbreaks or high risk of outbreaks, it is still important that government, prison officials, judges, district attorneys, and policymakers consider interventions to keep people safe and save lives."

Even as prison populations decreased, prison deaths soared by 77 percent in 2020.[7] In many states, these high death rates continued through 2021. Not all deaths were caused by COVID, but some could have been prevented had people not been locked in isolation, denied health care, or had potentially life-saving medical treatment postponed again and again.

Knowing about high levels of sickness and death in carceral institutions—whether jails, prisons, immigrant detention centers, or other forms of confinement—could have compelled policymakers to further reduce the numbers held inside. It could, at the very least, have resulted in reinstating mask requirements among staff and testing asymptomatic individuals. But if these numbers are artificially lowered—by people hiding symptoms and avoiding tests or by prisons refusing to test people with symptoms—the opportunity for those interventions is lost. Meanwhile, outbreaks continue to rip through jails and prisons, then outside to the surrounding communities—a perpetually revolving door of contagion.

Data alone may not be enough to change hearts, minds, and, ultimately, policy. In 2016, a group of abolitionist artists and scholars started the Illinois Deaths in Custody Project. The all-volunteer team met regularly to scour media for news about custodial deaths, submitted Freedom of Information Act requests, and then published this information online. They also asked incarcerated people for eulogies, art, and letters about these deaths. They created public workshops, exhibits, papers, and essays to raise visibility of these deaths.

Seven years after its founding, and three years into the pandemic, members questioned whether the heightened focus on death behind bars had created a palpable shift. "Will these forms of research enable more people to get free or to stay alive? How and why does transparency, and data, matter? Can organizing that spotlights death in custody communicate to a wide public that life matters?" they asked. "We need more and better data about deaths in custody. . . . But only freedom, not more data, will save lives."[8]

The information black hole reflects the opaque nature of jails and prisons. Since 2008, the American Bar Association has called on federal and state governments to create and fund independent monitoring entities to oversee jails and prisons. These independent bodies should be able to access all aspects of a jail or prison's operations and conditions, including death records, and publish findings online.

Reforms, such as oversight bodies, seek to improve immediate conditions for incarcerated people. This is crucial, especially given that, as of 2022, jails and prisons confined nearly 1.9 million people in jails and prisons while immigrant detention locked in another thirty thousand people.[9] While youth incarceration plummeted during the two decades before the coronavirus exploded across the United States, there were still 25,000 young people in juvenile prisons in 2020.[10]

Some jurisdictions already had such oversight entities. In New York City, for instance, the Board of Correction, a decades-old city agency, is tasked with regulating jail conditions, including solitary, medical treatment, and mental health care. In Pittsburgh, the nine-member Allegheny County Jail Oversight Board does the same for its jail. Similarly, the nine-member Texas Commission on Jail Standards, which always includes two sheriffs and a county judge, has a similar role for the state's 252 jails.

Despite the presence of these oversight bodies, all three jail systems have been plagued for decades by abuse, violence, scandals, and preventable deaths. The agencies lack the authority to sanction sheriffs and administrators for egregious violations or to force them to comply with their oversight. And, in 2020, their ability to visit, inspect, and speak directly to those working or confined within was curbed by the pandemic.

The inability of oversight bodies to rein in horrific abuses or improve life-threatening conditions points to the larger limitations of reforms. Prisons themselves emerged as the more humane reforms to floggings, banishment, and executions. While confinement is frequently preferable to death, we should remember Angela Y. Davis's reminder that incarceration aims to disappear social problems from public view and, in doing so, aggravates rather than solves them.[11]

The limits of oversight and reform demonstrate how little we can realistically improve a system that has always been intended to confine, isolate, dehumanize, and degrade those society has labeled as unwanted. That does not mean we should not be outraged or give up mobilizing to end these brutal and barbaric conditions. For the nearly 1.9 million people confined in jails, prisons, immigrant detention, and juvenile jails—and the many others who churn through these institutions each year—reforms that ameliorate any of these myriad injustices and abuses are welcome.

In 1967, the French-Austrian theorist André Gorz coined the term *non-reformist reforms* as a challenge to examine what is "conceived not in terms of what is possible within the framework of a given system or administration, but in view of what should be made possible in terms of human needs and demands."[12] Ruth Wilson Gilmore, a co-founder of Critical Resistance, connected this concept explicitly to prison abolition when she challenged abolitionists to work toward non-reformist reforms and seek out "changes that, at the end of the day, unravel rather than widen the net of social control through criminalization."[13]

Non-reformist reforms can, and do, include campaigns to address urgent needs that cannot wait for a restructuring of society. These campaigns include ending the shackling of pregnant people, limiting solitary, ensuring adequate medical treatment, releasing elderly or infirm people who have already spent decades behind bars, and mounting defense campaigns for people currently facing criminal charges. These address immediate needs but do not further strengthen a carceral response that sucks up money and resources that could be redirected to sustain individuals, families, and communities.

In 2022, federal lawmakers introduced a bill to expand compassionate release based on COVID vulnerability. Compassionate release allows for an early—and immediate—release of a person based on "extraordinary and compelling reasons," typically a terminal illness or debilitating medical condition. Forty-nine states (except Iowa) and the Federal Bureau of Prisons allow people to apply for compassionate release. Still, securing it is nearly as unlikely as clemency. Many prison systems require that a person be near death before considering their application—and even then may still not approve it. Between March 2020 and September 2022, the Federal Bureau of Prisons received 27,656 requests for compassionate release. The agency approved 16 percent of them.[14]

Even less is known about compassionate release among state prisoners, who make up the majority of the nation's prison population. Only thirteen states are required by law to track and report compassionate release statistics—and not all make that information public.[15] Even if they had, the Illinois Deaths in Custody Project has already demonstrated that data alone does not galvanize the outrage necessary to compel legislative or policy changes to prevent people from spending their last weeks of life locked behind metal doors or shackled to prison hospital beds.

The limits of data to galvanize action were apparent on the congressional floor the previous year. In 2021, federal lawmakers introduced three bills requiring prisons to publicly report COVID numbers, institute measures to stem the spread behind bars, and mandate federal prison staff to obtain immediate medical attention for those in custody. This last bill, had it been law in 2020, might have held someone accountable for the death of Heather, the trans woman who died after one month of medical neglect in federal prison. The medical staff who repeatedly ignored her calls for help would have been criminally liable for their inaction. And, with that sanction looming over their heads, they might have taken her complaints more seriously and brought her to the clinic for diagnosis and treatment.

Although deaths in federal prisons had increased 144 percent from 366 in 2019 to at least 526 in 2020, and COVID had ravaged prisons nationwide, those 2021 bills languished without a vote—or even substantial discussion in Congress.[16]

Similarly, prison officials who made decisions about parole, compassionate release, clemency, and other forms of early release either had access to institutional data about COVID spread or, at the very least, knew that keeping people behind bars during a plague escalated their risks for avoidable debilitation and death. Yet they still denied the vast majority of applicants, condemning them to what had truly become death-making institutions.

※

"Who's everybody?" Kwaneta wondered, as she read Biden's proclaimation that everybody seemed to be "in pretty good shape."

"I may appear outwardly healthy, but I'm having problems invisible to the naked eye," she told me. After her COVID infection in February 2021, symptoms had been lingering for months. Her vision began declining—rapidly. Black spots began floating in her right eye. Kwaneta typically reads, both to escape the despair of indefinite isolation and to keep her mind from atrophying. But the floaters required her to take more frequent breaks. Without reading, she could not drown out the cacophony bouncing through the corridors and the interior clamor of worries churning through her brain.

Her sense of smell remained off. Months after her illness, she could smell only sweet scents, like her soap and shampoo, but not the cheesy smell of Doritos or other foods. Over a year after her initial bouts with COVID, a neighbor commented on the tang of her spicy vegetable ramen soup. Another time, guards commented on the nachos she had made from chicken chili, ranch dressing, ramen seasoning, and jalapeño cheese. Both times, Kwaneta smelled nothing.

Kwaneta feared that she had long COVID, like the COVID long-haulers she had heard about on the radio. As early as spring 2020, people who had contracted the virus began publicly sharing their lingering symptoms, including fatigue, shortness of breath, and cognitive dysfunction. They had difficulty concentrating, confusion, and memory problems. The World Health Organization now acknowledges that between 10 to 20 percent of people who had the virus may develop long COVID.[17] Globally, 49 percent of people who have had COVID reported persistent symptoms four months after their initial diagnosis.[18] By February 2022, long COVID affected an estimated 16 million adults in the United States, forcing between 2 and 4 million out of the workforce.[19]

Kwaneta's prolonged isolation within a tiny, unchanging environment exacerbated the brain fog that many have attributed to long COVID. While writing a letter, she tried to use the word *puritanical*, but for twenty minutes, her brain insisted that the word she needed was *pilgrimage*. Finally, she reached for her dictionary and read through the entries starting with "p" until she found the correct word. She has had to repeat this process for multiple words.

She also began experiencing sharp chest pains. Twenty-five skips on her homemade jump rope left her heart pounding as if it would jump out of her chest. Some days, it felt like someone was stabbing her as she moved around her cell. Some days, the pain shot through her chest even when she sat still.

From years of nursing and reading medical journals, she knew that, while men often describe heart attacks as an elephant on their chests, women experience milder signs, such as shortness of breath, nausea, vomiting, fainting, light-headedness, and mild discomfort in one or both arms.

During her first year in solitary, she watched staff ignore two women who displayed textbook signs of heart attacks. Only after they passed out and remained unresponsive did guards call 911. Neither woman ever returned. To this day, Kwaneta does not know what happened to them. Were they shipped to the medical prison? Did they die?

Kwaneta worried that her ongoing chest pains indicated more dire problems. Evolving research indicates a substantial basis for her fears. A 2022 study of 150,000 veterans who had survived COVID found a substantially higher risk of heart disease than in the millions of veterans who had never been infected. They were also 52 percent more likely to have a stroke and 72 percent more like to experience heart failure.[20] Even those who had not been hospitalized were at higher risk for cardiovascular complications. This included people under age sixty-five and those who lacked the typical risk factors, such as smoking, obesity, or diabetes.

Black people have higher odds of developing conditions associated with long COVID, including blood clots in their lungs. Black patients who had been hospitalized for COVID were twice as likely to develop diabetes or be diagnosed with chest pain in the first six months after their hospital stays.[21]

As both a nurse and a Black woman, Kwaneta already knew that Black women face more obstacles when seeking medical care for diseases that diagnostic tests can confirm. The Food and Drug Administration has yet to approve a diagnostic test for long COVID. Outside the prison system, even for those with health insurance and conscientious doctors, the lack of an approved test has resulted in practitioners dismissing patients' complaints as psychosomatic, directing them to physical therapy or psychotherapy.

Inside the Texas prison system, the lack of a diagnostic test, coupled with the staff's prevalent disbelief about COVID, means that Kwaneta has no hope of receiving any type of medical treatment. Whenever a woman reports any concern, medical staff issue three recommendations—drink more water, lose weight, take Tylenol. "That's the standard protocol for *everything*," she told me. When another woman complained of long COVID symptoms, she overheard the prison's physician assistant tell her, "You're not gonna get a disability check out there by pretending to be sick in here." (After hearing him say that, Kwaneta filed a complaint with the Texas Medical Board.)

Behind prison walls, no one can request or consult a doctor who has experience with long COVID, nor can they sign up for any of the emerging clinical trials for evaluations and potential new treatments. Instead, Kwaneta has to navigate prison bureaucracy for authorization to evaluate her most severe symptoms, like the chest pains and heart palpitations. It's a process that requires her to submit multiple requests before officials will approve a visit with a specialist. And behind bars, even over-the-counter medicines such as aspirin may require a prescription. When Kwaneta told the physician's assistant about her chest pains and her concerns that they might be a symptom of a heart attack, he prescribed generic Tylenol rather than aspirin, which thins the blood and prevent blood clots and heart attacks. The blood work that he ordered did not include tests to assess her heart.

In July 2021, the Americans with Disabilities Act codified long COVID as a disability if it substantially limited one or more major life activities. While the act technically applies to all state prisons and local jails, the reality is far different. Even those with visible disabilities, such as Malakki, who needs a wheelchair, frequently face multiple hurdles in accessing accommodations.

In Texas, Kwaneta knows that no accommodation will be made for a person with long COVID. And having long COVID might also impede her release.

"Stop. Rest. Pace." is the approach increasingly recommended by those researching and treating long COVID. But it's not an approach that Kwaneta, or anyone in prison, can adopt without severe consequences. Texas remains one of a handful of states that requires its captive population to work without pay.[22] If Kwaneta is transferred to general population, she will be assigned a prison job. And, as she already learned from her winter working in the fields, she cannot take a day off no matter how gravely ill. If she does, staff will issue a disciplinary ticket for refusing to work, and when she finally gets a chance to appear before the parole board, that ticket could be their reason for denying her release.

At the same time, Texas prisons, like many other systems, have done nothing to minimize risk of COVID transmission. The showers remain unventilated, people in solitary continue to lack access to cleaning supplies, and even as numbers continue to spike, incarcerated people are no longer given masks unless medical staff determine that they have COVID symptoms. Moreover, in the rare instance that a person is tested and tests positive, staff place them in segregation, where they use the same showers and share the same vents as those around them. Each placement increases Kwaneta's chances of contracting COVID again and of developing chronic health issues like diabetes, kidney disease, organ failure, and mental health disorders. Kwaneta remains fully aware that, if she develops any of these, she is more likely to die a slow and painful death than receive timely and adequate medical treatment.

Despite their higher odds of developing conditions associated with long COVID, Black people and other people of color were less likely to be released from jail or prison early during the pandemic. In 2020, the number of incarcerated people decreased by at least 17 percent—the largest and fastest decrease of the nation's prison population in history.[23] But white people benefited disproportionately from decarceration efforts. In Arkansas, for instance, white people comprised 57 percent of the pre-pandemic prison population, but represented 72 percent of those eligible for early release during the pandemic. Conversely, people of color comprised just under 43 percent of state prisoners, but only 28 percent of them qualified for early release as a COVID precaution.[24]

These startling disparities are caused by several systemic factors. Prosecutors seek more severe charges against people of color. Courts mete out longer sentences to Black people and other people of color.[25] And when disasters compel policymakers to decarcerate, those serving shorter sentences for less serious (and often nonviolent) convictions are the ones likely to be released. Those with years or decades remaining or with violent felony convictions are often left behind.

Meanwhile, prisons have continually reported chronic understaffing. In August 2022, Texas prisons had only 70 percent of guard positions filled—and many were running with even fewer actual guards. Lane Murray had two-thirds of its guard positions filled, while Mountain View, where Jack had been transferred, had even more vacancies. Some prisons had as little as 30 percent of positions filled.[26] Lack of staff caused even more delays in handing out meals and medications. Staff were unavailable to escort people to the showers, recreation, their quarterly call home, or even to outside medical appointments.

That month, when Kwaneta and two other women were brought to an outside optometrist, guards refused to let them use the bathroom or even get a drink of water. The explanation? Lack of staff. The trip, which normally takes two hours, lasted six, during which the women remained in handcuffs and leg irons. When they finally returned to the prison, they had missed lunch. The guards told them to wait for dinner. When they begged for water, desperate after six hours in the Texas summer, the guards on duty told them, "We're short staffed. We'll give you water with dinner. Drink out of your sink." As always, the sink water was tepid and tasted funny.

While they claimed to be too busy to distribute water, short staffing didn't keep guards too busy to pull down the fabric that Kwaneta had hung over the window of her cell door so that she could change her soaked sanitary pad and soiled panties in private. "You can't cover your door," the guards scolded. But at least she'd had her long-awaited optometry appointment. Later, the prison canceled both her annual dental visit and the podiatry appointment for the foot pains she had been suffering since 2015. They also canceled the 2022 cardiology appointment that could have diagnosed and treated her recurring chest pains. Officials said that no guards were available to drive her to her appointments.

The term *short staffing* is a euphemism to divert attention from the state's continued addiction to incarceration. "Words matter. It's not too little staff, but too many people incarcerated," Kwaneta reminded me. "If they released all the Q-tips [elderly white-haired women], then there would be someone to take me to my hospital appointments," she told a guard who groused about the lack of staff. But instead of seeking ways to reduce its bloated prison population, Texas lawmakers continued with the "lock 'em up" policies of previous decades.

At the same time, lawmakers cut funding for these very same prisons where thousands continue to languish under the politicians' continuing tough-on-crime zeal. In October 2022, Texas governor Greg Abbott announced that he was diverting nearly $360 million from the state's prison budget to fund Operation Lone Star, his border-militarization project to station state troopers and National Guard members along the Texas-Mexico border.[27]

Meanwhile, the state refused to significantly reduce its prison population. At the end of 2020, 121,128 people were confined in Texas prisons.[28] One year later, at the end of 2021, the state prison population had fallen only slightly to 118,000, in large part because the pandemic had delayed sentencing and new admissions, not because lawmakers had decarcerated or repealed tough-on-crime measures.[29] By 2022, prison numbers rose to nearly 122,000 people.[30] Prisons, now more crowded than ever, continued many of the same careless practices that fueled earlier outbreaks.

In the spring of 2022, Mountain View staff confiscated masks, including Jack's, during routine cell searches. "I expect us to go full blown infected very soon," he predicted. That August, his prediction came true. Staff placed a person with COVID in the adjoining cell. Each cough—and there were many—made Jack cringe at the possibility of a virus-laden particle being propelled through the vent, into his cell, and into his lungs. Despite her positive status, the woman shouted at her neighbors through her door, projecting droplets into the hallway. Soon after, a second person who had tested positive for COVID was placed on Jack's unit. The unit was locked down yet again for medical isolation.

To Jack, the placements made no sense. "They already had a dorm locked down for COVID," he noted. "Why not put the two [positive] people there instead of down here with us?" In August 2023, staff once again placed a person with COVID on the unit and—once again—refused to distribute masks or take other precautions to prevent transmission. It was yet another example of lessons not learned from the prolonged pandemic.

Jack fervently hoped that the vaccine and boosters would keep him from contracting severe COVID. Staff had stopped masking altogether. Incarcerated people were brought to court and outside medical appointments while women from other prisons were brought, temporarily, to Mountain View for medical treatment. Every time he heard a person coughing, sneezing, or even clearing her throat, Jack worried that they had COVID—and that he would, once again, get sick. His fears were echoed by some of the nation's public health experts. "In the US, COVID is still on pace to kill more than a hundred thousand people per year," warned Dhruv Khullar, the physician and Weill Cornell Medical College professor. "Many of us share the reasonable worry that some future reinfection will be the one that causes longer-term harm to our health and quality of life."[31]

The 2022 study of veterans also suggested that those who have contracted COVID more than once are more likely to experience a range of medical problems, including heart attacks, strokes, breathing problems, kidney disorders, and mental health problems. They are twice as likely to die as those who have not been reinfected.[32] Khullar cautioned that the study had not yet been published in a peer-reviewed journal and that it drew from US veterans, many of whom are older men with multiple medical conditions. But many in prison—such as Malakki, Jack, Mary, and Kwaneta—are also aging and, even if they didn't enter prison with multiple medical conditions, years of poor nutrition and even worse medical care have undoubtedly damaged their health.

While both veterans and people in prison have multiple health problems, experience a higher prevalence of mental illness, and face dysfunctional medical systems with lengthy waits, Kwaneta reminded me that veterans are able to reduce their potential exposure. In prisons, people who are not in segregation must attend assigned programs. The assignment might be a job paying pennies, an educational class, a self-help group, or some combination. "You can't miss a day because you're sick. You will be written a disciplinary ticket, which will cause a parole denial," Kwaneta explained. "You're forced to attend crowded groups, live in shared crowded spaces—all without social distancing or mask wearing." Basically, the choice in prison boils down to one question: How badly do you want to go home?

Khullar lamented the public's widespread discarding of common sense precautions such as masking, social distancing, and vaccinations, as well as policymakers' unwillingness to fund robust testing and treatment programs, invest in public health infrastructure, support paid sick leave, and improve ventilation. "Has our battle with COVID-19 come to such a standstill that a slow burn of disruption, debility, and death will continue for years to come?" he asked.[33] Inside prisons, the answer to that question seemed to be a resounding yes.

"The pandemic was an opportunity to reevaluate policies so that people who live and work in prisons can be safe," reflected Kwaneta. "They didn't."

⁂

Prison pandemic protection measures became weaponized into punitive cudgels. When Washington State resumed in-person visits, its prisons initiated rapid testing for all visitors. Visitors had previously been allowed to give their incarcerated loved one a quick kiss at the start and end of each visit. But now even these brief pecks were prohibited. This new rule was buried within a forty-page COVID policy report but not directly communicated to visitors upon arrival.

In one men's prison, officials suspended a woman's visiting privileges for ninety days when she kissed her incarcerated fiancé at the end of their visit. Although she had tested negative before entering the visiting room, officials moved her fiancé between three different units for a ten-day isolation period during which he could not call her. He himself was never tested, even when officials returned him to his housing unit.[34]

At San Quentin, 94 percent of the incarcerated population got vaccinated against COVID-19. "We took the vaccine because we were told it would get us back to normal," wrote Rahsaan Thomas. By then, more than 2,200 people at the prison had gotten COVID and twenty-eight had died. But even with the high vaccination rate, some of the hypervigilant protocols that had failed to keep them safe during the pandemic remained in place. If three or more people in a unit tested positive for COVID, visits and activities, including jobs, were canceled until the entire unit tested negative for fourteen days. These rolling lockdowns have become the new normal. "I could understand if the lockdowns prevented San Quentin from repeating 'the worst epidemiological disaster in California correctional history,' as the state appeals court called the 2020 outbreak in a landmark ruling," Thomas reflected. "But they are making the same mistakes."

The lack of quarantining newly transferred men has historically and recently been the root of the prison's mass outbreaks, yet officials have not seemed to learn. The nearby prison in Susanville was slated for closure and, while the men transferred to San Quentin were tested before boarding the bus, they were not isolated upon arrival. Meanwhile, the prison remained at 111 percent capacity despite an earlier court order to cut the population by half. (A superior court judge later concluded that vaccinations and new procedures were enough and that the prison no longer needed to reduce its head count.)[35]

The vast majority of COVID-19 cases in California prisons occurred after lockdown procedures became routine. But mass vaccinations without large-scale decarceration still failed to stop outbreaks. Between September 2021 and February 2022, California prisons had more than two hundred thousand new cases despite its 80 percent vaccination rate.

※

Another lockdown ushered in the start of 2023 at Corcoran. By then, the prison was only testing men before in-person visits or if a staff member on their unit or at their job had tested positive. Mwalimu had become distrustful, telling me that people tested positive and were quarantined even when they had no symptoms. Mwalimu didn't believe that asymptomatic people could be positive. Instead, he suspected that staff used COVID to deny programs, visits, and recreational activities. Compounding his skepticism were his past experiences with the prison's medical department.

It bears repeating that these experiences, accumulated over years and decades and shared by hundreds in each prison, create a nocebo effect, in which a person's negative expectations cause them to feel harmed by treatment. The nocebo effect was repeated in prisons across the country, especially as incarcerated people saw their free-world counterparts removing their masks, returning to work and school, crowding into concerts, and living as if the pandemic had passed. The ongoing lockdowns and cancelations of visits and programs seemed like punitive deprivation, not preventive health measures.

At the start of March 2020, Frank M. Snowden, a Yale professor of the history of medicine and the author of *Epidemics and Society: From the Black Death to the Present*, cautioned that the use of the cordon sanitaire, or wholesale quarantine, could backfire and cause widespread distrust of authority figures. "The problem with the cordon sanitaire is that it's clumsy. It's a sledgehammer. It arrives too late and it breaks down that fundamental element of public health, which is information. That is to say that, threatened with the lockdown, people don't cooperate with authorities," he told the *New Yorker*. "Authorities therefore no longer know what's going on and people take flight, which spreads the epidemic."[36] While Snowden was referring to China's pandemic response in quarantining Wuhan's 11 million citizens, and later the 60 million in the entire Hubei Province, the same is even more true in jails and prisons, where authority is always viewed with understandable suspicion and fear.

Three hundred miles south of Corcoran, people at the Richard J. Donovan Correctional Facility in San Diego, or RJD, decided to stop cooperating. "If we all don't test, we won't go back on lockdown!" Angel Unique, a twenty-nine-year-old trans woman in the men's prison, told me.

If they test positive, incarcerated people are moved to a different unit and isolated with no additional medical care and no guarantee of returning to the same cell. All cells at RJD have either two or six people assigned to one cell. For trans women, being moved can lead to physical and sexual violence should their new cellmate be transphobic or a sexual assailant. It's a common fear given that trans women in men's prisons are thirteen times more likely to be sexually assaulted than their cisgender counterparts.[37]

That likelihood is not abstract for Angel. While at a different prison in 2019, she had been repeatedly raped by a prison psychologist. Afraid of staff retaliation, she did not report the rapes. Instead, she saved her boxers that had been stained with his semen. Finally, she and another trans woman talked to a captain who was willing to help them request a transfer, though he was not willing to help file an official complaint. In March 2020, both women were transferred to another men's prison, where they attempted to report the psychologist's assaults. At first, supervisors refused to take their report. Worried that the psychologist, who supervised the previous prison's LGBTQ group, would victimize other trans women, they continued to press their complaint. Officials then accused them of fabricating the story and separated them. They moved Angel to an open dormitory full of cisgender men. There, she was physically assaulted by a man who told her, "We don't want your kind here."

Staff then placed her in solitary for five days. On the sixth day, the staff member responsible for housing assignments said that she did not believe that Angel had been assaulted and sent her back to the dormitory. Angel repeated her concerns to other staff. No one believed her. She was attacked twice more; one was a group attack by three men. Finally, staff placed her in administrative segregation.

She remained isolated for six months before being transferred to another prison.

At the next prison, Angel tested positive for COVID. She was moved to one of eight isolation tents. She was given Pedialyte for dehydration, but no medical care. What she did receive was the continual threat of sexual violence. Angel was the only trans woman in a tent of fifty men. One man repeatedly tried to rape her, groping her in the shower and while she slept. She reported the assaults and, while sexual assault complaints are supposed to remain confidential, word still got out. Both staff and incarcerated men called her a "rat" and a "snitch," labels that can lead to attacks and deaths.[38] When she told staff about these threats, they once again placed her in segregation. She remained isolated for months, a stay that was lengthened by multiple COVID lockdowns, which delayed transfers to another prison.

In March 2022, Angel was moved to RJD. There, she was reunited with the other trans woman, with whom she lives in a two-person cell. But the threat of being moved—to a six-person pod or another cell with a transphobic cellmate—loomed constantly. At RJD, she was closer to her family, who could visit more frequently. But visiting required COVID testing. The nurses seemed indifferent to ensuring that tests were conducted properly, telling incarcerated people to swab their own noses. That worked to Angel's advantage and, at first, she faked it. If she tested positive, not only would she be moved to isolation, but her entire unit would be placed under quarantine. "They will all blame me as the one who 'started it,' the reason others 'can't get no visits,' etc.," she explained. That blame would likely lead to physical attacks and ongoing abuse. "Why would I invite that?"

When the vaccine became available, she immediately signed up—and urged her peers to do likewise. Angel hoped that vaccination would end the mandatory tests and ensuing lockdowns. She also saw it as one of the few options that incarcerated people had to protect themselves in an environment where they had little control.[39]

Even with mass vaccination, testing requirements continued—and so did her fears of being blamed for a unit-wide quarantine. Eventually, Angel decided that even the fake swabs were too risky. For over a year, she asked her mother and other family not to visit. "I couldn't face the high consequences of that positive test," she explained. Not seeing her loved ones took a toll on Angel, especially since she had transferred to RJD to be closer to them. In January, as her thirtieth birthday approached, she began cutting her arm. She didn't feel suicidal, but the months of isolation had deepened her depression. Cutting had been an old coping mechanism, and her arm took the brunt of that month's despair.

In February 2023, the prison ended pre-visit testing. Angel began seeing her mother every other week. She stopped cutting, though seven deep scars remained gashed in her arm—a visual reminder of living through a pandemic in prison.

## Epilogue

# The Ghost of COVID

The start of 2023 delivered another devastating blow to Kwaneta. In the pre-dawn hours of mid-January, guards strip-searched, handcuffed, and shackled her before driving her to the Coryell County Courthouse.

In the United States, over 90 percent of convictions are the result of plea bargains. In 2009, Kwaneta had agreed to a plea bargain in her criminal case, in which she had fatally shot an abusive boyfriend, and been sentenced to fifty years. She was determined not to be cowed into pleading guilty to the 2016 prison forgery charge, certain that her innocence would prevail at trial.

That January, she met the assistant prosecutor. If Kwaneta pled guilty, the woman told her, she would be sentenced to seven years, or time served. But if she insisted on a trial, the prosecutor's office would seek a sentencing enhancement of twenty-five to life based on her previous conviction. And, in a county that was more than 90 percent white and conservative, chances were high that a jury would convict Kwaneta, a Black woman already in prison, no matter what the evidence showed. Faced with the prospect of a lifetime imprisoned in a state over one thousand miles from her children, Kwaneta pled guilty.

During her seven years in solitary, she had read countless books on the criminal justice system to both keep her mind sharp and understand the system that she was trapped within. She knew that prosecutors often struck Black members from potential juries, that racism reared its ugly head among predominantly white juries, and that justice prevailed only in a small sliver of cases, usually high-profile ones with lots of media. "I felt stupid to believe I could get impartiality," she wrote shortly after returning from court.

That same month, dozens (or hundreds, according to advocates) of men in Texas's solitary units went on hunger strike to challenge the state's practice of long-term isolation. Like Kwaneta and others at Lane Murray, the men described a lack of direct communication with loved ones, no access to GED programs, and poor conditions worsened by staff shortages. Men could shower once a week. In one unit, men had outside recreation time only five times in three years. Many had been isolated for decades after being labeled gang members, or security threat groups, by Texas prison officials.[1] Texas's gang policies are similar to the California policies that were overturned through the pressure applied by the repeated prison hunger strikes and class-action lawsuits. To be released from solitary, Texas requires that men leave their gang and inform on other members through its Gang Renouncement and Disassociation Program.[2]

The hunger strikers demanded that Texas end the practice of isolating people based on their administrative status rather than their actual behavior. They also demanded that the prison agency create a "step-down program" allowing them to gradually reenter general population. The strike lasted twenty-one days. It drew national media coverage but no substantial changes.

Although no one at Lane Murray had participated, officials withheld Kwaneta's incoming and outgoing mail and e-messages. With no word from family or friends, she had tossed and turned at night, unable to sleep. Every mass shooting and violent attack increased her worries. No matter what she did, she couldn't change the channel. All she could do was stop listening to the news—and even that didn't help.

On February 13, I received a short note in the mail that she had written eleven days earlier. She had tried to send multiple e-messages. Each time, Securus Technologies deducted the cost of an electronic stamp from her account, but did not send the message. Kwaneta had started the year with $300 in her media account. Hoping to get through to someone, she continued to buy electronic stamp packages, each costing $22.31. By the end of February, she had depleted her entire balance.

The communication blackout wasn't limited to her or those in segregation. The entire prison seemed to have been affected. On the day that she wrote to me, the assistant warden walked through the prison with a representative from Securus. Multiple women yelled through their windows about the problem. "Not part of my job," the representative yelled back.

When Kwaneta asked the warden about the lack of postal mail, the warden blamed staff shortages. On February 15, I received notices of fourteen separate e-messages. All had been sent at least twenty days earlier. Later, I would receive repeats of the same messages sent on different dates—her desperate attempt to reach the outside world.[3]

One was a January 21 request after NPR had reported the men's hunger strike. "Where are the female voices?" she asked. "We are silenced again. Whether it's the *New York Times*, the *Texas Observer*, or the solitary confinement 'experts,' they all *only* discuss men. Well, we got stuff to say too."

She reminded me that unlike the men's prisons, women's prisons didn't classify people as security threat groups. If they had, the woman who had forged her signature might have been classified as Aryan Brotherhood and placed in segregation away from Kwaneta. But even without these designations, some women remained in solitary for over a decade without any further disciplinary infractions. Could I reach out to the reporters covering the strike and put them in touch with her? I received that message twenty-five days later—and sixteen days after the Texas hunger strike had ended and the media had moved on to other stories.

Meanwhile, the prison classification committee voted to keep her in solitary for at least another year.

On March 2, Lane Murray began allowing people in segregation to make (and pay for) phone calls from their tablets. That afternoon, Kwaneta called her mother and, for the first time in seven years, talked for more than five minutes. Three days later, she talked to her youngest daughter, who had been a nursing baby when Kwaneta began her sentence. Autumn had recently turned sixteen and was starting to consider colleges.

In March, they had their first full conversation since Kwaneta had been sent to solitary. "She is nothing like I imagined. I had her frozen at age nine," Kwaneta recalled. She called back again and again, stretching their first conversation to six 30-minute calls. Kwaneta cried through all six calls.

For the past seven years, she had heard about her children through infrequent conversations with her mother. "Now, I can hear their voices catch and I know something is wrong. Hesitation on certain topics. It's not always what they say but how they say it and what is left unsaid. I feel relief," she told me. Still, seven years in solitary had left her unable to have a normal phone conversation. Kwaneta shouted into her tablet, as if projecting her voice through her cell vents. "Use your inside voice," Autumn repeatedly admonished.

That first month, she spent $580 on calls, making up for those lost years. She warned her children that, in the future, she would have to limit her calls to once a week. "If it was up to me, I'd talk all day," she told me. "I heard Chicago made all calls free and the first week, visitation room was record-breaking full. People reestablishing relationships." But Kwaneta is not in Chicago, or California, which established free prison phone calls in 2023. While Texas lawmakers pushed to reduce the cost of prison calls from twenty-six cents to the current six cents per minute, no bill is on the horizon to further ease the financial burden. She could not afford to spend hundreds each month, no matter how desperately she wanted to hear their voices. Still, Kwaneta is fortunate that she can call at all. Many others have no family or friends who can deposit funds. Some have no family or outside friends at all.

While Kwaneta was rebuilding her relationship with her children, Jack anxiously awaited his first parole hearing. He had spent most of 2022 in a state of depression from the constant near-isolation. He started taking antidepressants and briefly checked himself into the mental health unit.

The prospect of parole lifted his spirits. He asked various friends, a writing mentor, and me to send letters of support to the parole board. He sent me his photos and paperwork, including the novel that he had handwritten between 2015 and 2019, for safekeeping. He was optimistic about his file, which included certificates for various programs. In late June, however, his hopes were dashed. He appeared before the parole board, which questioned him about his extensive record, including a failure in 1994 to complete a misdemeanor probation sentence in California. They stated that he was a threat to the public, denied him parole, and set his next hearing for 2026.

Even if the board had granted him parole, Jack would not have walked out a free man. When he was arrested in 2013, he had been on federal probation for bank robbery. Arrest is an automatic violation of probation, which mandates additional prison time. When the Texas prison system releases him, Jack will be transferred to the federal prison system to spend two more years behind bars.

Jack lamented the denial for a few days. Then, he vowed to refocus on his writing. Two weeks later, he learned that Texas was following the trend of barring incoming mail and was contracting with a corporation—in this case, Securus, which already held phone and e-messaging contracts—to digitally scan letters and upload them to the recipient's tablet. He asked me to return the photos of his grandchildren—his only ones—and the hundreds of pages that made up his novel. He worried that, if the sole copies existed on his tablet, they could be wiped out in a single glitch—or if the state changed providers.

Soon after, he received more stunning news. His youngest daughter was in prison herself. Although she was fifteen minutes away at Lane Murray, officials denied parent and daughter permission for an in-person visit or even phone calls.

Several studies have found that children with incarcerated parents face more economic insecurity, family instability, stigma, and depression, all of which increase their own risk of engaging in criminalized activities. Some of these studies divorce parental incarceration from other environmental factors, such as poverty, racism, and the lack of opportunity characteristic of criminalized communities.[4] Still, Jack wonders how his own choices—and his multiple prison sentences—have affected his daughter's trajectory.

"I think all the time about how my incarceration influenced my daughter to take the same path," he reflected. "I know she didn't want this for her life but seeing me locked up a good portion of her life had to have an effect." Jack recalled that, when the girl was seventeen, she spent a year in a juvenile prison. "I thought she'd learned her lesson because she didn't get in trouble again until her thirties. But I know the way I lived my life directly caused her current incarceration. She saw me taking the easy way out and followed my path," he lamented.

Mary also worries about her sons. Two of those sons, the ones who were ages ten and eleven when she was arrested and were in their thirties when the pandemic hit, were arrested and jailed on separate criminal charges. Despite multiple requests, Mary was not given permission to write to them. Both men, she told me, have anger issues with women, anger that she attributes to her lengthy absence. "They are living proof that putting mothers in prison for over twenty years harms children," she reflected. From prison, she can only get periodic updates when she calls her oldest son.

Mary started the new year by filing her second clemency application.

Five months later, as all Oklahoma prisons went on lockdown yet again after a fight at a men's prison, the board denied her application. She was condemned to spend another year in a dorm with sixty-two other pandemic-weary women sleeping less than three feet apart.

In February 2024, as I was finishing the copy edits for this book, Mary called. Her voice boomed with an excitement that I hadn't heard in years. She had been told that her release date was in June. She had also heard that other women were being sent home earlier than their scheduled release dates. "They're just kicking them out," she reported gleefully. Still, her decades-long incarceration has dulled her excitement about reuniting with her family. When I asked what she wanted to do first, she told me that she wanted to make a dental appointment to fix her teeth, something she had been unable to do during her decades behind bars. She also wanted to sign up for social security. "I should be wanting to see my children," the 71-year-old admitted, "but I haven't been around my kids for 26 years."

While I was writing this book, Malakki and I agreed to meet via video visit once a month. During our forty-five-minute video calls, Malakki would answer my questions or fill in the blanks about anecdotes he'd shared—his participation in the rolling hunger strike or the restorative justice program. We also talked about his health and ongoing struggles for medical care. Sometimes these visits supplemented his written answers to my ongoing barrage of questions. Other times, when his condition deteriorated between treatments, video calls were our only form of communication.

In early February 2023, Malakki didn't show up for his visit. I spent ten minutes staring at the orange wall of the video visiting booth before the system logged me out. That, in itself, no longer alarmed me. On previous occasions, he had been transferred to another unit and hadn't been able to alert me. "When you schedule a visit, it will be for the place I am IN THAT MOMENT," he later explained. "If I change location, the visit will still broadcast at the OLD LOCATION because the prison's system is archaic. Once I relocate, you have to cancel, then reschedule."

What especially irked me was that, if I logged on during that time slot, the prison counted it as one of the six video calls he was allowed each month. But that morning, Malakki hadn't shown up for a more ominous reason. Despite his recent treatment for multiple sclerosis, his body had shut down and he had been rushed to the hospital earlier that week. He had been feeling ill for several days, his friend Pearl later told me. But though Malakki had signed a medical release form that authorized her to speak with prison and hospital staff about his health and medical treatment. Prison staff claimed not to have that authorization, leaving her in agonizing ignorance.

Malakki spent ten days at the hospital, where medical staff inserted multiple IVs to keep him alive. He has foggy snippets of memories from that time. He remembered a tube inserted through his nose to his intestines to relieve the pressure. He recalled waking to doctors discussing the possibility of surgery. His overwhelming memory is of thirst. Nurses sponged his lips to alleviate the dryness, but for four days, he could not have any water. His lips were so chapped and cracking that they felt like Brillo pads. On the fifth day, he was finally allowed water and half a piece of bread. On the sixth day, they gave him a turkey sandwich. He forced himself to eat half.

Although he could barely move, prison policy dictated that he be restrained to the hospital bed. Guards handcuffed his left hand and chained his right leg to the bed. When the nurse needed to change his catheter, guards removed his leg iron. When it was time to eat, they removed his handcuffs. But they were immediately refastened once he was finished. Two guards remained with him at all times—one inside the hospital room, the other in the doorway. Both carried guns.

Malakki spent another month in the prison infirmary. He required the help of several men to get to the toilet, use the shower, and even get out of bed. Ten days after his return from the hospital, he wasn't sure that he could remain engaged for our usual forty-five-minute video visit.

Throughout this latest ordeal, he had been unable to shake off an overwhelming fear of abandonment. "It lingered like a ghost in my mind—that everyone was going to evaporate," he told me. Having been sentenced to life without parole, he was already condemned to die in prison. And now, he could hardly do anything by himself. "I just saw everyone slowly disappear, like they had had enough," he said. He had spent twenty-nine years in prison. He had seen others, who had spent the past thirty-five, forty, and forty-five years in prison, slowly lose connections as their loved ones moved away or simply moved on with their lives while others aged and died.

To assuage those fears, he prayed. He read history books— David Walker's *Appeal*, Marcus Garvey's *Message to the People*, and Joy DeGruy's *Post Traumatic Slave Syndrome*. He played music on his tablet, turning to the rap and hip-hop artists that had inspired him as an up-and-coming DJ, like Grandmaster Flash, Run-DMC, and Queen Latifah. He wrote a poem for the women in a nearby Pennsylvania prison where staff had confiscated their red, black, and green flags, claiming that these symbols of African pride were symbols of hate. Getting his words onto paper was a painstaking process, but he pushed himself, handwriting draft after draft. When he was finally satisfied, he typed his words onto a clean sheet and mailed them off.

One morning in mid-July, a guard told him to pack everything. "You're moving after breakfast," he said. Four years earlier, Malakki had requested a transfer to a prison that provides better medical services for chronic conditions. That request had lingered in bureaucratic limbo but, now that it was approved, he barely had time to finish his breakfast. "You're still eating? We gotta go!" the guard barked minutes later. Malakki had no time to go through his accumulated possessions and give away what he no longer needed, including multiple books from a college course he had finished. Instead, with the help of his prison-assigned aide, he packed everything except for his television and hygiene items, which he was allowed to take with him. Then he had to pay over $100 to ship those boxes via UPS, an expense that tipped his prison account into negative numbers. But with no advance notice, he had no choice.

Riding alone in the prison's handicap van, he kept his mask on his chin, unsure of what awaited him at the next prison. He pulled the mask over his nose and mouth when he arrived and kept it on until he was assured that there were no COVID cases. He was neither tested nor quarantined before being placed in a dormitory with ninety-nine other men. They were separated into cubicles, or bays, with two to four sets of bunk beds. A handful of handicap cells had one bed in each corner. The bathrooms were down the hall, making his middle-of-the-night bathroom visits more taxing.

Every morning, Malakki wakes and immediately sees his three cellmates. If they watch game shows on television, he hears them shouting answers at the screen. If they strike up a conversation, he has no way not to hear them. But at dusk, he told me, he could peek over the three-foot wall separating his cubicle from the hallway and watch the setting sun peek through the windows.

At the previous prison, the cafeteria had been closed and meals were delivered to each person's cell. But at this prison, men had to go to the cafeteria. Pushing his wheelchair to the cafeteria was sometimes tiring, but the meals, which frequently included fresh fruit, were much better. "I had a peach today!" he told me excitedly when we spoke three weeks after his transfer. "The last time I had a peach, Obama was still a senator!"

Three times a week, Malakki has physical therapy, which had been unavailable at the previous prison. After a few days, he noticed that his pain had lessened. After a month, he had fewer flare-ups.

The prison yard had two trees. He spent one of his first afternoons staring at them. Worried, another man asked if he was okay. "I haven't been this close to a tree in thirty years!" Malakki told him.

Having been imprisoned since the 1990s, Malakki has met many men in many different prisons. Word spread about his arrival and they soon came to greet him. They showered him with candy, snacks, and other items as welcoming gifts, and ensured he had what he needed during the week and a half that his belongings were in transit. Some of his former think tank colleagues talked about forming a new one. Sharing what he has learned about restorative justice has given him purpose, even if he never again sets foot outside of prison. "What I learned most is that we are not useless. What we have realized from our poor choices can help so many not make the same mistakes we did," he reflected. Being able to do so at the new prison gave him a renewed sense of purpose.

That didn't mean he was giving up on walking out of prison. The governor, Tom Wolf, had already commuted the sentences of forty-five people who had been sentenced to life without parole, a total six times greater than the previous four governors combined.[5] But Malakki's clemency application continued to languish.

Malakki doesn't let himself think about his hopes and fears for the future. If he does, his anxiety kicks in. "It's like my stomach is full from trying to eat too much," he told me, his voice cracking and his eyes filling with tears. "Whenever I go on a visit or go to the hospital, that door is right there." That door to the outside world both beckons and taunts him. "To be able to walk out the door and not come back . . . ," he said, his voice trailing off into a wistful silence.

※

Despite the lockdown, 2023 began more hopefully for Mwalimu. He still felt as if he were looking through fogged eyeglasses, making out shapes without clear details. Even so, his future seemed much brighter. California Proposition 57, passed in 2016, had moved his first parole hearing from 2025 to November 2023. Then in 2022, state lawmakers had passed AB 109, allowing people with nonviolent convictions to serve half rather than 85 percent of their sentence.

While in prison, Mwalimu had been charged with having a manufactured weapon, which he said was simply a broken spoon handle. But because he was already in the SHU and validated as a gang associate, he received an additional eight years. If not for that additional charge, he would have been released in 2019. But the weapon charge postponed his first parole hearing to February 2025 and his maximum release date to March 2027. With AB 109, his new release date was set for December 18, 2023.

He planned to continue writing, relishing the prospect of emailing editors directly. While he planned to leave prison in his past, he wanted to help develop resources in the inner city to prevent other young Black men from joining gangs and ending up in prison.

He also looked forward to getting to know his four children, all of whom had grown up without him. In 2020, he connected with his third child over the newly established video visits. The last time they had seen each other, she had been twelve years old. When they reconnected, she was nearly thirty with three children. He has yet to find his other children.

Two days before his release, after he had given away most of his belongings, Mwalimu learned that Orange County, where he had lived previously, had issued a bench warrant against him for failing to complete probation.

Four days before Christmas, Orange County deputies loaded him onto a van and drove him to jail, where he spent Christmas weekend. The day after Christmas, the judge dismissed his probation warrant. His girlfriend picked him up and the pair drove home, stopping briefly for a double cheeseburger and fries.

When they got to Los Angeles, Mwalimu saw familiar streets dotted with unfamiliar new restaurants. The next day, he met his parole officer, bought a phone, and, for the first time in over a decade, went grocery shopping. In spite of the many big adjustments he's had to make since his release, he feels that surviving the SHU has made him able to bounce back from disappointment and loss. Now out of prison, he planned to find a way to find and build relationships with his children and figure out how to make a difference in the world he had rejoined.

Many of the problems that plagued prisons before the pandemic remain unchanged. Just as the crisis laid bare the racial and economic inequalities of US society, it also unmasked the human toll of the country's commitment to remaining a prison nation.

During the first year of the pandemic, prisons released 648,400 people. While that might seem like a staggering number, only 37,700 (or 6 percent) were expedited releases. The majority were people who would have been released regardless of whether a pandemic was bearing down.[6]

Fourteen states, including Texas, issued no early releases in response to the pandemic.[7] In fact, when a handful of Texas judges released people without bail at the start of the pandemic, Governor Abbott issued an executive order to stop further releases. His order prohibited judges from releasing anyone who had a previous conviction for violence, no matter how long ago. For those facing charges for violence, the order prohibited release unless they paid bail. Judges also could not release them on electronic monitoring or personal bond—which, in Texas, entailed submitting their government identification and promising to return to court—without them paying bail.[8] Abbott also forbade mayors and directors of jails and prisons from issuing releases. At the start of the pandemic, the state's jails confined roughly sixty-eight thousand people; more than forty thousand were awaiting trial in courtrooms that were closed by COVID. His order meant that those who could afford to pay bail could wait for their day in court at home. Those who couldn't would ride out the pandemic behind bars.

Nationwide, prison admissions slowed during the pandemic's first few months. Through a combination of releases and delayed admissions, the prison population dropped. By the end of February 2021, 215,800 fewer people were incarcerated than the previous February.[9]

Still, prisons reported a COVID rate of 228 per 1,000 prisoners in 2020, a figure that was most likely an undercount with differing testing, or lack of testing, policies.[10]

Although prison populations had dropped, the 2021 prison COVID rate was higher—394,066 confirmed cases, or 30,780 for every 100,000 people.[11] In contrast, the general US population reported 9,350 cases for every 100,000 people.[12]

The death toll shows how much more severely the virus ravaged those behind bars. During 2020, deaths in prison rose more than 50 percent (compared with a 19 percent rise across the country).[13] COVID deaths accounted for 200 deaths for every 100,000 people behind bars. In comparison, the United States reported nearly 81 deaths for every 100,000 residents.[14]

The numbers kept rising. As of July 3, 2023, state, federal, and immigration prisons reported nearly three thousand COVID deaths since the start of the pandemic, a figure that researchers caution is likely an undercount.[15]

Jack and Kwaneta were right to be worried about the pandemic—and the government's lackadaisical response. Texas has the nation's largest prison population. Overall, the state's prison death rate rose dramatically—from 28 deaths for every 10,000 imprisoned people in 2019 to 48 deaths per 10,000 in 2020.[16] Between March 1, 2020 and February 28, 2021, its prisons had 255 COVID-related deaths, the highest of any prison system. Texas also had the highest COVID deaths—ten—among US women's prisons. These deaths were not color-blind—the COVID-19 prison mortality rate was 1.6 times higher for Black people than that of white people, while Latinx people died at twice the rate of their white counterparts.[17]

Furthermore, many prisons are in conservative, rural small towns where the prison is the main employer, and residents distrust both medical experts and Democrats, making future outbreaks inevitable.

California has the nation's second largest prison population. It also had the second highest number of COVID-related deaths with 219 deaths, or 43 deaths for every 10,000 incarcerated people, between March 2020 thru February 2021.[18] Mwalimu had been lucky—he escaped every new outbreak and variant. But others around him were not. The COVID case rate at Corcoran State Prison was 312 for every 1,000 people, or one-third of all incarcerated people. That was nearly double the rate in the surrounding community, which reported 160 COVID cases for every 1,000 residents.[19] The discrepancy between prison and outside was even higher in other areas. On average, the COVID case rate within California prisons was triple that of the surrounding county.[20]

By 2022 these swelling numbers no longer registered as a potential health crisis. People no longer feared that a positive case would result in hospitalization or death. Instead, they feared that it would trigger another lockdown—and so, many avoided testing. Many also shed their masks. The few who continued masking did so less to avoid COVID, but to hide facial hair growing from the lack of shaving equipment or broken dentures that prisons refused to replace.

COVID cases weren't the only rising numbers that year. Despite there being no rise in crime, prison populations increased for the first time in more than a decade. So did jail populations. Both have continued to rise in 2023.[21]

The pandemic could have been an opportunity to rethink the flawed logic of the US criminal legal system. Instead, it made clear the extreme harms of a country set on perpetual punishment. It was a stark lesson that informed the responses of people held within as each new variant worked its way behind bars.

"It's always a warning before the storm. COVID-19 was our warning," Kwaneta told me. "Society has decided by their inaction that our lives aren't valued because of mistakes and bad choices. They've proven they won't save us."

As I was finishing this book in August 2023, COVID surged once more. Suddenly, I knew nearly a dozen people, some of whom had escaped all the earlier waves, who were struck by the new Eris variant. Throughout the country, hospitalizations rose.[22] Two days before my book deadline, a bright red line blared at me ninety seconds into a home test.

But by that summer, states had stopped widespread testing, and the extent of the spread remained largely unknown. Most prisons, too, had stopped testing. Some, including Pennsylvania and Texas, had removed their COVID dashboards, as if no virus had ever torn through the concrete corridors.

California was an exception, continuing to publish both the cumulative number of prison cases and the numbers confirmed within the previous fourteen days. Corcoran, which had had 2,626 cases over the past three years, reported no active COVID cases in August. No one had said anything to the men about rising numbers outside, no one had distributed masks, and staff had long discarded any pretense of mask wearing. Programs were running regularly again and everything seemed back to normal. "We have no COVID problems," Mwalimu said that summer. "We figure it's over."

But COVID wasn't over. "I have been sick the past few days with what I thought was strep throat, since that is what my boss claimed she had," a woman in California wrote me in mid-August. "After realizing today I can't taste, I know what it is. But I won't type it for fear of the wrong person reading it and doing me how I have previously explained how people get done. So, I am staying in cell with fever, chills, headache, sinus pressure."

From his Pennsylvania dorm, Malakki wasn't sure what to say about the resurgence. The ghost of COVID hovered over daily interactions. Men went from greeting one another with hugs or handshakes to briefly tapping knuckles. Even now, when someone coughs or sneezes, Malakki backs away. In the cafeteria and day-room, he always sits at the table furthest from others.

He keeps his mask in the bag behind his wheelchair. But he knows that, while he can take precautions, he cannot keep himself totally insulated should the virus arrive. He constantly washes his hands, but in a dormitory, he shares the toilet and sink with dozens of others. In September, he requested the latest booster. The prison had none.

Two months later, in November, COVID hit his dormitory. The men were initially quarantined for five days. Then another man tested positive, extending the quarantine another five days. Then another man tested positive and the quarantine extended again. Malakki thinks he might have caught COVID during that time. For days, he lay in bed, unable to move. But he did not ask for a test, and no staffer noticed that the immobilized man might need one. He recovered enough to video visit with me shortly before Christmas. He was still waiting for that booster.

Kwaneta still wears her mask whenever she leaves her cell. When guards order her to remove it, she tells them that she has a cold and is trying not to infect them. "They leave me alone as long as I say a *cold* and not mention COVID," she explained.

She was pessimistic about the rising COVID numbers. "The government will double down on the wrong lessons learned," she predicted. "They learned what they can get away with. I fear they will continue to discourage reporting symptoms to keep numbers low." The policies and procedures implemented in the early days were continually ignored. Nationwide, lawmakers refused to reduce jail and prison populations in numbers significant enough to save lives. They failed to invest in ventilation systems or other structural changes for the next pandemic, which is inevitable. "We, as a country, have collectively decided by virtue of inaction that all prisons can be death sentences," Kwaneta reflected.

Earlier that year, Kwaneta had won two writing fellowships. She had been ecstatic. But since summer, prison officials had first refused to schedule, then canceled her increasingly urgent ophthalmology appointments. Each time, they claimed that there were not enough staff to drive her the five hours to the hospital. By December, her eyesight had deteriorated to the point where she could no longer read or write. Left untreated, her retina was in danger of detaching—requiring surgery or causing permanent vision loss. That was only one of seven different specialist appointments for conditions that she had developed while in prison. Her waning eyesight, chronic chest pains, dizziness, nausea, hearing loss, and severe foot pains were stark reminders of the ways in which incarceration dramatically corrodes a person's health—and the ways in which the ongoing COVID pandemic exacerbate this destruction.

Early in the pandemic, author Arundhati Roy reflected on the opportunities that a disaster of this magnitude presented amid the chaos and destruction. Likening the pandemic to a portal, she wrote, "We can choose to walk through it, dragging the carcasses of our prejudice and hatred, our avarice, our data banks and dead ideas, our dead rivers and smoky skies behind us. Or we can walk through lightly, with little luggage, ready to imagine another world. And ready to fight for it."[23]

As a nation, the United States could have stepped through the portal and embraced, or at least considered, the opportunity to reenvision and rebuild a society enabling everyone to thrive. Instead, it refused to shed the carcasses of racism, poverty, patriarchy, and all the ills that fuels its addiction to perpetual punishment.

But it need not stay that way. Abolition requires imagination—not just envisioning a world without prisons, but also reimagining societies so radically transformed that crime and criminalization become obsolete. That may seem impossible, but Ruth Wilson Gilmore put the possibility into perspective in a 2023 interview. The seventy-three-year-old carceral geographer and cofounder of multiple abolitionist organizations rejected the argument that abolition was unrealistic. "I say to people, 'Are you looking at me through a computer screen? That is a world entirely different from the world I was born into.'"[24]

As abolitionists Angela Y. Davis, Gina Dent, Erica R. Meiners, and Beth E. Richie remind us, we must "ask different questions *now*; consider alternative courses of action *now*; . . . [and] change our minds, apologize, recalibrate, and try again *now*."[25]

The coronavirus pandemic was an opportunity for the United States—as a whole—to change its mind about continuing as a prison nation. It was an opportunity to chart alternative responses to its many social failures and to envision better futures for everyone. As a country, or even as separate states, the United States did not seize that opportunity. But that doesn't cement our fate. We can always change our minds, change course, offer reparations for the harms that have been inflicted, develop resources that meet rather than suppress people's needs, and try again to imagine and build a world where we can help each other survive—and even prevent—the next disaster.

# Further Reading

## Books

Rhae Lynn Barnes, Keri Leigh Merritt, and Yohuru Williams, eds., *After Life: A Collective History of Loss and Redemption in Pandemic America* (Chicago: Haymarket Books, 2022).

Dan Berger, *Captive Nation: Black Prison Organizing in the Civil Rights Era* (Chapel Hill: University of North Carolina Press, 2015).

Alisa Bierria, Jakeya Caruthers, and Brooke Lober, eds., *Abolition Feminisms: Organizing, Survival, and Transformative Practice*, vols. 1 and 2 (Chicago: Haymarket Books, 2022).

Orisanmi Burton, *Tip of the Spear: Black Radicalism, Prison Repression, and the Long Attica Revolt* (Oakland: University of California Press, 2023).

Casper Cendre and Carla Cabral, eds., *Confined Before COVID-19: A Pandemic Anthology by LGBTQ Prisoners* (Oakland, CA: ABO Comix, 2020).

Angela Y. Davis, *Are Prisons Obsolete?* (New York: Seven Stories Press, 2003).

Angela Y. Davis, Gina Dent, Erica R. Meiners, and Beth E. Richie, *Abolition. Feminism. Now.* (Chicago: Haymarket Books, 2023).

Ejeris Dixon and Leah Lakshmi Piepzna-Samarasinha, *Beyond Survival: Strategies and Stories from the Transformative Justice Movement* (Oakland, CA: AK Press, 2020).

Nicole Eustace, *Covered with Night: A Story of Murder and Indigenous Justice in Early America* (New York: Liveright Publishing Corporation, 2021).

Ruth Wilson Gilmore, *Golden Gulag: Prisons, Surplus, Crisis, and Opposition in Globalizing California* (Berkeley: University of California Press, 2007).

Kelly Lytle Hernández, *City of Inmates: Conquest, Rebellion, and the Rise of Human Caging in Los Angeles, 1771–1965* (Chapel Hill: University of North Carolina Press, 2017).

Elizabeth Hinton, *From the War on Poverty to the War on Crime* (Cambridge, MA: Harvard University Press, 2018).

Mariame Kaba, *We Do This 'Til We Free Us: Abolitionist Organizing and Transforming Justice* (Chicago: Haymarket Books, 2021).

Mariame Kaba and Andrea J. Ritchie, *No More Police: A Case for Abolition* (New York: The New Press, 2022).

Alice Kim, Erica R. Meiners, Audrey Petty, Jill Petty, Beth E. Richie, and Sarah Ross, eds., *The Long Term: Resisting Life Sentences, Working Toward Freedom* (Chicago: Haymarket Books, 2018).

Victoria Law, *Resistance Behind Bars: The Struggles of Incarcerated Women*, 2nd ed. (Oakland, CA: PM Press, 2012).

Judith Levine and Erica R. Meiners, *The Feminist and the Sex Offender: Confronting Harm, Ending State Violence* (New York: Verso Books, 2020).

Lyle C. May, *Witness: An Insider's Narrative of the Carceral State* (Chicago: Haymarket Books, 2024).

Nicole Hahn Rafter, *Partial Justice: Women, Prisons and Social Control* (New Brunswick, NJ: Transaction Publishers, 1990).

Beth E. Richie, *Arrested Justice: Black Women, Violence, and America's Prison Nation* (New York: New York University Press, 2012).

Andrea J. Ritchie, *Invisible No More: Police Violence Against Black Women and Women of Color* (Boston: Beacon Press, 2017).

Hugh Ryan, *The Women's House of Detention: A Queer History of a Forgotten Prison* (New York: Bold Type Books, 2022).

Maya Schenwar, *Locked Down, Locked Out: Why Prisons Don't Work and How We Can Do Better* (San Francisco: Berrett-Koehler Publishers, 2014).

Maya Schenwar and Victoria Law, *Prison by Any Other Name* (New York: The New Press, 2020).

Aishah Shahidah Simmons, ed., *Love WITH Accountability: Digging up the Roots of Child Sexual Abuse* (Oakland, CA: AK Press, 2019).

Laura Spinney, *Pale Rider: The Spanish Flu of 1918 and How It Changed the World* (New York: PublicAffairs, 2017).

Steven Thrasher, *The Viral Underclass: The Human Toll When Inequality and Disease Collide* (New York: Celadon Press, 2022).

Homer Venters, *Life and Death in Rikers Island* (Baltimore: Johns Hopkins Press, 2019).

## Periodicals and Online Resources

The COVID Prison Project: COVIDprisonproject.com

*The Fire Inside: Newsletter of the California Coalition for Women Prisoners*: womenprisoners.org

Mariame Kaba, *Prison Culture* blog: usprisonculture.com

*Prison Health News*: prisonhealth.news

*Prison Legal News*: Select articles available online at prisonlegalnews.org

UCLA COVID Behind Bars Data Project: uclaCOVIDbehindbars.org

# Acknowledgments

**W**riting a book is often a solitary endeavor. Writing a book about—and during—an ongoing pandemic can feel even more isolating, particularly as the outside world begins to open and beckon.

I am always envious of the writers' salons and gatherings in bygone eras. What must it be like to emerge from the seclusion of writing to talk with a coterie of other writers and literary-minded creators and, over food and drink, bounce ideas—and unravel particularly knotty conundrums—with one another?

Each time I start a new book, I vow to create something like Zoe Norris Anderson's Ragged Edge Klub, a group of writers, filmmakers, performers, and politicians who met for weekly dinners.[1] (Well, minus the politicians.) Or, less ambitiously, at least invite a smaller group of writer friends over for dinner regularly.

During the writing of this book, I did neither of those. But even without these regular group meals, I am lucky to have many extraordinary people whom I can lean on for both sustenance and practical support:

First, many thanks and much appreciation go to Steven Englander for his never-ending support and patience during this and all of my previous books. Many men might balk at being left to solo parent for two weeks while their partners traveled around the country, but he has always encouraged me to grab every opportunity, whether delivering a keynote speech on women's transatlantic prison resistance at Oxford University or book touring around the

Midwest. He read early versions of my manuscript and gave feedback on how to shape this into a story rather than a long litany of terrible facts.

Hugs to Siuloong Englander, who has been on this journey of thinking and writing about prisons her entire life. She has visited prisons both in utero and as a rambunctious toddler. She has cheered and cried her way through many conferences (and many of her mother's presentations). Until her teenage years, she accompanied me on a number of events during my Never-Ending Book Tour (which will be entering Year 15 by the time this hits shelves); her presence ensured that we also took time to explore whatever city we found ourselves in and to eat the most delicious vegan food we could find. It's a practice that I continue to this day.

Profound gratitude to Dan Berger, who read the draft manuscript and offered invaluable feedback (and corrections). Thank you, too, for letting me eat up your last weekend of summer.

Thank you to Melissa Morrone for carving out the time to read over half my book as individual draft chapters and helping me shape them into a comprehensive narrative; to Anika Paris and Tomas Moniz for reading early chapters; and to Bryan Welton for reminding me that abolition isn't a narrow set of demands, ensuring that my recent history is correct, and making sure that the fried green tomatoes didn't burn.

I am very grateful to George Francisco for reading my draft manuscript. Although no longer a newcomer to US prison issues, he still challenged me to provide context and was always down for talking about books and current events over food and drink at the end of a long writing day.

Virtual flowers (and burned pesto) to Leigh Goodmark, who knows why she is thanked.

Much appreciation goes to Aaron Littman and Michael Everett at the Behind Bars Data Project (formerly known as the UCLA COVID Behind Bars Data Project) for documenting and making public COVID behind bars data, without which this would be a set of stories without larger context. Thank you, too, for answering all my questions (and for patiently walking me through how to read the spreadsheets).

I am much obliged to Brian Francisco for answering all my questions about long COVID and for reading draft passages to ensure they were as accurate as evolving research can be.

Finishing this manuscript would have been much more tedious and painful had Liz, Nina, and all the adorable (and at times distracting) residents of Overcliff not opened their castle for that last sprint. The views from their observatory and the sunsets over the Hudson, not to mention the nightly vegan feasts, were the fuel I needed to push me toward the finish line. (Plus, Kwaneta and Malakki loved my descriptions of the sunset on the castle patio when they called.)

Last winter, when it was too cold to work outside and I still wasn't comfortable working unmasked in indoor public spaces, Brooks Headley and the folks at Superiority Burger opened their back room before they opened their (newly renovated restaurant) doors to the general public. Thank you for the occasional off-line writing office that got me through most of chapter 7.

Thank you, as always, to Hannah Bowman, my incredible agent, for championing this book—and working with me through multiple partial drafts to tell the larger story.

Thank you to Anthony Arnove, Rory Fanning, Jameka Williams, and the team at Haymarket Books for recognizing the importance of memorializing this period in our history as a prison nation.

And of course, many thanks and appreciation to the people currently inside prisons across the United States. Some shared their experiences with me, some took the time to read and offer feedback on chapter drafts, some pointed me in the direction of books and articles that they'd heard about and thought might be useful. Thanks to Mary Fish, Kwaneta Harris, Jack, Malakki, Mwalimu Shakur, Tracy McCarter, Kayla Absher, Geneva

Phillips, Sarah Pender, Angel Unique, Elena House-Hay, Lee Doane, Rashad Clarke, Twinn, and the hundreds of others who informed me of prison conditions, injustices, and acts of resistance over the years.

# Notes

In describing incarcerated people's experiences, I drew extensively from letters, e-messages, phone calls, and video interviews.

## Introduction

1. Quoted in Jennifer E. James, Leslie Riddle, and Giselle Perez-Aguilar, "'Prison Life Is Very Hard and It's Made Harder If You're Isolated': COVID-19 Risk Mitigation Strategies and the Mental Health of Incarcerated Women in California," *International Journal of Prison Health*, November 21, 2022, https://www.ncbi.nlm.nih.gov/pmc/articles/PMC10129363/pdf/nihms-1894024.pdf.

2. Population of Mabel Bassett Correctional Center as of May 4, 2020: Oklahoma Department of Corrections, "Incarcerated Inmates and Community Supervision Offenders Daily Count Sheet," https://oklahoma.gov/content/dam/ok/en/doc/documents/population/count-sheet/2020/doc-oms-count-may-4-2020.pdf.

3. In 2020, the United States had 1,944 prisons and 3,134 jails. See Wendy Sawyer and Peter Wagner, *Mass Incarceration: The Whole Pie 2020*, Prison Policy Initiative, March 24, 2020, https://www.prisonpolicy.org/factsheets/pie2020_allimages.pdf.

4. Nicholas A. Christakis, *Apollo's Arrow: The Profound and Enduring Impact of Coronavirus on the Way We Live* (New York: Hachette Books, 2020), 192.

5. On April 13, 2020, the prison reported that six women were quarantined as a precautionary measure after returning from outside. Oklahoma Corrections, "COVID-19 Inmate Testing," https://web.archive.org/web/20200415002218/http://doc.publishpath.com/websites/doc/images/COVID-19/COVID-19%20stats%20report.pdf.

6. Adam Payne, "Iran Has Released 85,000 Prisoners in a Bid to Stop the Spread of the Coronavirus," *Business Insider*, March 17, 2020, https://www.businessinsider.com/coronavirus-COVID-19-iran-releases-eighty-five-thousand-prisoners-2020-3.

7. Katherine Bruce Lockhart, "More Than a Million Prisoners Have Been Released during COVID, but It's Not Enough," *The Conversation*,

November 9, 2021, https://theconversation.com/more-than-a-million-prisoners-have-been-released-during-COVID-19-but-its-not-enough-170434; Marcelo F. Aebi and Mélanie M. Tiago, "Prisons and Prisoners in Europe: An Evaluation of the Medium-Term Impact of the COVID-19 on Prison Populations," Council of Europe, 2020, http://www.antoniocasella.eu/nume/Aebi_Tiago_10nov20.pdf.

8. For more on the connections between the movement to abolish slavery and reshape society to include formerly enslaved people, and today's prison abolitionist movements, see *Abolition. Feminism. Now* by Angela Y. Davis, Gina Dent, Erica R. Meiners, and Beth E. Richie.

9. Mariame Kaba, "A Love Letter to the #NoCopAcademy Organizers from Those of Us on the Freedom Side," *Prison Culture* (blog), March 13, 2019, https://www.usprisonculture.com/blog/2019/03/13/a-love-letter-to-the-nocopacademy-organizers-from-those-of-us-on-the-freedom-side/.

10. Timothy Williams, Libby Seline, and Rebecca Griesbach, "Coronavirus Cases Rise Sharply in Prisons Even As They Plateau Nationwide," *New York Times*, June 16, 2020.

11. Victoria Law, "States Say They're Decarcerating, Yet 1 in 5 Prisoners Has Had COVID," *Truthout*, December 25, 2020, https://truthout.org/articles/states-say-theyre-decarcerating-yet-1-in-5-prisoners-has-had-COVID/.

12. Katie Park, Keri Blakinger, and Claudia Lauer, "A Half-Million People Got COVID-19 in Prisons. Are Officials Ready for the Next Pandemic?" *The Marshall Project*, June 30, 2021.

13. Elena House-Hay, undated letter to author.

14. Victoria Law, "17 States and DC Have Stopped Reporting Active COVID Cases behind Bars," *Truthout*, August 5, 2022, https://truthout.org/articles/17-states-and-dc-have-stopped-reporting-active-COVID-cases-behind-bars/.

15. Arundhati Roy, "The Pandemic Is a Portal," in *Azadi: Freedom. Fascism. Fiction.* (Chicago: Haymarket Books, 2020).

16. Eric Reinhart, interview with author, April 18, 2022.

17. Gregory Hooks and Wendy Sawyer, "Mass Incarceration, COVID-19, and Community Spread," Prison Policy Initiative, December 2020, https://www.prisonpolicy.org/reports/COVIDspread.html.

18. I am indebted to the editors I worked with at *The Appeal, Gothamist, The Guardian, Ms. Magazine, The Nation, Positively Aware, The Progressive, Radcliffe Magazine, Truthout,* and *Vox* for recognizing the importance of exposing how the pandemic was affecting people behind bars.

19. Jacob Kang-Brown, Chase Montagnet, and Jasmine Heiss, "People in Jail and Prison in 2020," Vera Institute of Justice, January 2021, https://www.vera.org/downloads/publications/people-in-jail-and-prison-in-2020.pdf.

20. "Pandemic Diaries," New York Public Library event, March 15, 2023, https://www.nypl.org/events/programs/2023/03/15/pandemicdiaries.
21. Mariame Kaba, "Conversation with Mariame Kaba and Stevie Wilson," *Sostre at 100*, Schomburg Center for Research in Black Culture, March 23, 2023.
22. Angela Y. Davis, *Are Prisons Obsolete?* (New York: Seven Stories Press, 2003).
23. Alejandra Oliva, *Rivermouth: A Chronicle of Language, Faith, and Migration* (New York: Astra House, 2023), 5.

## Chapter 1: The Pandemic Begins

1. For sorting cotton, see Karen Altom, "A Day in the Life: TDCJ Assistant Warden," *Postcards Magazine*, December 30, 2015, https://www.postcardslive.com/a-day-in-the-life-tdcj-assistant-warden/.
2. Kwaneta Harris, "Working in Prison Fields Didn't 'Correct' Me, It Revealed the System's Brutality," *Truthout*, August 15, 2022, https://truthout.org/articles/working-in-prison-fields-didnt-correct-me-it-revealed-the-systems-brutality/.
3. Harris, "Working in Prison Fields."
4. Deborah Netburn, "A Timeline of the CDC's Advice on Face Masks," *Los Angeles Times*, July 27, 2021.
5. Keri Blakinger: "TIMELINE: The Spread of COVID-19 in Texas Prisons," *WFAA*, December 13, 2020, https://www.wfaa.com/article/news/local/investigates/no-way-out/timeline-spread-of-COVID-19-in-texas-prisons/287-bc71f61a-8b51-4795-a946-2514e88b2121.
6. This is not limited to Texas prisons. In October 2022, I received a letter and prison documentation from a trans man in Minnesota who was maced when a guard saw him attempting to hang himself. He was then charged with three rules violations—disruptive conduct, self-mutilation, and refusing to obey an order
7. Keri Blakinger, "'Pig Slop' No More? Texas Prisons Detail Plan to Improve Food," *The Marshall Project*, January 20, 2023, https://www.themarshallproject.org/2023/01/20/pig-slop-no-more-texas-prisons-detail-plan-to-improve-food.
8. The Lane Murray Unit's administrative segregation unit has three pods that can each house up to forty-two women at any given time. PME News Service, "35 Employees at Gatesville Prison Units Have Tested Positive for the Coronavirus," *Temple Daily Telegram*, April 23, 2020, https://www.tdtnews.com/news/coronavirus/article_d018e9f8-5c1f-5253-875c-fbc7fde50e2e.html.
9. Jack, "Birth of a Pandemic," August 30, 2022.
10. "Pottawatomie County, Oklahoma Coronavirus Cases and Deaths," USA Facts, https://usafacts.org/visualizations/coronavirus-COVID-19-

spread-map/state/oklahoma/county/pottawatomie-county.

11.  By February 9, 2021, the county had 7,462 confirmed COVID cases and 60 deaths. Oklahoma had a total of 77,701 cases and 633 deaths. "COVID-19 in Oklahoma," April 2020, https://oklahoma.gov/COVID19/newsroom/2020/april/situation-update-COVID-19-04062020.html#:~:text=As%20of%20this%20advisory%2C%20there,a%20female%20older%20than%2065.

12.  In January 2023, Congress passed the Martha Wright-Reed Just and Reasonable Communications Act of 2022, which empowers the Federal Communications Commission to regulate in-state calls from jails and prisons as well as prison video calls. "The Act directed the FCC to 'promulgate regulations no earlier than 18 months and no later than 24 months after its enactment.'" As of February 2024, the FCC has not released proposed regulations. See Wanda Bertram, "Since You Asked: What's Next for Prison and Jail Phone Justice Now That the Martha Wright-Reed Just and Reasonable Communications Act is Law?" *Prison Policy Initiative*, January 19, 2023, https://www.prisonpolicy.org/blog/2023/01/19/martha-wright-reed-act/"

13.  Elizabeth Kim, "Manhattan Woman Is First Confirmed Case in New York State, Second Infected Person in U.S. Dies," *Gothamist*, March 1, 2020, https://gothamist.com/news/coronavirus-update-manhattan-woman-first-confirmed-case-new-york-state.

14.  Former Rikers doctor Rachael Bedard estimates that the first positive tests were found on March 17, 2020. Rachael Bedard, "The Disillusionment of a Rikers Island Doctor," *New Yorker*, March 24, 2022; Nick Pinto, "Coronavirus Has Arrived at Rikers Island: Inside New York City Jails, Where the Pandemic Is Set to Explode," *The Intercept*, March 18, 2020, https://theintercept.com/2020/03/18/coronavirus-rikers-island-jail/.

15.  "Televisit Request Form," New York City Department of Correction, https://www1.nyc.gov/site/doc/inmate-info/video-visit-request-form.page.

16.  In early September 2020, after Tracy filed repeated complaints via 311, the city's hotline for non-emergency calls, and outside advocates pressured the jail to change the policy, officials stopped requiring strip searches for video visits. Days later, Tracy was released on electronic monitoring. In December 2022, after a sustained campaign and increasing media attention, the district attorney agreed to dismiss the charge against her. I covered her pretrial proceedings for *The Nation* throughout 2022: "'The Worst Abuser You Could Ever Have,'" *The Nation*, July 18, 2022, https://www.thenation.com/article/society/tracy-mccarter-suvived-punished/; "A Judge Dismisses the Murder Charge Against a Domestic Violence Survivor," *The Nation*, December 2, 2022.

17. Jonathan Kirkpatrick, "Recollections of Solitary Confinement During the HIV Epidemic," *Filter Magazine*, January 9, 2023, https://filtermag. org/hiv-solitary-confinement.

18. American Civil Liberties Union and Human Rights Watch, *Sentenced to Stigma: Segregation of HIV-Positive Prisoners in Alabama and South Carolina*, April 2010, p. 13, https://www.aclu.org/sentenced-stigma-segregation-hiv-positive-prisoners-alabama-and-south-carolina?redirect=hiv-aids-prisoners-rights/sentenced-stigma-segregation-hiv-positive-prisoners-alabama-and-south-caro.

## Chapter 2: Dire Predictions for a Prison Nation

1. World Prison Population List (12th edition), Institute for Crime and Justice Policy Research, https://www.prisonstudies.org/highest-to-lowest/prison-population-total?field_region_taxonomy_tid=All

2. Beth E. Richie, *Arrested Justice: Black Women, Violence, and America's Prison Nation* (New York: New York University Press, 2012), 3.

3. For more about precolonial Indigenous practices and the injustices inflicted by colonizers, see Kelly Lytle Hernández, *City of Inmates: Conquest, Rebellion and the Rise of Human Caging in Los Angeles, 1771–1965* (Chapel Hill: University of North Carolina Press, 2017); and Nicole Eustace, *Covered with Night: A Story of Murder and Indigenous Justice in Early America* (New York: Liveright, 2021).

4. Hernández, *City of Inmates*.

5. Mary Ellen Curtin, *Black Prisoners and Their World, Alabama, 1865–1900*, Carter G. Woodson Institute Series in Black Studies (Charlottesville: University Press of Virginia, 2000), 6.

6. Margie Mason and Robin McDowell, "Locked Up: The Prison Labor that Built Business Empires," *Associated Press* and *Reveal* at the Center for Investigative Reporting, September 22, 2022, https://apnews.com/article/ap-investigation-convict-leasing-reveal-podcast-71bcdbeff840ff4bfbbea48ea50a1cb5.

7. Nancy Kurshan, "Women and Imprisonment in the U.S.: History and Current Reality," Freedom Archives, http://www.freedomarchives.org/Documents/Finder/DOC3_scans/3.kurshan.women.imprisonment.pdf.

8. Curtin, *Black Prisoners and Their World*, 7.

9. Hernández, *City of Inmates*.

10. Eastern State Penitentiary, "Audio Tour Transcript," https://easternstate. org/audio-tour-transcript.

11. In early 2017, after waves of protests against Trump policies, the construction of the Dakota Access Pipeline, and police violence, twenty states enacted thirty-six laws penalizing protests. Eric Halliday and Rachael Hanna, "State Anti-protest Laws and Their Constitutional Impacts," *Lawfare*, October 25, 2021, https://www.lawfareblog.com/

state-anti-protest-laws-and-their-constitutional-implications.

12. Ruth Wilson Gilmore, *Golden Gulag: Prisons, Surplus, Crisis, and Opposition in Globalizing California* (Berkeley: University of California Press, 2007).

13. Elizabeth Hinton, "Excerpt: 'Making Mass Incarceration,'" Humanities New York, March 5, 2018, https://humanitiesny.org/making-mass-incarceration/.

14. Hinton, "Excerpt: 'Making Mass Incarceration.'"

15. Elizabeth Hinton, *From the War on Poverty to the War on Crime: The Making of Mass Incarceration in America* (Cambridge, MA: Harvard University Press, 2018), 130.

16. Hinton, *From the War on Poverty*, 137–38.

17. Dan Baum, "Legalize It All," *Harper's Magazine*, April 2016, https://harpers.org/archive/2016/04/legalize-it-all/.

18. Farnsworth Fowle, "Study Shows Prison Population Rose 13 Percent in 1976 to Set a Record," *New York Times*, February 18, 1977.

19. Hinton, *From the War on Poverty*, 163.

20. Hinton, *From the War on Poverty*, 258.

21. Hinton, *From the War on Poverty*, 259.

22. Michelle Alexander, *The New Jim Crow: Mass Incarceration in the Age of Colorblindness* (New York: The New Press, 2010), 50.

23. Human Rights Watch, "The Impact of the War on Drugs on U.S. Incarceration," in *Punishment and Prejudice: Racial Disparities in the War on Drugs*, May 2000, https://www.hrw.org/reports/2000/usa/Rcedrg00-03.htm; Center for American Progress, "Ending the War on Drugs: By the Numbers," June 27, 2018, https://www.americanprogress.org/article/ending-war-drugs-numbers/.

24. Steven W. Thrasher, *The Viral Underclass: The Human Toll When Inequality and Disease Collide* (New York: Celadon Books, 2022), 160.

25. Allen Beck, *Correctional Populations in the United States, 1995*, US Department of Justice, Bureau of Justice Statistics, June 1997, https://bjs.ojp.gov/content/pub/pdf/cpius951.pdf.

26. Keri Blakinger and Beth Schwartzapfel, "The 1990s Law That Keeps People in Prison on Technicalities," *The Marshall Project*, May 26, 2022, https://www.themarshallproject.org/2022/05/26/the-1990s-law-that-keeps-people-in-prison-on-technicalities.

27. Jenni Gainsborough and Marc Mauer, "Diminishing Returns: Crime and Incarceration in the 1990s," The Sentencing Project, September 2000, https://www.prisonpolicy.org/scans/sp/DimRet.pdf.

28. Allen J. Beck, *Prisoners in 1999*, US Department of Justice, Bureau of Justice Statistics, August 2000, https://bjs.ojp.gov/content/pub/pdf/p99.pdf.

29. John Gramlich, "America's Incarceration Rate Falls to Lowest Level

Since 1995," Pew Research Center, August 16, 2021, https://www. pewresearch.org/short-reads/2021/08/16/americas-incarceration-rate-lowest-since-1995/.

30. Sheldon Silver and Herman D. Farrell, "Perspectives from the New York State Assembly's Committee on Ways and Means," Occasional Paper No. 9, March 1998, https://assembly.state.ny.us/Reports/WAM/Perspectives/199803/.

31. Alex Felker, "Failure of the Rockefeller Drug Laws," *Criminal Justice*, December 13, 2015, https://scholarsarchive.library.albany. edu/cgi/viewcontent.cgi?article=1010&context=honorscollege_ cj#:~:text=Drucker's%20data%20led%20to%20some,of%20the%20 Rockefeller%20drug%20laws.

32. "A Primer: Three Strikes—the Impact After More Than a Decade," Legislative Analyst's Office, October 2005, https://lao.ca.gov/2005/3_ strikes/3_strikes_102005.htm.

33. Ryan S. King and Marc Mauer, *Aging Behind Bars: "Three Strikes" Seven Years Later*, The Sentencing Project, August 2001, https://www. prisonpolicy.org/scans/sp/inc_aging.pdf.

34. Ryan S. King and Marc Mauer, *Aging Behind Bars: "Three Strikes" Seven Years Later*, The Sentencing Project, August 2001, https://www. prisonpolicy.org/scans/sp/inc_aging.pdf. The Sentencing Project, "Fact Sheet: Incarcerated Women and Girls," November 2020, https://www. cmcainternational.org/wp-content/uploads/2020/11/Incarcerated-Women-and-Girls_Fact_Sheet_11.2020.pdf. While women's imprisonment numbers decreased in 2020, they increased another ten percent in 2021. Niki Monazzam and Kristen M. Budd, "Fact Sheet: Incarcerated Women and Girls," The Sentencing Project, April 3, 2023, https://www.sentencingproject.org/fact-sheet/incarcerated-women-and-girls/]

35. "Race and Ethnicity in the United States: 2010 Census and 2020 Census," US Census Bureau, August 12, 2021, https://www.census.gov/ library/visualizations/interactive/race-and-ethnicity-in-the-united-state-2010-and-2020-census.html; E. Ann Carson, *Prisoners in 2020 Statistical Tables*, US Department of Justice, Bureau of Justice Statistics, December 2021, Table 6, https://bjs.ojp.gov/content/pub/pdf/p20st.pdf.

36. Council on Criminal Justice, "Racial Disparities in State Imprisonment Declined Substantially from 2000 to 2020," press release, September 22, 2022, https://counciloncj.org/racial-disparities-national-trends/; Michael Winerip, Michael Schwirtz, and Robert Gebeloff, "For Blacks Facing Parole in New York State, Signs of a Broken System," *New York Times*, December 4, 2016; Kristen Bell, "A Stone of Hope: Legal and Empirical Analysis of California Juvenile Lifer Parole Decisions," *Harvard Civil Rights – Civil Liberties Law Review* 54 (2019), https://philpapers.org/

go.pl?id=BELSOH&aid=BELSOHv1.

37. The Office of Minority Health at the US Department of Health and Human Services estimated that, in 2020, 9.7 million people (or 2.9 percent of the US population) identified as American Indian and/or Alaskan Native. "American Indian/Alaskan Native," https://minorityhealth.hhs.gov/omh/browse.aspx?lvl=3&lvlid=62#:~:text=In%20 2020%2C%20an%20estimated%203.7,Native%20and%20another%20 race%20group. For rates of incarceration, see Carson, *Prisoners in 2020*, Table 5.

38. "Racial Disparities Are Rising in Oklahoma Prison Admissions During the COVID-19 Pandemic," Fwd.us, 2020, https://www.fwd.us/wp-content/uploads/2020/12/FWD-BlackIncarceration-OK-2020-v2.pdf.

39. Melissa Rosenfelt, "Like the Drum, Native American Women Are the Heartbeat of Their Oklahoma Communities," *The Oklahoman*, April 5, 2021, https://www.oklahoman.com/story/special/2021/04/05/native-american-women-heartbeat-their-oklahoma-communities/4698946001/; Isabel Coronado, "What's Happening to Our Native Women in Oklahoma?" *The Next 100*, October 22, 2020, https://thenext100.org/whats-happening-to-our-native-women-in-oklahoma/.

40. Maya Schenwar and Victoria Law, *Prison by Any Other Name: The Harmful Consequences of Popular Reforms* (New York City: The New Press, 2020).

41. Critical Resistance, "What Is the PIC? What Is Abolition?" https://criticalresistance.org/mission-vision/not-so-common-language/#:~:text=PIC%20abolition%20is%20a%20 political,alternatives%20to%20punishment%20and%20imprisonment.

42. Matthew Karp, "In the 1850s, the Future of American Slavery Seemed Bright," *Aeon*, November 1, 2016, https://aeon.co/ideas/in-the-1850s-the-future-of-american-slavery-seemed-bright.

43. Gloria Anzaldúa, *Borderlands/La Frontera: The New Mestiza* (San Francisco: Aunt Lute Books, 1999), 109.

44. Orisanmi Burton, *Tip of the Spear: Black Radicalism, Prison Repression, and the Long Attica Revolt* (Oakland: University of California Press, 2023), 14, 158.

45. Eric Reinhart, interview with author, April 18, 2022.

46. Jessica MacNeil, Mark Lobato, and Marisa Moore, "An Unanswered Health Disparity: Tuberculosis Among Correctional Inmates, 1993 Through 2003," *American Journal of Public Health* 95, no. 10 (October 2005), https://ajph.aphapublications.org/doi/pdf/10.2105/AJPH.2004.055442.

47. For more about the MRSA outbreaks in the Los Angeles jail system and Georgia and Texas prisons, see "Methicillin-Resistant *Staphylococcus aureus* Infections in Correctional Facilities – Georgia, California, and Texas, 2001–2003," *MMWR Weekly*, October 17, 2003, https://www.cdc.

gov/mmwr/preview/mmwrhtml/mm5241a4.htm.

48. Brad Lander, "Doctors in NYC Hospitals, Jails, and Shelters Call on the City to Take More Aggressive Action to Combat the Spread of Coronavirus," *Medium*, March 12, 2020, https://medium.com/@bradlander/doctors-in-nyc-hospitals-jails-and-shelters-call-on-the-city-to-take-more-aggressive-action-to-fb75f0b131c2.

49. Bedard, "The Disillusionment of a Rikers Island Doctor," *New Yorker*, March 24, 2022.

## Chapter 3: Deadly Inadequacies Amidst an Uncertain Spring

1. Malakki asked that his legal name be withheld to avoid retaliation. Pearl asked to not be identified by her legal name to avoid possible employment repercussions.

2. Kevin McCarthy, "Challenging Gladiator Fights in the CDCR," *UCLA Law Review*, May 10, 2021, https://www.uclalawreview.org/challenging-gladiator-fights-in-the-cdcr/.

3. Maria Dinzeo, "California Prison Officials on Hook for COVID Outbreak at San Quentin," *Courthouse News Service*, July 18, 2022, https://www.courthousenews.com/california-prison-officials-on-hook-for-COVID-outbreak-at-san-quentin/.

4. Office of the Inspector General (OIG), *COVID-19 Review Series*, part 3, February 2021, p. 38, https://www.courthousenews.com/wp-content/uploads/2021/02/SanQuentin_COVID-IGreport.pdf.

5. Ada Kwan et al., *Prisons During the COVID-19 Pandemic: A Report by the CalPROTECT Project*, CalPROTECT (California Prison Roadmap for Targeting Efforts to Address the Ecosystem of COVID Transmission), May 1, 2022, 132, https://amend.us/wp-content/uploads/2022/05/2022-0501-CalPROTECT-Report.pdf.

6. OIG, *COVID-19 Review Series*, part 3, 48.

7. OIG, *COVID-19 Review Series*, part 3, ii.

8. Kim Christensen, Richard Winton, and Anita Chabria, "Prison Officials Ignored Warnings Before Inmate Transfer That Led to Virus Outbreak, Watchdog Says," *Los Angeles Times*, February 1, 2021; Eileen Guo, "'Obsessed with Staying Alive': Inmates Describe a Prison's Piecemeal Response to a Fatal COVID-19 Outbreak," *Stat News*, June 12, 2020, https://www.statnews.com/2020/06/12/california-institution-for-men-COVID19-outbreak/.

9. Lonnie Williams, "What These Walls Won't Hold," Beyond the Bars conference, March 26, 2023.

10. Hernández, *City of Inmates*.

11. Nancy Tomes, "'Destroyer and Teacher': Managing the Masses During the 1918–1919 Influenza Pandemic," *Public Health Reports* 125, no.

3, supplement (2010), https://www.ncbi.nlm.nih.gov/pmc/articles/PMC2862334/.

12. L. L. Stanley, "Influenza at San Quentin Prison, California," *Public Health Reports (1896–1970)* 34, no. 19 (May 1919), 997, https://cssh.northeastern.edu/pandemic-teaching-initiative/wp-content/uploads/sites/43/2020/10/Stanley-1919.-Influenza-at-San-Quentin-Prison-California.pdf.

13. Stanley, "Influenza at San Quentin Prison," 999.

14. Stanley, "Influenza at San Quentin," 999.

15. Stanley, "Influenza at San Quentin," 1001.

16. None of these three outbreaks affected the prison's women's unit, which confined thirty women that year. Stanley, "Influenza at San Quentin," 1005.

17. Matthew Rae et al., "The Burden of Medical Debt in the United States," *Health System Tracker*, March 10, 2022, https://www.healthsystemtracker.org/brief/the-burden-of-medical-debt-in-the-united-states/; Mona Chalabi, "Will Losing Health Insurance Mean More US Deaths? Experts Say Yes," *The Guardian*, June 24, 2017.

18. Larry M. Maruschak and Marcus Berzofsky, "Medical Problems of State and Federal Prisoners and Jail Inmates, 2011–12," US. Department of Justice, Office of Justice Programs, October 2016, Tables 1 and 2, https://bjs.ojp.gov/content/pub/pdf/mpsfpji1112.pdf.

19. Rebecca Vallas, *Disabled Behind Bars: The Mass Incarceration of People with Disabilities in America's Jails and Prisons,* Center for American Progress, July 2016, https://cdn.americanprogress.org/wp-content/uploads/2016/07/15103130/CriminalJusticeDisability-report.pdf.

20. Lauren Brinkley-Rubenstein, interview with author, April 22, 2022.

21. "The Most Significant Criminal Justice Policy Changes from the COVID-19 Pandemic," Prison Policy Institute, https://www.prisonpolicy.org/virus/virusresponse.html#copays. In 2019, organizing and advocacy by formerly incarcerated people pushed the California legislature to pass—and the governor to sign—a bill eliminating co-pays in the state's jails and prisons.

22. Mark Martin, "San Quentin Warden Fired Over Health Care. State Investigated Conditions at Prison," *San Francisco Chronicle*, July 8, 2005, https://www.sfgate.com/news/article/san-quentin-warden-fired-over-health-care-state-2657070.php.

23. California Prison Health Care Receivership Corp, "San Quentin Under the Microscope," press release, August 2, 2007, https://cchcs.ca.gov/wp-content/uploads/sites/60/2017/08/PR_080207.pdf?emrc=f7b665.

24. American Civil Liberties Union, *At America's Expense: The Mass Incarceration of the Elderly*, June 2012, p. 8, https://www.aclu.org/sites/default/files/field_document/elderlyprisonreport_20120613_1.pdf.

25. Supreme Court of the United States, *Brown v. Plata*, May 23, 2011, p. 9,. https://www.law.cornell.edu/supct/pdf/09-1233P.ZO

26. Supreme Court of the United States, *Brown v. Plata*.

27. Amanda Chicago-Lewis, "The Prisoners Fighting California's Wildfires," *BuzzFeed*, October 30, 2014, https://www.buzzfeed.com/amandachicagolewis/the-prisoners-fighting-californias-wildfires.

28. Paige St. John, "Federal Judges Order California to Expand Prison Releases," *Los Angeles Times*, November 14, 2014.

29. California Department of Corrections and Rehabilitation (CDCR), *Weekly Population Report As of March 11, 2020*, https://www.cdcr.ca.gov/research/wp-content/uploads/sites/174/2020/03/Tpop1d200311.pdf.

30. Erica Bryant, "19 People Have Died from New York City Jails in 2022," Vera Institute of Justice, December 12, 2022, https://www.vera.org/news/nyc-jail-deaths-2022.

31. Victoria Law, "Health Care in Jails and Prisons Is Terrible. The Pandemic Made It Even Worse," *Vox*, June 28, 2022, https://www.vox.com/23175978/health-care-prison-jail-COVID-pandemic.

32. "Joint Case Management Conference Statement," in Marciana Plata, et al. v. Gavin Newsom, et al., Prison Law Office, March 30, 2022, https://prisonlaw.com/wp-content/uploads/2022/04/22.03.28-Doc-3796-Joint-Case-Management-Conference-Statement.pdf.

33. Isabel Song Beer, "DOC Failed to Facilitate Nearly 40,000 Medical Appointments," *amNY*, June 8, 2022, https://www.amny.com/politics/doc-failed-to-facilitate-medical-appointments/.

34. Jake Offenhartz, "City Ordered to Pay Rikers Detainees Who Were Denied Medical Appointments," *Gothamist*, August 10, 2022, https://gothamist.com/news/city-ordered-to-pay-rikers-detainees-who-were-denied-medical-appointments.

35. Homer Venters, interview with author, April 25, 2022.

36. Eric Reinhart, interview with author, April 18, 2022.

37. A study from the Yale School of Public Health put the number of deaths that could have been prevented by universal health care between March 2020 and March 2022 at 338,594. Jenny Blair, "Study: More Than 335,000 Lives Could Have Been Saved During Pandemic If U.S. Had Universal Health Care," Yale School of Public Health, June 20, 2022, https://ysph.yale.edu/news-article/yale-study-more-than-335000-lives-could-have-been-saved-during-pandemic-if-us-had-universal-health-care/.

## Chapter 4: Long Hot Summer in Lockdown

1. In early 2020, I received e-messages from several women at New York's Bedford Hills Correctional Facility. They had been ordered to wear their blue surgical masks inside out because blue was the color worn by prison guards. The women wanted to know if wearing masks inside out would

protect them from the coronavirus. The prison rescinded this ill-thought requirement after calls from advocates and concerned family members.

2. Unlock the Box, *Solitary Confinement Is Never the Answer: A Special Report on the COVID-19 Pandemic in Prisons and Jails, the Use of Solitary Confinement, and Best Practices for Saving the Lives of Incarcerated People and Correctional Staff*, June 2020, https://solitarywatch.org/wp-content/uploads/2020/06/UTB-Report-6.2020.pdf.

3. Rachel Aviv, "Punishment by Pandemic," *New Yorker*, June 15, 2020.

4. Taylor Majewski, "'We Went from Almost No Lockdowns to Daily Lockdowns': The Mental Health Crisis Inside California Women's Prisons," *Stat News*, April 28, 2023, https://www.statnews.com/2023/04/28/lockdowns-prisons-mental-health/.

5. This averaged out to nearly seventy thousand state and federal prisoners and another twenty thousand of people in jails (4.4 percent and 2.7 percent, respectively, of the jail and prison populations). Solitary Watch, "FAQ: Solitary Confinement in the United States," 2018, https://solitarywatch.org/wp-content/uploads/2019/05/Solitary-Confinement-FAQ-2018-final.pdf.

6. Laura Sullivan, "Timeline: Solitary Confinement in U.S. Prisons," *NPR*, July 26, 2006, https://www.npr.org/templates/story/story.php?storyId=5579901.

7. Rory Carroll, "California Prison Hunger Strike Leader: 'If Necessary We'll Resume. This Is War,'" *The Guardian*, September 27, 2013, https://www.theguardian.com/world/2013/sep/27/california-prison-hunger-strike-todd-ashker.

8. Solitary Watch, "Inside Pelican Bay State Prison," https://solitarywatch.org/resources/multimedia/photography/inside-pelican-bay-state-prison/.

9. Dan Berger, *Captive Nation: Black Prison Organizing in the Civil Rights Era* (Chapel Hill: University of North Carolina Press, 2015).

10. Todd Ashker was also convicted in criminal court, turning his six-year sentence for burglary into a life sentence for murder.

11. Alyssa Newcomb, "California Prison Hunger Strike Leader Is Convicted Murderer with Alleged Aryan Brotherhood Ties," *ABC News*, July 29, 2013, https://abcnews.go.com/US/california-prison-hunger-strike-leader-convicted-murderer-alleged/story?id=19805895.

12. Victoria Law, "What Does a Book Have to Do with a Movement?" *Waging NonViolence*, September 15, 2015, https://wagingnonviolence.org/2015/09/what-does-a-book-have-to-do-with-a-movement/.

13. Paige St. John, "Inmates End California Prison Hunger Strike," *Los Angeles Times*, September 5, 2013.

14. Victoria Law, "Two Years After Hunger Strike, California Settlement May Release 2,000 Prisoners from Solitary," *Truthout*, September 2, 2015, https://truthout.org/articles/two-years-after-hunger-strike-

california-settlement-may-release-2000-prisoners-from-solitary/. In August 2023, a federal appeals court ruled that the CDCR did not have to disclose reasons for placing a person in the SHU. Bob Egelko, "Ninth Circuit Expands California's Use of Solitary Confinement as Lawmakers Work to End It," *San Francisco Chronicle*, August 24, 2023, https://www.sfchronicle.com/politics/article/california-solitary-confinement-18329231.php.

15. The alias "Nancy" is used here because she did not want her experiences of sexual assaults published under her legal name.

16. Aviv, "Punishment by Pandemic."

17. David Cloud et al., "The Ethical Use of Medical Isolation—Not Solitary Confinement—to Reduce COVID-19 Transmission in Correctional Settings," AMEND, April 9, 2020, https://amend.us/wp-content/uploads/2020/04/Medical-Isolation-vs-Solitary_Amend.pdf.

18. AMEND, "Urgent Memo: COVID-19 Outbreak: San Quentin Prison," 3, https://amend.us/wp-content/uploads/2020/06/COVID19-Outbreak-SQ-Prison-6.15.2020.pdf.

19. Unlock the Box, *Solitary Confinement Is Never the Answer*.

20. David Ditto, "COVID-19 Kills 28 San Quentin Incarcerated," *San Quentin News*, December 31, 2020, https://sanquentinnews.com/COVID-19-kills-28-san-quentin-incarcerated/.

21. Ditto, "COVID-19 Kills."

22. CDCR, *San Quentin State Prison Adjustment Center: Condemned Inmate/Ad-Seg Inmate Orientation Handbook*, March 2013, https://caitlinkellyhenry.com/wp-content/uploads/2016/02/SQ-Adjustment-Center-Orientation-Handbook.pdf.

23. *San Quentin State Prison Adjustment Center*, 3.

24. Juan Moreno Haines and Katie Rose Quandt, "San Quentin Is Still Punishing People for Being Sick," *Type Investigations*, September 19, 2022, https://www.typeinvestigations.org/investigation/2022/09/19/san-quentin-death-row-COVID-quarantine/.

25. Haines and Quandt, "San Quentin."

26. Gregory Hooks and Wendy Sawyer, *Mass Incarceration, COVID-19, and Community Spread*, Prison Policy Initiative, December 2020, https://www.prisonpolicy.org/reports/COVIDspread.html .

27. Typewritten affidavit, October 26, 2020.

28. Handwritten affidavit, November 20, 2020.

29. Connor Brooks and Sean E. Goodison, "Federal Deaths in Custody and During Arrest, 2020—Statistical Tables," U.S, Department of Justice, Bureau of Justice Statistics, July 2022, Tables 1 and 4, https://bjs.ojp.gov/content/pub/pdf/fdcda20st.pdf.

30. Terry Allen Kupers, *Solitary: The Inside Story of Supermax Isolation and How We Can Abolish It* (Oakland: University of California Press, 2017), 88.

31. Physicians for Human Rights, "Background Brief: Alternatives to Solitary Confinement," May 2023, p. 3, https://www.phr.org.il/wp-content/uploads/2023/05/5298_SolitaryBrief_paper_Eng.pdf.

32. Terry Kupers, "Repetitive Self-Harm in Solitary Confinement," *Correctional Health Care Report* 24, no. 3 (Summer 2023), 1, https://solitarywatch.org/wp-content/uploads/2023/07/CHC-2403-01-Kupers-Self-Harm.pdf.

33. Jennifer Gonnerman, "Three Years on Rikers Without Trial," *New Yorker*, September 29, 2014; Amy Drozdowska, "Kalief Browder, in His Own Words," *WNYC*, June 3, 2016, https://www.wnycstudios.org/podcasts/tnyradiohour/segments/kalief-browder-his-own-words; Gonnerman, "Kalief Browder, 1993–2015," *New Yorker*, June 7, 2015.

34. Lauren Brinkley-Rubinstein, Josie Sivaraman, and David L. Rosen, "Association of Restrictive Housing During Incarceration with Mortality After Release," *JAMA Network Open*, October 4, 2019, https://jamanetwork.com/journals/jamanetworkopen/fullarticle/2752350.

35. Jennifer Gonnerman, "The Purgatory of Parole Incarcerations During the Coronavirus Crisis," *New Yorker*, April 11, 2020.

36. The California prison system is designed to incarcerate a maximum of 89,663 people. CDCR, *Weekly Report of Population*, April 1, 2020, https://www.cdcr.ca.gov/research/wp-content/uploads/sites/174/2020/04/Tpop1d200401.pdf.

37. Aviv, "Punishment by Pandemic."

38. Kelly Lyn Mitchell et al., *Examining Prison Releases in Response to COVID: Lessons Learned for Reducing the Effects of Mass Incarceration*, Robina Institute of Criminal Law and Criminal Justice, July 2022, p. 79, https://robinainstitute.umn.edu/sites/robinainstitute.umn.edu/files/2022-07/Examining%20Prison%20Releases%20in%20Response%20to%20COVID%20-%20July%202022.pdf.

39. North Carolina Department of Public Safety, "Prison Population, Entries and Exits," https://www.ncdps.gov/media/6638/download.

40. Mitchell et al., *Examining Prison Releases*, iii.

41. *Prisoners in 2020*, Tables 9 and 19, https://bjs.ojp.gov/content/pub/pdf/p20st.pdf.

42. David Sears et al., "Substance Abuse and Treatment Facility (SATF) Corcoran Site Visit Report," Berkeley Public Health/AMEND, March 5, 2021, p. 7, https://amend.us/wp-content/uploads/2021/03/SATF-December-2020-Visit-Report_3.7.21.pdf.

43. Sears et al., "SATF Corcoran Site Visit Report."

44. COVID Prison Project, "California Prison System COVID-19 Data," https://COVIDprisonproject.com/data/california/; CDCR, "Population COVID-19 Tracker," https://www.cdcr.ca.gov/COVID19/population-status-tracking/ ; CDCR, "Weekly Report of Population As of Midnight,

July 5, 2023," https://www.cdcr.ca.gov/research/wp-content/uploads/
sites/174/2023/07/Tpop1d230705.pdf; Centers for Disease Control and
Prevention, National Center for Health Statistics, "California," https://
www.cdc.gov/nchs/pressroom/states/california/ca.htm.

## Chapter 5: The Twin Pandemics

1.  COVID-19 Policing Project, quoted in Mariame Kaba and Andrea J.
    Ritchie, *No More Police: A Case for Abolition* (New York: The New Press,
    2022), 48.

2.  American Public Health Association, "Addressing Law Enforcement
    Violence as a Public Health Issue," Policy No. 201811, November 13,
    2018, https://www.apha.org/policies-and-advocacy/public-health-
    policy-statements/policy-database/2019/01/29/law-enforcement-
    violence.

3.  Josiah Bates, "The Black Prison Population Increased During the Height
    of the COVID-19 Pandemic, Report Finds," *The Grio*, May 1, 2023,
    https://thegrio.com/2023/05/01/the-black-prison-population-increased-
    during-the-height-of-the-COVID-19-pandemic-report-finds/. See also
    Brennan Klein et al., "COVID-19 Amplified Racial Disparities in the
    U.S. Criminal Legal System," *Nature*, April 19, 2023, https://www.
    nature.com/articles/s41586-023-05980-2.

4.  Liz Szabo, "Study Reveals Staggering Toll of Being Black in America: 1.6
    Million Excess Deaths over 22 Years," *NBC News*, May 16, 2023, https://
    www.nbcnews.com/health/health-news/study-reveals-staggering-toll-
    black-america-16-million-excess-deaths-2-rcna84627.

5.  "'Weathering,' the Life's Work of Arline Geronimus," Institute for Social
    Research: Population Studies, University of Michigan, March 23, 2023,
    https://psc.isr.umich.edu/news/a-monumental-new-book-weathering-
    arline-geronimuss-lifes-work/.

6.  Regina Mahone, "Linda Villarosa on the Impact of the Racist Health
    Care System on 'Every Body,'" *The Nation*, June 14, 2022, https://www.
    thenation.com/article/society/linda-villarosa-health-race/.

7.  Latoya Hill, Samantha Artiga, and Nambi Ndugga, "COVID-19 Cases,
    Deaths, and Vaccinations by Race/Ethnicity as of Winter 2022,"
    *KFF Health News*, March 7, 2023, https://www.kff.org/coronavirus-
    COVID-19/issue-brief/COVID-19-cases-deaths-and-vaccinations-by-
    race-ethnicity-as-of-winter-2022/.

8.  Larry Buchanan, Quoctrung Bui, and Jugal K. Patel, "Black Lives Matter
    May Be the Largest Movement in U.S. History," *New York Times*, July 3,
    2020.

9.  Delan Devakumar et al., "Racism, the Public Health Crisis We Can No
    Longer Ignore, *The Lancet*, June 11, 2020; Zinzi D. Bailey, Justin M.
    Feldman, and Mary T. Bassett, "How Structural Racism Works—Racist

Policies as a Root Cause of U.S. Racial Health Inequities," *New England Journal of Medicine*, December 16, 2020.

10. E. Ann Carson, *Prisoners in 2020—Statistical Tables*, US Department of Justice, Bureau of Justice Statistics, December 2021, Table 5, https://bjs.ojp.gov/content/pub/pdf/p20st.pdf.

11. US Census Bureau, "Race and Ethnicity in the United States: 2010 Census and 2020 Census," August 12, 2021, https://www.census.gov/library/visualizations/interactive/race-and-ethnicity-in-the-united-state-2010-and-2020-census.html; Carson, *Prisoners in 2020*, Table 3.

12. Because "Autumn" is still a minor, Kwaneta and I agreed that we would not publish her legal name. Antonio and Alana are the names of her two older children.

13. For more about Devil's Night and Detroit residents' efforts, see Cale Weissman, "How Detroit Exorcised Devil's Night," *Atlas Obscura*, October 16, 2015, https://www.atlasobscura.com/articles/how-detroit-exorcised-devils-night, and Jake Rossen, "'Just for the Hell of It': A History of Detroit's 'Devil's Night,'" *Mental Floss*, October 20, 2022, https://www.mentalfloss.com/posts/detroit-devils-night-history#:~:text=Every%20October%2030%2C%20hundreds%20of,refer%20to%20as%20Devil's%20Night.

14. Jack, "The Murder and the Defunding," unpublished essay, postmarked November 22, 2022.

15. Will Stone, "Tear-Gassing Protesters During an Infectious Outbreak 'A Recipe For Disaster,'" *KHN*, June 5, 2020, https://khn.org/news/tear-gassing-protesters-during-an-infectious-outbreak-a-recipe-for-disaster/.

16. Stone, "Tear-Gassing Protesters."

17. Stone, "Tear-Gassing Protesters."

18. Niki Kapsambelis, "Six Inmates Escape from State Prison in Pittsburgh," *Associated Press*, January 9, 1997, https://apnews.com/article/349d95274945e11ccfaf09a5fc1f1926.

19. At the women's prison in Muncy, Pennsylvania, administrators also confiscated the window shades that women used for privacy while changing clothes or using the toilet. See House of Representatives, Commonwealth of Pennsylvania, *Hearing on Inmate Escape*, October 14, 1999, pp. 188–89, https://www.legis.state.pa.us/WU01/LI/TR/Transcripts/1999_0125T.pdf.

20. Matt Munoz, "Women Detainees Suddenly Released from Mesa Verde Find Relief Through Safety Network," *Kern Sol News*, May 19, 2020, https://southkernsol.org/2020/05/19/women-detainees-suddenly-released-from-mesa-verde-find-relief-through-safety-network/.

21. Rebecca Plevin, "Immigrants in California Detention Centers Launch Hunger Strikes to Call for COVID-19 Protections, Advocates Say," *Desert Sun*, April 19, 2020, https://www.desertsun.com/story/news/

health/2020/04/19/immigrants-california-detention-centers-launch-
hunger-strikes-call-COVID-19-protections-advocates-sa/5162354002/;
Andrea Castillo, "Advocates Say Hundreds of Immigrants Detained in
California Are on Hunger Strike. ICE Says Only Two," *Los Angeles Times*,
April 19, 2020.

22. Rebecca Plevin, "'This Death Was Preventable': Family Asks State
    to Probe 74-Year-Old's Suicide in ICE Detention," *Desert Sun*,
    August 7, 2020, https://www.desertsun.com/story/news/politics/
    immigration/2020/08/07/family-asks-newsom-probe-choung-woohn-
    ahn-suicide-ice-mesa-verde/5504694002/.

23. Qazi was released from ICE detention in August 2020. By then, more
    than half of people detained at Mesa Verde had tested positive for
    COVID. Asif Qazi, "Opinion: During Six Months of ICE Detention,
    I Saw COVID-19 Spread," *Mercury News*, September 1, 2020,
    mercurynews.com/2020/09/01/opinion-during-six-months-of-ice-
    detention-i-saw-COVID-19-spread/.

24. Interfaith Movement for Human Integrity, "United in the Fight for
    Liberation," YouTube video, June 8, 2020, https://www.youtube.com/
    watch?v=QlQnjqDPkMw.

25. Madi Bolanos, "Mesa Verde on Hunger Strike Again amid Positive
    COVID-19 Cases," *KVPR*, July 7, 2020, https://www.kvpr.org/
    news/2020-07-07/mesa-verde-on-hunger-strike-again-amid-positive-
    COVID-19-cases; Eric Westervelt, "COVID-19 Outbreak Devastates
    California's San Quentin Prison," *NPR*, July 4, 2020, https://www.
    npr.org/2020/07/04/887239267/COVID-19-outbreak-devastates-
    californias-san-quentin-prison.

26. Victoria Law, "Incarcerated People Are Challenging Deadly Pandemic
    Conditions in Prisons," *Truthout*, September 6, 2020, https://truthout.
    org/articles/incarcerated-people-are-challenging-deadly-pandemic-
    conditions-in-prisons/.

27. Adams et al. v. Koenig et al., p. 5, https://www.courthousenews.com/
    wp-content/uploads/2021/02/AdamsEtal_CDCR-COMPLAINT.pdf.

28. Claude Marks, "Prisoners Sue California Prison System Following
    Targeted Raid Against Black People," *ScheerPost*, December 20, 2021,
    https://scheerpost.com/2021/12/20/inmate-sues-california-prison-
    system-following-targeted-raid-against-black-people/.

29. In August 2023, a federal court ruled that prison officials could utilize
    confidential information to place people in solitary.

30. Asaf Shalev, "Soledad Prison Sees First COVID-19 Cases after a 3
    am Raid by Outside Officers," *Monterey County Now*, August 5, 2020,
    https://www.montereycountyweekly.com/news/local_news/soledad-
    prison-sees-first-COVID-19-cases-after-a-3am-raid-by-outside-officers/
    article_6fce5570-d738-11ea-bda2-9ff4ae1bae12.html.

31. CDCR, *Population COVID-19 Tracking* (institution view tab), https://www.cdcr.ca.gov/COVID19/population-status-tracking/ (accessed August 27, 2023).

32. Mary Duan, "Black Prison Inmates in Soledad Sue Over a July 2020 Raid That Resulted in a Mass Spread of COVID-19," *Monterey County Now*, February 25, 2021, https://www.montereycountyweekly.com/news/local_news/black-prison-inmates-in-soledad-sue-over-a-july-2020-raid-that-resulted-in-a/article_c2566682-76db-11eb-bde2-c745a02ac24a.html.

## Chapter 6: Pandemic Summer: Outbreaks, Overheating, and Organizing

1. Joshua Connor, "Op-Ed: COVID-19 Has Invaded San Quentin Prison. To Save Lives, People Must Be Released," *Los Angeles Times*, July 8, 2020.

2. That October, an appeals court ordered San Quentin to reduce its prison population by 50 percent. Kevin Sawyer, "'They Want to Do Me In': The Prisoner Who Fought COVID Overcrowding," *Filter Magazine*, February 8, 2021, https://filtermag.org/prisoner-COVID-overcrowding-california/.

3. Empowerment Avenue, "Our History," https://www.empowermentave.org/our-histroy.

4. Stop San Quentin Outbreak, "Who We Are," https://stopsqoutbreak.org/about/.

5. "Activists Call on Governor Newsom to Address San Quentin Outbreak," *ABC7 News*, July 9, 2020, https://abc7news.com/san-quentin-prison-outbreak-COVID-19-in-prisons-coronavirus-state/6309072/.

6. "Activists Call on Governor Newsom."

7. Elliot Almond, "Bay Area Activists Say Prisoners Deserve COVID-19 Relief in New Protest Sunday," *Mercury News*, January 31, 2021, https://www.mercurynews.com/2021/01/31/activists-say-prisoners-deserve-COVID-19-relief-in-new-protest-sunday/.

8. J. Clark Kelso, "Transferring COVID High-Risk Patients to Safer Housing," California State Assembly Committee on Budget, October 21, 2020, p. 8, https://abgt.assembly.ca.gov/sites/abgt.assembly.ca.gov/files/Transferring%20COVID%20High-Risk%20Patients%20to%20Safer%20Housing.pdf.

9. CDCR, "Release Occurrences from CDCR's In-Custody Population Released Early Due to COVID-19 Between July 1 to November 25, 2020," version 24, November 26, 2020, https://calmatters.org/wp-content/uploads/2020/12/Expedited-release-demographics-to-Nov.-25.pdf.

10. CDCR, "Weekly Report of Population As of Midnight, November 18, 2020," https://www.cdcr.ca.gov/research/wp-content/uploads/

sites/174/2020/11/Tpop1d201118.pdf.

11. Jennifer E. James, Leslie Riddle, and Giselle Perez-Aguilar, "'Prison Life Is Very Hard and It's Made Harder If You're Isolated': COVID-19 Risk Mitigation Strategies and the Mental Health of Incarcerated Women in California," *International Journal of Prison Health*, November 2022, 12, https://pubmed.ncbi.nlm.nih.gov/36394281/.

12. Kiera Feldman, "California Kept Prison Factories Open. Inmates Worked for Pennies an Hour as COVID-19 Spread," *Los Angeles Times*, October 11, 2020.

13. Jonah Valdez, "'We Are Terrified': Coronavirus Outbreak Reported in Prison," *Daily Bulletin*, May 17, 2020, https://www.dailybulletin.com/2020/05/17/we-are-terrified-coronavirus-outbreak-reported-at-chino-womens-prison/.

14. Feldman, "California Kept Prison Factories Open."

15. James, Riddle, and Perez-Aguilar, "'Prison Life Is Very Hard,'" 7.

16. Eileen Guo, "Inmates Witnessed a Suicide Attempt. They Received Coloring Pages Instead of Counseling," The Fuller Project in partnership with the *Washington Post*, July 27, 2020, https://fullerproject.org/story/prison-mental-health-COVID-confinement/.

17. April Harris, "Coronavirus Chronicles," *Abolition Feminisms*, vol. 1, *Organizing, Survival, and Transformative Practice*, ed. Alisa Bierria, Jakeya Caruthers, and Brooke Lober (Chicago: Haymarket Books, 2022), 112.

18. Harris, "Coronavirus Chronicles," 115.

19. Harris, "Coronavirus Chronicles," 109. While California prison policy allows media representatives to contact incarcerated people through postal mail, phone, or in-person visits, it does not allow official media interviews with incarcerated people.

20. Harris, "Coronavirus Chronicles," 118.

21. Victoria Law, "Erika Rocha's Suicide Brings Attention to the Dire Need for Mental Health Care in Prison," *Rewire News*, May 20, 2016, https://rewirenewsgroup.com/2016/05/20/erika-rochas-suicide-brings-attention-dire-need-mental-health-care-prison/.

22. Christopher Zoukis, "Epidemic of Suicides in California Women's Prison," *Prison Legal News*, June 30 2017, https://www.prisonlegalnews.org/news/2017/jun/30/epidemic-suicides-california-womens-prison/.

23. Victoria Law, "Erika Rocha's Suicide Brings Attention to Dire Need for Mental Health Care in Prison," *Rewire News Group*, May 20, 2016, https://rewirenewsgroup.com/2016/05/20/erika-rochas-suicide-brings-attention-dire-need-mental-health-care-prison/.

24. California Senate Bill 960, signed into law in September 2018, requires the CDCR to provide annual reports on plans to reduce suicide risk factors. CIW warden Kimberly Hughes retired in 2016 after extensive media coverage about the spate of suicides and suicide attempts. Don

Thompson, "Two California Women's Prison Wardens Retire amid Abuse, Suicide Claims," *KQED*, August 5, 2016, https://www.kqed.org/news/11042222/two-california-womens-prison-wardens-retire-amid-abuse-suicide-claims.

25. James, Riddle, and Perez-Aguilar, "'Prison Life Is Very Hard,'" 11.

26. James, Riddle, and Perez-Aguilar, "'Prison Life Is Very Hard,'" 13.

27. Barbara Hoberock, "Women's Prison in Taft Declared a COVID-19 'Hot Spot,'" *Tulsa World*, August 28, 2020, https://tulsaworld.com/news/local/womens-prison-in-taft-declared-COVID-19-hot-spot/article_c6e767e0-e960-11ea-9593-eb6d0755ba6e.html.

28. Oklahoma Department of Corrections, "COVID-19 Stats Report," results as of August 27, 2020, archived on https://web.archive.org/web/20200831124323/http://doc.publishpath.com/Default.aspx?shortcut=COVID-19-stats-report.

29. Justin Wolf, communications director of Oklahoma Department of Corrections, email to author, December 17, 2020.

30. Gregory Hooks and Wendy Sawyer, "Mass Incarceration, COVID-19 and Community Spread," *Prison Policy Initiative*, December 2020, Appendix Table 1, https://www.prisonpolicy.org/reports/COVIDspread_appendix1.html.

31. Chris Polansky, "'They Don't Deserve to Die': Families Rally at Prison Where Almost Every Inmate Has Caught COVID," *Public Radio Tulsa*, September 13, 2020, https://www.publicradiotulsa.org/local-regional/2020-09-13/they-dont-deserve-to-die-families-rally-at-prison-where-almost-every-inmate-has-caught-COVID.

32. Matt Trotter, "Many Fewer Inmates Being Released After Commutations Than Governor's Office Announced," *Public Radio Tulsa*, April 15, 2020, https://www.publicradiotulsa.org/local-regional/2020-04-15/many-fewer-inmates-being-released-after-commutations-than-governors-office-announced.

33. Jeanine Santucci, "Most US States Don't Have Universal Air Conditioning in Prisons. Climate Change, Heat Waves Are Making It 'Torture,'" Phys.org, September 12, 2020, https://phys.org/news/2022-09-states-dont-universal-air-conditioning.html. In July 2023, after thirty-two people, including two at the Murray Unit, died during the previous month, the Texas prison system installed air conditioning in the facility's segregation unit. The newly installed system cooled the cells to approximately 85 degrees during the triple-digit summer.

34. July 4, 2023, was the hottest day on Earth since record keeping began more than forty years ago.

35. Alexi Jones, "Cruel and Unusual Punishment: When States Don't Provide Air Conditioning in Prison," Prison Policy Initiative, June 18, 2019, https://www.prisonpolicy.org/blog/2019/06/18/air-

conditioning/.

36. Xinbo Lian et al., "Heat Waves Accelerate the Spread of Infectious Diseases," *Environmental Research* 231 (May 2023), https://www. ncbi.nlm.nih.gov/pmc/articles/PMC10191724/#:~:text=The%20 collision%20between%20the%20pandemic,to%20human%20health%20 and%20life.

37. "Texas Spent $7 Million to Fight Against A/C in a Prison. It May Only Cost $4 Million to Install," *Texas Tribune*, September 1, 2018, https:// www.news-journal.com/texas-spent-7-million-to-fight-against-a-c-in-a-prison-it-may-only/article_bc067dc6-ae5b-11e8-9dd2-97ab9f1062d4. html.

38. Prison officials charged Kwaneta with fraud after a journalist attempted to register her own number, listed under her husband's name, to Kwaneta's phone list. Justine van der Leun, "I Hope Our Daughters Will Not Be Punished," *Dissent Magazine*, June 29, 2020, https://www. dissentmagazine.org/online_articles/i-hope-our-daughters-will-not-be-punished.

39. Bryce Newberry, "Families of Texas Prisoners Call for Release As COVID-19 Affects Thousands Behind Bars," *KVUE*, May 23, 2020, https://www.kvue.com/article/news/local/families-texas-prisoners-release-COVID19-protest/269-39eedcae-4d06-4aec-9b2a-d607d96779bb.

40. Harris, "Coronavirus Chronicles," 120.

41. Victoria Law, "As Some States Reopen, People in Prison Continue to Face Harmful Lockdowns," *Truthout*, July 29, 2020, https://truthout. org/articles/as-some-states-reopen-people-in-prison-continue-to-face-harmful-lockdowns/.

42. UCLA COVID Behind Bars Data Project, historical data, downloaded from https://github.com/uclalawCOVID19behindbars/data/blob/ master/historical-data/historical_facility_counts.csv; CDCR, "Timeline, Final Update: September 2022," https://www.cdcr.ca.gov/COVID19/ updates/.

43. Aishah Abdala et al., *Hidden Hazards: The Impacts of Climate Change on Incarcerated People in California State Prisons*, Ella Baker Center for Human Rights, June 2023, 10.

## Chapter 7: Winter, Dashed Hopes, and a Deadly Second Wave

1. United States Census, "Quick Facts: Oklahoma," https://www.census. gov/quickfacts/OK; Carson, *Prisoners in 2020*; Allison Herrera, "Why Oklahoma Has the Highest Female Incarceration in the Country," *The World*, October 3, 2017, https://theworld.org/stories/2017-10-03/why-

oklahomas-female-incarceration-rate-so-high.

2. I use the term *nations* to indicate that the Kickapoo and the Potawatomi are both sovereign nations with their own systems of government. See Dr. Twyla Baker, *How to Talk About Native Nations: A Guide*, Native Governance Center, https://nativegov.org/resources/how-to-talk-about-native-nations/.

3. Victoria Law, "Efforts to Decrease Prison Populations Are Leaving Women Behind," *Truthout*, February 7, 2018, https://truthout.org/articles/efforts-to-decrease-prison-populations-are-leaving-women-behind/.

4. Ethan Shaner to Oklahoma Department of Corrections, Re: Attorney General Opinion Request No. W-14, October 12, 2020, https://acrobat.adobe.com/link/review?uri=urn:aaid:scds:US:1ae3e29c-9743-4726-a337-1a8c31bbd0fe.

5. State of Oklahoma, House Bill No. 2342, 1994, http://www.oklegislature.gov/cf_pdf/1993-94%20INT/hb/HB2342%20INT.pdf.

6. Kim Bellware, "Oklahoma Approves Largest Single-Day Commutation in U.S. History," *Washington Post*, November 3, 2019, https://www.washingtonpost.com/nation/2019/11/03/oklahoma-approves-largest-single-day-commutation-us-history/.

7. "The Process," Pennsylvania Board of Pardons, https://www.bop.pa.gov/application-process/Pages/Process.aspx.

## Chapter 8: Vaccination and Insurrection

1. Mike German, "The FBI Warned for Years That Police Are Cozy with the Far Right. Is No One Listening?" *The Guardian*, August 28, 2020, https://www.theguardian.com/commentisfree/2020/aug/28/fbi-far-right-white-supremacists-police.

2. Rhae Lynn Barnes, Keri Leigh Merritt, and Yohuru Williams, eds., *After Life: A Collective History of Loss and Redemption in Pandemic America* (Chicago: Haymarket Books, 2022), 304.

3. Howard Goodman, "Studying Prison Experiments Research: For 20 Years, a Dermatologist Used the Inmates of a Philadelphia Prison as the Willing Subjects on Shampoo, Foot Powder, Deodorant, and, Later, Mind-Altering Drugs," *Baltimore Sun*, July 21, 1998.

4. Jordan Parker, "UCSF Apologizes for 'Unethical' Experiments with Mosquitoes and Pesticides on Prisoners Decades Ago," *San Francisco Chronicle*, December 21, 2022.

5. Floreal-Wooten v. Washington County Detention Center, filed in the US District Court, Western District of Arkansas, Fayetteville Division, January 13, 2022, https://www.acluarkansas.org/sites/default/files/field_documents/complaint-_file_marked.pdf. In 2023, the court ruled that experimenting on incarcerated people without their knowledge was

a violation of their due rights. https://www.acluarkansas.org/en/press-releases/aclu-arkansas-celebrates-victory-landmark-case-against-wcdc-doctors-controversial.

6. Floreal-Wooten v. Washington County Detention Center, filed in the US District Court, Western District of Arkansas, Fayetteville Division, January 13, 2022, https://www.acluarkansas.org/sites/default/files/field_documents/complaint-_file_marked.pdf.

7. Casey Cep, "Johnson & Johnson and a New War on Consumer Protection," *New Yorker*, September 12, 2022.

8. Laura Spinney, *Pale Rider: The Spanish Flu of 1918 and How It Changed the World* (New York: PublicAffairs, 2017), 125.

9. Carlos del Rio, Preeti N. Malani, and Saad B. Omer, "Confronting the Delta Variant of SARS-CoV-2, Summer 2021," *JAMA* 326, no. 11 (2021), 1001, doi:10.1001/jama.2021.14811.

10. Texas Board of Criminal Justice, Minutes from 217th Meeting, June 25, 2021, p. 4, https://www.tdcj.texas.gov/documents/tbcj/TBCJ_Summary_2021-06.pdf; Texas Department of Criminal Justice, *Annual Review: Fiscal Year 2021*, p. 18, https://www.tdcj.texas.gov/documents/Annual_Review_2021.pdf.

11. Alexi Jones, Michele Deitch, and Alycia Welch, *Canary in the Coal Mine: A Profile of Staff COVID Deaths in the Texas Prison System*, University of Texas at Austin, Lyndon B. Johnson School of Public Affairs, Prison and Jail Innovation Lab, February 2022, p. 14 (Figure 9).

12. Jones, Deitch, and Welch, *Canary in the Coal Mine*, 14 (Figure 9).

13. Dhruv Khullar, "How Many Times Will You Get COVID?" *New Yorker*, October 8, 2022.

## Chapter 9: What Has (Not) Been Learned

In describing incarcerated people's experiences, I drew extensively from letters, e-messages, phone calls, and video interviews.

1. David Cohen and Adam Cancryn, "Biden on '60 Minutes': 'The Pandemic Is Over,'" *Politico*, September 18, 2022, https://www.politico.com/news/2022/09/18/joe-biden-pandemic-60-minutes-00057423.

2. "Coronavirus in the U.S.: Latest Map and Case Count," *New York Times*, January 14, 2022 (accessed November 3, 2022).

3. Martha Lincoln and Anne S. Sosin, "Ending Free COVID Tests, US Policy Is Now 'You Do You,'" *The Nation*, September 9, 2022, https://www.thenation.com/article/society/COVID-tests-end-pandemic/.

4. Joshua Manson and Liz DeWolf, "The Federal Bureau of Prisons Is Even Less Transparent Than We Thought," UCLA COVID Behind Bars Data Project, April 2, 2021, https://uclaCOVIDbehindbars.org/blog/bopdata.

5. Victoria Law, "17 States and DC Have Stopped Reporting Active COVID Cases Behind Bars," *Truthout*, August 5, 2022, https://truthout.org/

articles/17-states-and-dc-have-stopped-reporting-active-COVID-cases-behind-bars/.

6.  Alice asked that she not be publicly identified for fear of retaliation. Law, "17 States and DC Have Stopped Reporting."

7.  In contrast, death rates in the general US population rose 23 percent. Naomi F. Sugie et al., "Excess Mortality in U.S. Prisons During the COVID-19 Pandemic," *Science Advances* 9, no. 48 (2023), https://science.org/doi/10.1126/sciadv.adj8104?adobe_mc=MC-MID%3D3665319679113272781024088368286382982998%7C-MCORGID%3D242B6472541199F70A4C98A6%2540Ado-beOrg%7CTS%3D1701373274.

8.  Therese Quinn et al., "Data and Liberation," *Inquest*, February 28, 2023, https://inquest.org/data-and-liberation/.

9.  Jacob Kang-Brown et al., "People in Jail and Prison in 2022," Vera Institute of Justice, June 2023, https://www.vera.org/downloads/publications/People-in-Jail-and-Prison-in-2022.pdf; TRAC Immigration, "Immigration Detention Quick Facts," https://trac.syr.edu/immigration/detentionstats/pop_agen_table.html (accessed August 26, 2023).

10. Joshua Rovner, "Youth Justice by the Numbers," The Sentencing Project, May 16, 2023, https://www.sentencingproject.org/policy-brief/youth-justice-by-the-numbers/.

11. Angela Y. Davis, *Are Prisons Obsolete?* (New York: Seven Stories Press, 2003).

12. André Gorz, *Strategy for Labor: A Radical Proposal* (Boston: Beacon Press, 1964), 7.

13. Ruth Wilson Gilmore, *Golden Gulag: Prisons, Surplus, Crisis, and Opposition in Globalizing California* (Berkeley: University of California Press, 2007), 242.

14. US Sentencing Commission, *Compassionate Release Data Report: Fiscal Years 2020 to 2022*, December 2022, https://www.ussc.gov/sites/default/files/pdf/research-and-publications/federal-sentencing-statistics/compassionate-release/20221219-Compassionate-Release.pdf.

15. Mary Price, *Everywhere and Nowhere: Compassionate Release in the States*, Families Against Mandatory Minimums, June 2018, 12, https://famm.org/wp-content/uploads/Exec-Summary-Report.pdf.

16. In 2019, the US Department of Justice, which tracks and analyzes data about prisons deaths, experienced bureaucratic changes. Since then, its death counts often do not match the complete data. E. Ann Carson, *Prisoners in 2020—Statistical Tables*, US Department of Justice, Bureau of Justice Statistics, Tables 9 and 19, https://bjs.ojp.gov/content/pub/pdf/p20st.pdf; COVID Prison Project, "COVID Prison Hotspots: June 26 to July 9, 2020," https://COVIDprisonproject.com/data-visualizations/.

17. World Health Organization, "Post COVID-19 (Long COVID)," December

7, 2022, https://www.who.int/europe/news-room/fact-sheets/item/post-COVID-19-condition#:~:text=Definition,months%20with%20no%20other%20explanation.

18. Mary Van Beusekom, "Global Data Reveal Half May Have Long COVID Four Months On," Center for Infectious Disease Research and Policy at the University of Minnesota, April 18, 2022, https://www.cidrap.umn.edu/global-data-reveal-half-may-have-long-COVID-4-months.

19. Stephani Sutherland, "Long COVID Now Looks Like Neurological Disease, Helping Doctors to Focus Treatments," *Scientific American*, March 1, 2023, https://www.scientificamerican.com/article/long-COVID-now-looks-like-a-neurological-disease-helping-doctors-to-focus-treatments/.

20. Saima May Sidik, "Heart-Disease Risk Soars After COVID—Even with a Mild Case," *Nature*, February 10, 2022, https://www.nature.com/articles/d41586-022-00403-0.

21. Bridget Kuehn, "Long COVID Symptoms Vary Among Racial and Ethnic Groups," *Cornell Chronicles*, February 20, 2023, https://news.cornell.edu/stories/2023/02/long-COVID-symptoms-vary-among-racial-and-ethnic-groups.

22. In 2022, voters in Alabama, Oregon, Tennessee and Vermont approved changing their state constitutions to prohibit involuntary labor and slavery as punishment for a criminal conviction. Victoria Law, "Forced Prison Labor Was Also on the Ballot," *The Nation*, November 10, 2022, https://www.thenation.com/article/society/forced-prison-labor-was-also-on-the-ballot/.

23. Brennan Klein et al., "COVID-19 Amplified Racial Disparities in the US Criminal Legal System," *Nature* 617 (April 2023), https://www.nature.com/articles/s41586-023-05980-2.

24. Klein et al., "COVID-19 Amplified Racial Disparities," Figure A.23, https://static-content.springer.com/esm/art%3A10.1038%2Fs41586-023-05980-2/MediaObjects/41586_2023_5980_MOESM1_ESM.pdf.

25. Klein et al., "COVID-19 Amplified Racial Disparities," Figure A.23, https://static-content.springer.com/esm/art%3A10.1038%2Fs41586-023-05980-2/MediaObjects/41586_2023_5980_MOESM1_ESM.pdf.

26. Keri Blakinger, "0822 CO Report," *The Marshall Project*, https://www.documentcloud.org/documents/23168882-0822-co-report.

27. Karen Brooks Harper, "Texas Diverts $359.6 Million from Prisons to Keep Greg Abbott's Border Mission Operating," *Texas Tribune*, October 27, 2022, https://www.texastribune.org/2022/10/27/operation-lone-star-greg-abbott-budget/.

28. Texas Department of Criminal Justice, *Annual Review FY2020*, 18, https://www.tdcj.texas.gov/documents/Annual_Review_2020.pdf.

29. Texas Department of Criminal Justice, *Annual Review FY2020*, 18.
30. Texas Department of Criminal Justice, *Statistical Report: FY 2022*, 1, tdcj. texas.gov/documents/Statistical_Report_FY2022.pdf.
31. Khullar, "How Many Times Will You Get COVID?," *The New Yorker*, October 8, 2022.
32. Ziyad Al-Aly, Benjamin Bowe, and Yan Xie, "Outcomes of SARS-CoV-2 Reinfection," *International Journal of Environmental Research and Public Health*, June 17, 2022, https://www.ncbi.nlm.nih.gov/pmc/articles/ PMC9961977/pdf/ijerph-20-03335.pdf
33. Khullar, "How Many Times Will You Get COVID?," *The New Yorker*, October 8, 2022.
34. Raymond Williams, "Inside Prison, COVID Protections Are Weaponized," *The Progressive*, January 3, 2023, https://progressive.org/ latest/inside-prison-COVID-protections-weaponized-williams-3123/#. Y7UTBv05APQ.twitter.
35. Rahsaan Thomas, "San Quentin's Rolling Lockdowns Are Not Keeping Anyone Safe," *The Appeal*, February 7, 2023, https://theappeal.org/san-quentin-COVID-lockdowns-rahsaan-thomas/.
36. Isaac Chotiner, "Q&A: How Pandemics Change History," *The New Yorker*, March 3, 2020.
37. US Department of Justice, National Institute of Corrections, *Policy Review and Development Guide: Lesbian, Gay, Bisexual, Transgender, and Intersex Persons in Custodial Settings*, 2nd ed., 2014, https://info.nicic.gov/sites/ info.nicic.gov.lgbti/files/lgbti-policy-review-guide-2_0.pdf.
38. Mwalimu Shakur confirmed that those labeled rats or snitches are subject to beatings, assaults, and even murder by others in prison. He said that, in California prisons, people are expected to address problems on their own or appeal to others in the same racial group for help. He said that the same code was expected of trans women who had been sexually harassed, abused, or assaulted by others. He added that there were no trans women on his housing unit so he could not give an example of how incidents of sexual abuse and harassment might be handled.
39. Angel Unique, "I Encourage You to Get Your COVID-19 Vaccine," *Prison Health News* 47 (Fall 2021), 13.

## Epilogue: The Ghost of COVID

1. Paul Flahive, "Hunger Strike in Texas Prison Continues," Texas Public Radio, January 13, 2023, https://www.tpr.org/criminal-justice/2023-01-13/hunger-strike-in-texas-prisons-enters-day-4.
2. John Yang and Karina Cuevas, "Texas Prisoners Stage Hunger Strike to Protest Solitary Confinement," *PBS NewsHour*, January 18, 2023, https:// www.pbs.org/newshour/show/texas-prisoners-stage-hunger-strike-to-protest-use-of-solitary-confinement.

3. In August 2023, I was still receiving repeat messages that Kwaneta had previously sent. The messages had been dated as if they had just been written. But I had already gotten the original messages up to one month earlier, sometimes repeatedly. Kwaneta was still charged for each of these repeats. Meanwhile, Securus updated its terms of service to include a disclaimer stating that the company made no promises that its products would meet a user's expectations or requirements, that the website would be error-free, and that access to its website or products would always be available without interruption or secure from unauthorized access. Securus Technologies, "General Terms and Conditions," version 1.7, effective August 23, 2023, https://securustech.net/friends-and-family-terms-and-conditions/index.html.

4. Peggy C. Giordano et al., "Linking Parental Incarceration and Family Dynamics Associated with Intergenerational Transmission: A Life Course Perspective," *Criminology* 57, no. 3 (August 2019), https://www.ncbi. nlm.nih.gov/pmc/articles/PMC8021139/#:~:text=Through%20our%20 analyses%2C%20we%20find,family%2Drelated%20risks%20linked%20to.

5. Jacob Deemer, "Pennsylvania's Clemency Application System Undergoing Most Extensive Update in Decades, Aims to Improve Public Access," *Explore Jefferson*, April 5, 2023, https://www.explorejeffersonpa.com/ pennsylvanias-clemency-application-system-undergoing-most-extensive-update-in-decades-aims-to-improve-public-access/.

6. Ann E. Carson, Melissa Nadel, and Gerry Gaes, "Impact of COVID-19 on State and Federal Prisons, March 2020 to February 2021," US Department of Justice, Bureau of Justice Statistics, 7, https://bjs.ojp.gov/content/pub/ pdf/icsfp2021.pdf.

7. The fourteen states were Alabama, Alaska, Arizona, Idaho, Mississippi, Missouri, Nebraska, Nevada, New Hampshire, South Carolina, South Dakota, Tennessee, Texas, and Wyoming. Kelly Lyn Mitchell et al., "Examining Releases in Response to COVID: Lessons Learned for Reducing the Effects of Mass Incarceration," Robina Institute of Criminal Law and Criminal Justice, July 2022, Appendix E, p. 64, https:// robinainstitute.umn.edu/publications/examining-prison-releases-response-COVID-lessons-learned-reducing-effects-mass.

8. Greg Abbott, Executive Order No. GA-13, March 29, 2020, https:// gov.texas.gov/uploads/files/press/EO-GA-13_jails_and_bail_for_ COVID-19_IMAGE_03-29-2020.pdf.

9. *Impact of COVID-19 on State and Federal Prisons*, 1.

10. *Impact of COVID-19 on State and Federal Prisons*, 17, Table 7.

11. Neal Marquez et al., "COVID-19 Incidence and Mortality in Federal and State Prisons Compared with the U.S. Population, April 5, 2020, to April 3, 2021," *JAMA*, October 6, 2021, https://jamanetwork.com/journals/ jama/fullarticle/2784944. For the total prison population in 2021 see

Jacob Kang-Brown, Chase Montagnet, and Jasmine Heiss, People in Jail and Prison Spring 2021, Vera Institute of Justice, 1, https://www.vera.org/downloads/publications/people-in-jail-and-prison-in-spring-2021.pdf.

12. Marquez et al., "COVID-19 Incidence and Mortality."

13. Jennifer Valentino-DeVries and Allie Pitchon, "As the Pandemic Swept America, Deaths in Prison Rose Nearly 50 Percent," *New York Times*, February 19, 2023.

14. Marquez et al., "COVID-19 Incidence and Mortality."

15. The COVID Prison Project reported 2,933 deaths in state, federal, and ICE prisons as of July 3, 2023: https://COVIDprisonproject.com/data/national-overview/. This figure excluded COVID deaths in local jails, juvenile facilities, or other forms of confinement. The UCLA COVID Behind Bars Data Project reported 3,181 COVID deaths in state, federal, and ICE prisons and some county jails and youth facilities: https://uclaCOVIDbehindbars.org/.

16. Valentino-DeVrise and Pitchon, "As the Pandemic Swept America."

17. Amanda Klonsky and Neal Marquez, "Opinion: Texas Should End Medical Copays in Its Prisons," *Austin American-Statesman*, December 4, 2022, https://www.statesman.com/story/opinion/columns/guest/2022/12/04/opinion-to-avoid-more-tragedy-texas-should-end-medical-copays-in-prisons/69692612007/.

18. Carson, Nadel, and Gaes, *Impact of COVID-19 on State and Federal Prisons*, 21; Valentino-DeVrise and Pitchon, "As the Pandemic Swept America." In 2019, there were 31 deaths in California prisons for every 10,000 prisoners.

19. Kwan et al., *California State Prisons During the COVID-19 Pandemic*, 63, Table 4.8, https://amend.us/wp-content/uploads/2022/05/2022-0501-CalPROTECT-Report.pdf.

20. These were the average case rates as of October 2021.

21. Wendy Sawyer, "Why Did Prison and Jail Populations Grow in 2022—and What Comes Next?" Prison Policy Initiative, December 19, 2023, https://www.prisonpolicy.org/blog/2023/12/19/bjs_update_2022/.

22. In mid-January 2022, the United States reported a record high number of nearly 151,000 COVID hospitalizations in one week. That figure dropped dramatically, then rose several times. In January 2023, there were 44,410 hospitalizations, a figure that declined through mid-July. By late August, hospital admissions had risen to slightly above 15,000. Centers for Disease Control and Prevention, "COVID Data Tracker," https://COVID.cdc.gov/COVID-data-tracker/#trends_weeklyhospitaladmissions_select_00.

23. Arundhati Roy, "The Pandemic Is a Portal," *Azadi: Freedom. Fascism. Fiction.* (Chicago: Haymarket Books, 2020), https://rethinkingschools.org/articles/the-pandemic-is-a-portal/.

24. Sonali Kolhatkar, "Envisioning a New World Through Abolition Geography," *Yes Magazine*, February 7, 2023, https://www.yesmagazine.

org/social-justice/2023/02/07/ruthie-wilson-gilmore-abolition-geography%EF%BF%BC.

25. Angela Y. Davis et al., *Abolition. Feminism. Now.* (Chicago: Haymarket Books, 2022), 168.

## Acknowledgments

1. Ann Lewinson, "Meet Zoe Anderson Norris, the 'Nellie Bly You've Never Heard Of,'" *HellGate*, February 28, 2023, https://hellgatenyc.com/meet-zoe-anderson-norris-the-nellie-bly-youve-never-heard-of.

# Index

"Passim" (literally "scattered") indicates intermittent discussion of a topic over a
cluster of pages.

# About the Author

**Victoria Law** is an author and freelance journalist focusing on the intersections of incarceration, gender, and resistance. Her books include *Resistance Behind Bars: The Struggles of Incarcerated Women, Prison By Any Other Name: The Harmful Consequences of Popular Reform*, and *"Prisons Make Us Safer" and 20 Other Myths About Mass Incarceration*. Her writings about prisons and other forms of confinement have appeared in the *New York Times, The Nation, Wired, Bloomberg Businessweek,* the *Village Voice, The Guardian, In These Times, HellGate,* and *Truthout.* She is a cofounder of Books Through Bars—NYC and the zine *Tenacious: Art and Writings by Women in Prison.*

# About Haymarket Books

Haymarket Books is a radical, independent, nonprofit book publisher based in Chicago. Our mission is to publish books that contribute to struggles for social and economic justice. We strive to make our books a vibrant and organic part of social movements and the education and development of a critical, engaged, and internationalist Left.

We take inspiration and courage from our namesakes, the Haymarket Martyrs, who gave their lives fighting for a better world. Their 1886 struggle for the eight-hour day—which gave us May Day, the international workers' holiday—reminds workers around the world that ordinary people can organize and struggle for their own liberation. These struggles—against oppression, exploitation, environmental devastation, and war—continue today across the globe.

Since our founding in 2001, Haymarket has published more than nine hundred titles. Radically independent, we seek to drive a wedge into the risk-averse world of corporate book publishing. Our authors include Angela Y. Davis, Arundhati Roy, Keeanga-Yamahtta Taylor, Eve Ewing, Aja Monet, Mariame Kaba, Naomi Klein, Rebecca Solnit, Olúfẹ́mi O. Táíwò, Mohammed El-Kurd, José Olivarez, Noam Chomsky, Winona LaDuke, Robyn Maynard, Leanne Betasamosake Simpson, Howard Zinn, Mike Davis, Marc Lamont Hill, Dave Zirin, Astra Taylor, and Amy Goodman, among many other leading writers of our time. We are also the trade publishers of the acclaimed Historical Materialism Book Series.

Haymarket also manages a vibrant community organizing and event space in Chicago, Haymarket House, the popular Haymarket Books Live event series and podcast, and the annual Socialism Conference.

Printed in the USA
CPSIA information can be obtained
at www.ICGtesting.com
JSHW011053290724
67053JS00006B/6